Divine Zodiac Messages

Guidance from Angels, Tarot, Genies, Animals, Runes, Crystals, Numbers, Chakras, Devas, Gods & Goddesses for each Star Sign

Lani Sharp

Copyright © 2018

All rights reserved. This book or any portion thereof may not be reproduced or used in any manner whatsoever without the express written permission of the author except for the use of brief quotations in a book review.

Printed in Australia
First Printing, 2018
ISBN: 978-0-6483447-9-7

White Light Publishing House
Harkness, VIC, Australia 3337
whitelightpublishing.com.au

*Dedicated to The Universe ~
My Divine Source.*

Thank you, thank you, thank you.

The whole world is you.
Yet you keep thinking there is something else.

Hsueh-Feng I-Ts'un

CONTENTS

Introduction ~ Why I wrote this book	9
A little bit about my Divine Self	13
Angel Messages	
About Angels	17
Angel Messages for the Signs	
Aries	25
Taurus	28
Gemini	32
Cancer	35
Leo	39
Virgo	42
Libra	46
Scorpio	50
Sagittarius	54
Capricorn	57
Aquarius	61
Pisces	65
Tarot Messages	
About Tarot	69
The Tarot & Astrology	72
Tarot Messages for the Zodiac	
Aries	74
Taurus	78
Gemini	82
Cancer	85
Leo	87
Virgo	90
Libra	93
Scorpio	97
Sagittarius	101
Capricorn	105
Aquarius	107
Pisces	110
Genie Messages	
About Genies	115
Genies by your Birthdate	115
Animal Spirit Messages	
About Spirit Animals	119

Spirit Animal Messages for the Zodiac	122
Aries	122
Taurus	123
Gemini	124
Cancer	125
Leo	126
Virgo	127
Libra	128
Scorpio	130
Sagittarius	131
Capricorn	132
Aquarius	133
Pisces	134
Rune Messages	
About Runes	137
The Rune Calendar	139
Rune Messages for the Zodiac	
Aries	140
Aries & Taurus	140
Taurus	141
Taurus & Gemini	142
Gemini	143
Gemini & Cancer	144
Cancer	145
Cancer & Leo	146
Leo	147
Leo & Virgo	148
Virgo	148
Virgo & Libra	149
Libra	150
Libra & Scorpio	151
Scorpio	152
Scorpio & Sagittarius	153
Sagittarius	154
Sagittarius & Capricorn	155
Capricorn	156
Capricorn & Aquarius	157
Aquarius	157
Aquarius & Pisces	158

Pisces	159
Pisces & Aries	160
Crystal Messages	
About Crystals	163
Zodiac Crystals	165
Mystical Birthstones of the Zodiac	166
Crystal Messages for the Zodiac	
Aries	166
Taurus	167
Gemini	168
Cancer	169
Leo	170
Virgo	171
Libra	172
Scorpio	173
Sagittarius	174
Capricorn	176
Aquarius	177
Pisces	178
Numeric Messages	
About Numbers & Numerology	179
The Music of the Spheres	181
Other important numbers for your Life's Journey	182
Numeric Messages for the Zodiac	
Aries	184
Taurus	186
Gemini	187
Cancer	189
Leo	190
Virgo	192
Libra	194
Scorpio	195
Sagittarius	198
Capricorn	199
Aquarius	201
Pisces	202
Chakra Messages	
About Chakras	205
Chakra Messages for the Zodiac	207

Aries & Leo	207
Taurus & Libra	209
Gemini & Virgo	211
Cancer & Scorpio	213
Sagittarius & Pisces	215
Capricorn	218
Aquarius	220
Deva Messages	
About Devas	223
Making a Wish Using your Deva	225
Deva Messages for the Zodiac (By Element)	
Fire ~ Aries, Leo & Sagittarius	226
Earth ~ Taurus, Virgo & Capricorn	228
Air ~ Gemini, Libra & Aquarius	231
Water ~ Cancer, Scorpio & Pisces	233
God & Goddess Messages	
About Gods & Goddesses	237
Invoking your God or Goddess	238
God & Goddess Messages for the Zodiac	
Aries	239
Taurus	241
Gemini	242
Cancer	244
Leo	246
Virgo	248
Libra	250
Scorpio	251
Sagittarius	254
Capricorn	256
Aquarius	258
Pisces	260
Divine Affirmations	**263**
Special Message from the Universe for all Zodiac Signs	266

★ ★ ★

INTRODUCTION ~ WHY I WROTE THIS BOOK

Do not feel lonely. The entire Universe is inside you.

Rumi

Millions of spiritual creatures walk the Earth unseen, both when we wake, and when we sleep.

John Milton, *Paradise Lost*, **Book IV**

The doorway to all-knowing: There is no such thing as 'my' consciousness; there is just consciousness acting as a continuity that is moving across all forms of evolution, from mineral to man.

Pir Vilayat Khan

★ ★ ★

Let's get one thing straight before we begin our journey into the ethereal realms of the Universe and the Divine, that sacred, infinite space of dreams, whims, magic and wonder:

You and the Divine are one and the same!

You are not separate from the Divine Source. There is no 'out there' and 'in here'. All Divine entities and energies reside *within you*, not outside of you. According to quantum physicists and law of attraction experts, the external does not exist, despite our perception of it as an 'outside force', as tangible, material or solid. All perceived reality is merely a projection, an illusion, something created by the observer: *You*. Everything you see in the apparent outside world, is a reflection of your own inner workings. While this is an intricate and complex concept, it is well worth noting before we begin so that you are made aware of the beautiful fact that *you are indeed the entire Universe and the entire Universe is you*.

Spend all the time you need to grapple with this, if indeed it can be grappled with and grasped, and yet it will still bring you home to the base essence of the principle that every single message in this book already exists within you. Indeed, all the Divine power and messages that this book contains, can be accessed within the boundless mechanisms of your own inner worlds.

Essentially what I am saying here is that you don't need a book called *Divine Zodiac Messages* to impart these ethereal messages to you. Everything this book contains is already imprinted on the collective unconscious, already downloaded into the Universe's database for All to access at anytime and anywhere, and forms the most part of the Akashic Records, the Infinite Spirit, the Cosmic Field, the Ancient Archives, the Gateways Beyond, and the knowledge of the Timeless Wise Ones.

Everything throughout these pages pervades and transcends time and space. The channels I received the messages through have always existed, exist now, and will always exist, for they are like invisible cords that connect All That Is with yourself, the eternal and immortal *you*.

It is not necessary for me to even relay these messages for you, because if you have enough practice, self-attunement, dissolution of ego and fear, and connection to your higher intuitive faculties, you can just as easily access all this information yourself. But many of us feel a little lost, confused, and frayed from time to time, which is when guideposts are called for.

So by all means, read this book! After all, the essence of reading is a precious gem woven into the fabric of life, and it is always nice to read someone else's words, to enjoy experiencing a different perspective, a refreshing take on things, a new wave of energy. Just know that you *can* access everything contained within these pages yourself, too, if you so desire and choose. In fact, you may resonate with certain messages contained herein, and decide on a whim and a prayer to investigate that genie, rune, goddess, spirit animal or Tarot card in more depth so that it may deeper permeate your soul.

The main basis I had for writing this book is that I believe we as Divine beings on an Earthly plane all have one common thread: We are all seekers of the Truth; we are all seekers of the Light. The Truth and the Light can mean different things to different people, and that is why our search is so influenced by our individual tendencies, desires, characteristics, spiritual blueprints, and soul plans.

However we go about finding both or either, is a highly individual thing and is such a very powerful task to undertake, yet many of us do not even know where to begin. And that is why I wrote this book, for I am here to set you on that Path, a beautiful journey that ultimately leads to the self-actualisation of your Highest Self, your truest purpose and your spirit's noblest quest. One of the beings, powers or entities of your zodiac sign may step out of the page and into your life, to help guide, encourage, support and empower you, and I sincerely hope that all these Divine essences speak to you as they have to me.

Throughout this book, I offer Divine Messages for each zodiac sign so that each individual may find their way to at least the beginning of their own special Path, which can and does lead to their most wondrous, evolved, enlightened Self if they follow it with conviction and a certain level of discipline, focus, intention, purpose, and mastery.

First and foremost, I am a writer, an architect of words. But I am also a born magician, witch, spell-caster, astrologer, healer, light-worker, metaphysician, dream-believer, star-gazer, goddess and Divine Messenger, which is how I've come to deliver these words to the page that you are now reading.

As everyone on this spinning sphere is, I was born with a very special soul purpose and mission, and I possess a deep knowing that I was incarnated into this life experience so that I may assist and enlighten others along their own deeply personal journeys. Everyone is working on special soul-growth lessons in this lifetime, and everyone's set of lessons is as unique as a fingerprint. For the obvious reasons of time and logistics, I can't possibly counsel each and every person in the world around what their life purpose is, even though I would dearly love to, as I come across so many in my daily interactions who yearn and indeed seek to know more about what the Divine Sources have to say to them.

What this tells me is two things: (1) That a great many of us are seeking a deeper meaning, a more profound purpose in our lives; and (2) That many of us desire a Divine nudge in the right direction, in the form of a message or another human being to impart this knowledge to us so that we may use it to enjoy a more fulfilling, satisfying life experience.

Sadly, too many of us live our lives by default, that is, we may plod along aimlessly, trying our best no doubt, but still not quite reaching the heights we intuitively know deep down that we are capable of achieving. We are capable of so much more than we dare to believe we are, and although it is only ourselves that can ultimately move us in any direction, some external guidance is always helpful.

Yet it is here that I should make a distinction: because every living being is part of an almost unfathomably intricate, interconnected and holographic Universe, in which everything and everyone is a part of the Whole, integrated system, it means that we as Earthly human beings, are not separate from that which is Divine, mystical, or of the Universe. In fact, we are profoundly and eternally connected to it, and some would say, *are* it. But this doesn't mean that the occasional bit of advice, assistance, guidance or pointer in the right direction from a Source we perceive to be outside of ourselves is impotent. In fact, your seeking of and receiving a Divine message, whether it be through your own intuition, trance work, a shaman, or through a channeller such as myself, is further proof that you are deeply connected to everything and everyone around you. Always keep in mind, throughout this journey, that All is One, and One is All.

And this brings me back to why I wrote this book - to give *you*, a Child of the Universe, special messages in order to re-connect with you through the invisible cord that binds you to the wider Universe.

Because so many of us have deviated from our true selves and authentic Path - or have never even uncovered who we actually are - we can often feel struck, trapped, limited, helpless, lacking, dissatisfied, unable to cope. There are many reasons for this, which are beyond the scope of this book, but suffice to say that many of us are not reaching our pure, unlimited potential for reasons such as fear, self-imposed limitations, lack of money or resources, low self-confidence, and in many cases, because we simply do not know how to access the deepest parts of ourselves which have the answers about our true-life purpose.

Furthermore, we don't know where or how to search for these answers. Sometimes we may feel lost or fearful, not quite knowing that *all* the answers we seek are *inside of ourselves*. External answers such as the words written in this book may guide you, but you will find that some messages resonate while others may not, which further affirms that those messages you connect most with contain the answers that you have known all along. Always keep in mind that as a Divine Child, you were actually born with all the answers already inside of you, you just needed to be reminded of them so that they may guide your Soul Path. Like a baby girl born with all her eggs already in existence, just waiting to be fertilised when she reaches a child-bearing age, so too is our Divine Spark already within us, awaiting fertilisation.

Time and logistical reasons don't allow me to enjoy a soul connection and provide a channel for Divine assistance for each and every one of you individually, and thereby reveal to you some ideas about your ultimate life purpose, so I decided to write a book that covers all twelve zodiac signs, in the hope that you may find something among the words that resonates with you. Self-exploration can be a wonderful and wholly liberating journey to undertake, and even though I may share my words and my knowledge with you, only you can find the deeper truths within them that apply to *you*.

And so, it is my sincere wish, objective and hope that through reading each of your zodiac sign's special messages from different Divine sources - angels, runes, numbers, spirit animals, etc. - you may even find your own deeper meanings within these messages and then go on to explore their meanings more deeply if they hold particularly true or meaningful for you. Remember, there is a reason for something that jumps out at you as an especially powerful message; it is obviously something you are needing to hear and learn at this stage of your soul's journey and evolution.

I absolutely adore the embrace of the angels, the whims of the genies, the cosmic dance of the gods and goddesses, the power of the runes, the alchemy of the numbers, the elemental force of the devas, the energy of the charkas, the essence of crystals, the mystique of the tarot, and the sacred whispers of the animal spirits, and I sincerely hope that their messages echo out from these pages profoundly to you as well.

Their presence and meanings have endured for many centuries - indeed since time began because this knowledge was born along with the Universe - and this alone lends them a power beyond my verbal and written expression. In many cases, their force and essence can only be felt with the heart. I wish that for you too, to *feel* them with your heart. After all, feeling is everything, for it creates your entire world and re-connects you with your Divinity.

My life's passion and indeed my life's work, lies in relaying Divine messages to others, through my work as an astrologer, author, crystal therapist, aura interpreter, tarot scholar, and Akashic Record reader, and above all, an intuitive empath who seeks to enlighten others through my writing and all manner of complementary healing pathways that holistically treat a person's mind, body and spirit.

The following is a snapshot of my journey so far, some of which you may be able to relate. I do hope it inspires you to move beyond any limitations you may be currently placing upon yourself, and into new realms of fulfilling experience, love and the Divine Light that is your birthright and you so deserve.

Blessings to you all for your uniquely personal journey. May your Divine forces ever propel you forwards and guide you *from within*.

A LITTLE BIT ABOUT MY DIVINE SELF

I am a born channeller * and messenger. One beautiful warm morning in the February of 1976, a little sunbeam was born ~ that sunbeam was me! I came forth with magic in me, a born lightworker you might say. Not only did I arrive in the much-revered Year of the Dragon, but I was born on February 2, a sacred day for witches, pagans, wizards, alchemists, magic-weavers, spell-casters and of course lightworkers of all kinds. In Pagan traditions in the northern hemisphere, February 2 is known as Imbolc, a time which celebrates the first signs of Spring and the awakening of the light in the Goddess; and in the southern hemisphere where I was born, it is known as Lughnasadh, a time which heralds the first harvest, and the blessings and prosperity this brings with it.

From the moment I took my first breath under the cosmically whimsical cocktail of an Aquarius Sun and Pisces Moon, I was well on my way to healing, guiding and assisting others. I have always had a deep affinity with symbolism, esoterism, mysticism, and the Divine, so being born on this truly magical day holds a very special and profound meaning for me and my life's path.

Here are a few magical things about me:

✯ I am a solitary eclectic witch who casts spells, worships the Sun, wishes on the Moon, basks in the rays of Venus, breathes in Jupiter beams, and can turn anyone into a frog or prince if I so desire.
✯ I am a mother, lightworker, astrologer, author, tarot reader, crystal healer, numerologist, magician, alchemist, traveller, seeker, guide, spiritual teacher, esoteric student, dream-believer, and Divine channeller and messenger.
✯ My numerology number is 9, which is a number of vision, compassion, imagination, humanitarianism, intuition and holistic perception, stirring one's deepest psychic self and innate healing and channeling potential. It also strengthens my connection with the Divine.
✯ Before breaking it down to 9, my birth date's numerology number is 27, a powerful number of the Universe, which is said to possess a sacred essence.
✯ The letters of my name add up to the number 44, which is an angelic vibration indicating that I am here for high purposes and to fulfill grand visions.
✯ My Sun in Aquarius is on the tenth house cusp in my birth horoscope, right on the midheaven, a prominent sign and position pointing me towards the lightworker, humanitarian, and global messenger's path.
✯ My Moon is in Pisces, giving me a deeply spiritual focus and belief system.
✯ I have every magical tool I need at my disposal, both inner and outer.
✯ I am rich, enriched, loved, loving, prosperous, abundant and blessed beyond measure
✯ I am doing what I love every single day and with each breath and step that I take. Delivering messages through my light-work is my passion and I believe that

assisting others to receive these Divine and cosmic messages, is the main reason I was born.
★ All messages I receive come from a place of Love.
★ I believe that all things, good and bad, are unfolding as they should be, and that everything happens for a reason, in order that everyone's spiritual evolution may unfold as part of their own Divine Plan. Nothing happens by chance.
★ I believe that Love is all there is.

As a lightworker and messenger, I simply provide the tool, channel and/or the information to the recipient and then they do the rest, whether they are aware of this or not. So, if someone walks away from a session or reading feeling somehow still unhealed or broken, then there is something within *them* that is blocking that healing from taking place and only they can do the necessary work and take the needed steps to begin the healing journey. I am merely the teacher and channel for healing, messages and lightwork.

Remember, healing is an inside job! No one can heal you but you. I am simply a channel that can pass this understanding onto you if you request it. Once it is in your hands, then what you choose to do with it is entirely up to you. That is the beauty of being a messenger, that I see so many wondrous examples of people healing themselves. They may try to thank me for any insights they have gained, any shifts they can sense or healing they feel has occurred, but I always remind them that they are the primary and ultimate master healer of themselves.

Some principles that I pass onto my clients, friends and family when they have chosen to undertake a healing journey or to receive a Divine message under my guidance are:

★ Love is a Universal vibration that communicates to all species, functions on all levels and expresses our true nature. Love is the foundation of all healing and is the core essence of the life force.
★ Healing is a skill that can be taught and that grows stronger with practice. Lightworkers and other wellbeing practitioners become stronger at running the energy in their healing ability over time.
★ The energy follows the natural intelligence of the body to do the necessary work.
★ Trusting the process is essential. The work may cause temporary pain, emotional issues to arise, or other distressing symptoms - and these are all part of the healing process. The life force and the healing steps work with a complexity and a wisdom that are beyond our conception and levels of comprehension.
★ Everyone is essentially a channeller of and receptacle for Divine forces. Each person's gifts in life, healing and channeling are unique.
★ It is important to realise that the channelling and healing practitioner is also receiving a healing by doing the work.

And so, as a lightworker, channeller and messenger for others, I receive the messages and the light myself; as a healer, I receive the healing myself. This is all just part of the nature of the work that I do. I am so blessed to have been given the gift of this very special and unique Path.

I believe everyone has Divine light in them, and all we need to do to tap into this is to ensure that our channels are open to receiving the messages and gifts that are meant just for us from the Universal mind, the All That Is, the Absolute. Our superconscious mind resides within each of us and embodies the '*perfect pattern*' spoken of by Plato, The Divine Design - for I sincerely believe there is a Divine Design for each and every person in this human incarnation.

This book and its messages may light the way somewhat through the power of words and affirmations, however they are not based upon individuals, but rather Sun signs or birth dates (which you share with millions of others, both past and present). Therefore, it is up to you and you alone to find your place in the Grand Universal scheme of things. Just know that you were born with a life purpose, came forth with a Divine mission, born to evolve into something, and you are here as an Eternal Light Being to live out your unfolding Self over this lifetime, or indeed many lifetimes.

In essence, by channelling and living through the messages I receive from the etheric Divine Source, I can say what my own deepest truths are: I have been enriched by suffering and blessed by adversity. And through it all, I have never given up. And in all this time, along my whole lightworker-messenger journey, I have never once laid down my life's weapons and tools, because of the biggest and deepest underlying truth of my soul: *I was born to do this*. And I want more than anything else for someone, even just one soul I may have touched, to say, "Because of you I didn't give up." I am in the ever-evolving process of deep and rich healing. And despite - or perhaps because of - everything, I am both the healer and the healed, all at once. After all, I am a born messenger and channel for the highest of Divine and cosmic forces and truths.

I pass them onto you, my dear readers, infused deeply with the essence of wild abundance, ageless wisdom, and infinite blessings. For you are all my co-travellers on this journey, we are all connected as One, and in reading this book, you are most certain to receive and heed the timeless messages contained herein simply by taking this journey alongside me.

* Channelling is the process of receiving information from a discarnate entity, symbol or higher spiritual being. As a channeller, I serve as a bridge between the spirit or spiritual intelligences that abound in the ethereal realms of the entire Universe, and as these messages come to me, I ground them here on our material plane in order to interpret them and relay them to you, the reader and receiver.

☆ ☆ ☆

Angel Messages

ABOUT ANGELS

Angels are our link to the Divine, helping us in our soul's journey and gently highlighting wisdom, beauty, benevolence and trust in our world. Everyone has a guardian angel aligned to their soul and their life's pathway.

Alicen & Neil Geddes-Ward

See, I am sending an angel ahead of you
to guard you along the way
and to bring you to the place
I have prepared.

Exodus 23:20

Live such that when you stumble,
An angel's hand may guide you to the goal,
That vanished before you.

Hafiz

The New Age movement offers spiritual paths accessible to all. As we reach out toward the timeless and the divine, the strength of those invisible helping hands is of untold value. We need our angels still.

David Ross

Throughout the string of your lives, close to and far from Earth, always by your head your angel holds your star.

Manfred Kyber

An angel is a celestial being who is considered to be a messenger of the Highest Power, whatever you conceive this Power to be - God, the Universe, the Supreme Creator, All That Is, the Higher Self, Spirit, the Light, the Tao, Cosmic Intelligence, Source, the Absolute, the Force, Truth, or an entity of your own conception. The word *angel* itself, derives from the Greek *angelos*, and translates to "messenger of God." To humans, angels are often seen as bringers as all sorts of messages. Angels in all their forms are believed to bring the message of 'spirit' into matter, carrying the blueprints of creation and the Source from the Divine into the manifest world.

Angels are not and never have been human; they, like fairies and nature spirits, are part of a different evolutionary pattern – but they do appear to us in human form (usually with wings) because that is what we most readily understand.

An angel can be in many different places at once, and with the same intensity and concentration. In that sense, they are omnipresent and omnipotent, and wish wholeheartedly for us to be aware of them and benefit from them.

An archangel is an angel of greater than ordinary rank. They possess a stronger, more powerful essence than the guardian angels, through overseeing and guiding the other angelic beings who are said to be with us here on Earth.

The nine-tiered hierarchy of angels is divided into three groups, known as triads *, spheres or choirs: the highest ones are involved in work that is intended to help the entire Universe. The angels in the lowest triad help look after the Earth and its inhabitants.

There are said to be three categories of angels, each with three subdivisions:

✶ The first sphere, the *Heavenly Counsellors*, comprises Seraphim, Cherubim & Thrones
✶ The second sphere, the *Heavenly Governors*, comprises Dominions, Virtues & Powers
✶ The third sphere, the *Heavenly Messengers*, comprises Principalities, Archangels & Angels

The most famous classification of angels was created by Dionysius in the sixth century and was included in his book *The Celestial Hierarchies*. His system contains the already listed nine ranks of angels, across three triads:

First Triad

The first hierarchy is that closest to the Divine Source and profoundly involved in the celebration of Divinity, creation, and the entire Universe.

1 ✶ Seraphim ~ Have six red wings that glow. Two wings cover their feet, two their faces, and the other two are used for flying. They carry flaming red swords

and chant. The name Seraphim is associated with shining or blazing, an indication of their closeness to the Divine Source.

2 ✶ Cherubim ~ Wear deep blue clothes and carry swords to protect the way to the Tree of Life at the east gate of Eden. They are described as having four faces and four wings. The Cherubim play a role chiefly of prayer and blessing, and wisdom is one of their special attributes.

3 ✶ Thrones ~ The judiciary angels who administer Divine judgment and ensure that Cosmic truths are imparted to everyone. The Thrones are akin to the wheeled chariots in *Book 1 of Ezekiel* and are the great supporters of the whole cosmos.

Second Triad

The second hierarchy protects Divine purpose.

4 ✶ Dominions ~ Work in heaven as middle-level executives, deciding what needs to be done and then issuing the necessary orders to ensure that the universe works the way it should. They determine what cosmic responsibilities need to be attended to and supervise the tasks and duties of each angel. Also known as the Dominations, the Dominions are defenders against ill forces.

5 ✶ Virtues ~ Work out the necessary strategy to get the responsibilities underway. They provide confidence, courage and blessings. The Virtues' main attributes are healing and restoration, and accordingly, they transmit the power to work miracles.

6 ✶ Powers ~ Carry out the plans. They also protect and watch over people's souls. The Powers strive against ill forces, like the Dominions, but also preside over birth and death, and are often associated with stars.

Third Triad

The third hierarchy cares for all created beings, especially for humankind with its glorious yet sometimes precarious gift of free will.

7 ✶ Principalities ~ Organise the tasks that need to be performed on Earth. They have a special interest in spiritual matters and the welfare of nations. The Principalities protect social structure and sound organisations.

8 ✶ Archangels ~ Carry out the tasks organised by the principalities. They are the most important of messengers. The Archangels care for all created beings.

9 ✶ Angels ~ The ones who are closest to us. They are the humblest angels, yet they have the huge responsibility of interacting between the Universe and humankind. Our guardian angels belong to this group. The Angels are the lowest order and have direct contact with humans. Caring for us is their main task.

* The number of orders, nine, or a trinity of trinities, is significant. For the Greek mathematician Pythagoras, eight, or a full chord, represented man, so nine stood for a higher order of being. From the nine worlds of Norse mythology to the nine Greek muses, the number nine is often significant in religion, spirituality, and legend.

Of course, all such classifications are a human construct, a way of placing order upon the unknowable and allowing us to perceive something about which we have no words to express. However, as long as we think of angelic hierarchies as a way of working with celestials, of remembering important attributes, and we are able to imagine and experience these beings, this order of angels will prove useful to those wishing to draw upon their messages and assistance.

'Angel' is the generic term and also relates specifically to those closest to the physical. Similarly, archangel may be taken to mean any of the higher orders, and indeed signifies the order just above ordinary 'angel'. Found in a number of religious traditions, the word 'archangel' itself is usually associated with the Abrahamic religions. The word archangel is of Greek origin and means literally 'chief angel'. All archangels end with the 'el' suffix, 'el' meaning 'in God' and the first part of the name meaning what each individual Angel specialises in. The archangel who governs your sign will likely be the one with whom you most resonate. The astrological sign is an energy signature, a matrix of a specific stellar pattern that will subtly affect and influence you, so it makes sense that there is a special angelic being and connection that harmonises with each particular zodiac sign.

Although there are many associations for the great archangels of the Universe, we must keep in mind there is great overlapping in their duties, purposes, and guidance. For example, we may say that one is for healing and another for protection, but they can all perform the functions of the others, it's just that each has areas of greater focus and responsibilities.

Four of the multitude of archangelic beings work intimately with the Earth. These are Raphael (Air), Michael (Fire), Gabriel (Water) and Uriel (Earth). Associated with each of these archangels are one of the four elements, specific colours, one of the four directions or quarters of the Earth, three signs of the zodiac, and a variety of other energies, qualities, essences, and powers. Understanding these associations and considering them in relation to our own paths, can help us determine with which of them we are more likely to resonate. Each sign, being of the one of four elements, vibrates to the essence of that element's archangel.

ZODIAC ARCHANGELS

From the moment of conception, and even before that, there is attached to the incarnating soul someone who volunteers to be his guardian.

Silver Birch

ANGELS OF THE ZODIAC *

Aries ✴ Chamuel, Ariel, Jophiel
Taurus ✴ Haniel, Chamuel, Sandalphon
Gemini ✴ Raphael, Zadkiel, Metatron
Cancer ✴ Muriel, Haniel, Gabriel
Leo ✴ Michael, Raziel
Virgo ✴ Raphael, Metatron
Libra ✴ Haniel, Jophiel, Chamuel
Scorpio ✴ Azrael, Chamuel, Jeremiel, Raziel
Sagittarius ✴ Zadkiel, Raguel
Capricorn ✴ Cassiel, Azrael, Asariel
Aquarius ✴ Uriel, Cassiel
Pisces ✴ Asariel, Zadkiel, Sandalphon, Tzaphkiel

Overseers of All Zodiac Signs ✴ Michael, Raphael, Haniel

* Different sources vary as to which angels are aligned with each zodiac sign. During my extensive study and research for this component of the book, I encountered much contradictory and conflicting information around the angelic resonances with the twelve signs; you could even say that each source was entirely different to all the other sources. Because of this very confusing and frustrating energy, I decided to stick with my own inner voice, as well as the angelic wisdom of the experts, scholars, and a couple of special friends of mine who are deeply connected with the angels in their everyday work and life. Their counsel, advice and suggestions were absolutely invaluable, and most of the angels they recommended are included in my *Angels of the Zodiac Angels* list. Ultimately though, it was me who decided which angels were assigned to each sign, based purely upon my instincts, research, insights, and the more consistent information I came across in my adventurous research 'travels'. You may or may not agree with my list, or certain angels, and that is fine. In any case, sometimes the best thing to do is just discover your own, by making a conscious connection to your specific birth guardian angel (see under following heading '*Individual Birth Guardian Angels*'). This to me, is far more personal and unique than any standardised, 'pop culture' list anyway. Enjoy the journey!

    Each sign is associated with a particular archangel. Such knowledge can help you to build up a relationship with these beings, based upon your strengths and needs. However, no link is rigid, and as you work and connect with the angelic realm, you will come to develop your own affinities. When invoking a specific archangel, a useful ritual to draw them closer is to light a candle in that angel's colour, burn some suitable oil or incense, and hold the appropriate crystal while focusing on what you are needing guidance on.

    It is useful to keep in mind that the Kabbalah suggests that although guardian angels and archangels can assist us anonymously, their powers are limited unless we specially request help. When we explicitly ask for assistance from the Divine and etheric realms, the ever-present angels are freer to perform loftier tasks and services on our behalf. This applies to other spirits, entities and powers also.

INDIVIDUAL BIRTH GUARDIAN ANGELS

Sometimes the guardian angels of our life fly so high
That we cannot see them any longer,
But they never lose track of us.

Jean Paul Richter

Your angel loves you unconditionally and honours your free will and will never override it unless it is a life-or-death situation. So, the only way you'll be able to experience your angel is by accepting that they are close to you and inviting them into your life. Know that every second your angel falls deeper and deeper in love with the light that you are.

Kyle Gray

It is said that we each have a specially-appointed guardian angel who has been looking after us and out for us from the day we were born onwards. This special being * is by our side throughout our entire life, constantly providing guidance, protection, support, and companionship, and even placing opportunities in our path and organising synchronicities so that our requests and desires may come true if they are for our highest good. You can summon your guardian birth angel by any number of methods, such as burning a candle, programming a crystal for this purpose, visualisation, or by simply asking your angel to communicate and connect with you by showing you a sign. Having said all this, many people yearn for communication with angels and feel they are not achieving this. Some may even achieve it without consciously desiring it. One thing is clear: angels, as spirits of good, cannot *really* be summonsed or invoked. Most angels, as agents of good, will only act or be simply sent to us as needed. For the most part they visit and send messages only at times when their intervention or communication is critical and providential.

Although there are many methods for connecting with your birth angel, in short, the following tips will help you to make a connection and communicate with your individual birth guardian angel:

* Ask for a sign. Don't give instructions or tell your angel how you want the sign to appear, simply ask them to offer a clear sign that they have heard you, and one that you can clearly recognise, such as finding a feather, encountering the number 44 (the angels' number), seeing a butterfly or a cloud formation, hearing a song, encountering a bird flying across your path, or seeing a flash of unexplained light around you.

* You can find out your angel's name through meditating for a short time and ask your birth angel his or her name before you go to sleep; you should have an answer when you wake up. Often the first name that pops into your head when you ask will be more or less right. Sometimes you angel will give you special clues. You

might hear a name the following day or read an unusual name that stands out for you somewhere, or you might be introduced to someone with a unique name that just fits. It may take more time than this, but it pays to be ever observant and aware of the ways of the spiritual world.

✯ Angels align with the synchronicity of three, so when something occurs in threes, you can safely rely on the information.

✯ Light a candle in a particular angel's colour (e.g. green for Raphael), or simply light an all-purpose white candle. Meditate by the candle's flame as you gently call your angel in.

✯ Affirm regularly: "*At every turn I am surrounded by my guardian angels and birth angel, who watch over me, protect me, open up the path for my desires, and help me to achieve my life purpose. I am always loved unconditionally and completely accepted as I am. I always receive assistance when and as I need it. I am never alone.*"

✯ Ask for help, surrender, turn it over, relax and trust. Trust that your birth angel is helping you carry your worries, but remember that you must specifically request help, as they will not interfere with your free will. If you specially ask for guidance, the angels are only too happy to provide it, and will even avert negative events or place opportunities in your path to let you know that they are working on your behalf. While it may take some practice or even convincing, asking your angel for help is simple and effective, and is also an exercise in faith. Once you have requested assistance, you can then trust that your angel has heard your message and has taken your concerns or request to the Higher powers for transmutation.

✯ The crystal rutile quartz, otherwise known as 'angel's hair', as well as one of your birthstones, can be used to connect with your birth guardian angel. You can program the crystals for this specific purpose to amazing effect. Rutile quartz is the most abundant mineral on Earth and is a type of titanium ore that occurs with granite, creating fine strands of titanium needles that are embedded within it. When held to the light, these pin-shaped inclusions look multidimensional and golden, hence the name 'angel's hair'. This powerful and enchanting stone can be used to connect with the angelic realms, and its potent amplifiers will release any blocked energies in the etheric and physical bodies, allowing for clearer connection to your angel. Rutile quartz can help usher in angelic care and protection, being linked so closely to the spiritual realms.

✯ To connect with angels, it is helpful to clear the channels through which you can receive, by purifying yourself first: dispel disbelief, discourage too much expectation, rid yourself of negative thoughts, be patient, let go, relax, surrender, and relinquish the need to control.

✯ Once you sense you have made a connection with your birth angel, you may wish to interpret your encounter. The form and content of angelic guidance may often surprise us. Sometimes, the message and encounter may feel too obscure or enigmatic to understand. Accept the first words or pictures that come to you, and in time their significance and meaning will emerge. You can always ask your angel later for clarification of their message. The more open, receptive, loving, and accepting to you are overall, the swifter your connections with your angel/s will be.

✷ Trust that your birth guardian angel will be a saviour who will be there for you at the eleventh hour. He or she will come when you are in grave danger. If fate throws you into the path of disaster and you are in the wrong place at the wrong time, he or she can, by the laws of the cosmos, intervene and save you.

Connecting with angels is easier for some than for others. Bear in mind that some people's minds are relatively receptive to angels, possessing a natural openness that allows them to sense things beyond the physical plane, while others need to train themselves and practice in order to perceive the hidden mysteries of the Universe. The more we can simplify our human frailties and complexities and accept things truly as they are, the more receptive we can become.

There is much that you can do to ensure that you are as open as possible to the presence and the messages of these light beings - indeed, there are as many ways of communicating with angels as there are angels themselves - and since angels are messengers from the spiritual realm, it is the higher, ethereal plane who ultimately chooses how they will appear to us, how their messages are delivered to us, or how we will hear them. All you really need to do is trust in their Divine omnipresence.

YOUR BIRTH ANGEL'S MESSAGE ✷ Your Special Angel wants you to always remind yourself of the following:

"You are a Child of the Universe, no less than the trees and the stars. You are loved. You are eternal. You are the All That Is."

* Are spiritual guides and angels one and the same? This is a common misconception, but an understandable one. The distinction is this: guides are people or animals in the spiritual realms who have lived on Earth, while angels have never had an Earthly experience because they are entirely heavenly, other-worldly, cosmic beings.

∾ ARIES ∾

ARIES'S ELEMENTAL ARCHANGEL ★ MICHAEL

♈

Element of Fire
The southern quarter of the Earth
The Autumn season
The colour red
The astrological signs of Aries, Leo and Sagittarius

Michael, meaning "Who is like God or the Divine," is the leader of all the archangels and is in charge of courage, truth, strength and integrity. He protects us physically, emotionally and psychically. Michael helps us to follow our truth without compromising our integrity and helps us find our true natures, so we can be faithful to who we really are. Michael encourages us to fight for just and noble causes; he gives us the courage and strength to stand up for what is right, especially when persecuted. Overall, Michael is the archangel of protection, peace, safety, clarity, balance, and moving forward. This being works to bring patience and a safeguard against any psychic imbalances or dangers, and if your problem is a very powerful adversary, you can summon his help. Known as the Saint of protection, he is the angelic being who is dedicated to releasing the world from fear. Most images of him show him holding a sword made of fire and light, a powerful symbol of his ability to cut through fear and liberate us from it. In this way, Michael helps us to tear down the old and build the new. If we specially ask for it, he bestows upon us the courage to follow our Truth and live by the light of our Divine purpose. His halo colours are royal purple, royal blue, and gold.

MICHAEL'S MESSAGE FOR ARIES ★ "I am your special being of Divine Light. I offer you, Aries, the Divine gift of courage. You, the powerful Ram, lead others with your aura of supreme leadership and command. Be of sound mind and body, nurture your spirit, and approach your Great Work with both caution and determination, and you will succeed in opening doorways through which ever-greater opportunities can flow in. I will protect you in all your brave crusades and endeavours and endow upon you the strength to carry on when you are feeling depleted or overcome. Affirm to yourself: '*The yearnings and impulses of my soul are signs of my true soul purpose and I listen to them with deep, wild intuition. I deserve to realise my inner and outer dreams effortlessly, with joy, grace and willpower, and I will achieve my wildest ambitions and desires by invoking the assistance of my special angel, Michael.*' I am always here to envelope you with my powerful embrace. All you need to do is call on me and I will be your omnipresent All-Provider."

ARIES'S ZODIAC ARCHANGEL ★ JOPHIEL

Jophiel's name means 'beauty of God'. He is the Angel of creativity, patience and beauty, the bringer of sunshine, wisdom and joy, and is the patron archangel of artists and artistic projects. He carries the flame of intuition, and his blessings include creativity and inspiration. Jophiel is believed to have guarded the Tree of Knowledge in the Garden of Eden, Jophiel is one of the princes of Divine Presence and is said to be a close friend of Metatron. He has a strong interest in beauty and can be called upon by anyone involved in creating beauty in any form. Jophiel helps people who are using their creativity and can be invoked by those who need help with a creative project. Jophiel can be called upon for beautifying and uplifting your thoughts and feelings, as well as clearing clutter out of your life, helping in clearing out clutter from your home, space, or life in general. He also is the dispeller of clouds of doubt and thereby increases self-esteem, courage, vitality and strength.

HALO COLOUR ★ Dark pink
CANDLE COLOUR ★ Gold
CRYSTALS ★ Citrine, rubellite or deep pink tourmaline

Jophiel's Message for Aries ★ *"Please be patient with yourself, because deep down in your heart is the certainly that everything happens at the right time. Allow yourself to pause on your Path of growth in order to radiate peace and beauty, and to simply be."*

OTHER SPECIAL ANGELS FOR ARIES ★ Malahidae, Machidiel (Ariel *), Chamuel & Lamach ^

* Ariel is the Angel of Aries and the month of March and is also known as Machidiel.
^ Lamach is the ruler of the planet Mars

MALAHIDAE ★ Malahidae is known as the angel of courage and is a protective angel who rules over the sign of Aries. He brings the gift of bravery, and inspires blessings, liveliness, optimism, hope, enthusiasm and adventure.

Malahidae's Message for Aries ★ *"Always know that you are the Supreme Courageous One and that you have all the tools at your disposal at all times, to inspire within you the strength, hope and joy that you need to manifest your deepest desires. To access these resources, call on me at any time you need to and I will imbue you with a deep sense of bravery to face any adversities."*

CHAMUEL ★ Chamuel's name means 'he who sees God', and he is the ruler of Mars, the head of the choir of dominions and one of the seven great archangels. He is known as the Angel of self-Love, self-confidence, opening the heart, global peace, and of finding things and places. Chamuel encourages both universal and personal peace and helps you to find whatever it is you are seeking. Because he helps us to locate important components of our lives, he can be called upon to find new love, friendships, careers, or indeed any lost item or 'missing' soul fragments. He can be called upon for any matters involving tolerance, understanding, forgiveness and love. He rights wrongs, soothes troubled minds, and provides justice. You can call on him whenever you need additional strength, or are in conflict with someone else, as he provides courage, persistence and determination. Chamuel is also the relationship balancer and healer, enabling the heart to open and encouraging you to value yourself and realise what you have to offer. Chamuel brings comfort if a relationship is in distress, giving you the gift of insight that you still have much to offer and your love has not been wasted. He can also connect you with your soul mate.

Chamuel's Message for Aries ★ *"Where there is courage, hope is never lost. Trust in the flow and use your innate strength to light the way ahead. I serve to remind you that love is everything, for love is all there is, and everything is born from this power and emanates from its core. With love, the whole Universe is yours."*

ARIES'S INDIVIDUAL BIRTH GUARDIAN ANGELS

This is a personal guardian angel - not necessarily a zodiac essence - that was appointed to you at birth. You can connect with your birth guardian angel through employing many methods. Find one which works for you and know and trust that your angel has heard you and is answering you in any number of ways. Some methods that you can use to communicate with, connect to, and request help from your special guardian have already been outlined in the introduction to this chapter.

Summon your Birth Angel using one of your birthstones and a piece of rutile quartz, lighting a white candle, and by saying the following affirmation: *"My birth angel is by my side throughout my entire life, and never leaves my side. At every turn I am surrounded and embraced by my guardian angel's special energy and loving powers, and he/she watches over me, protects me, guides me, gently directs me towards my most authentic Path, and helps me to achieve my life purpose. I am always loved and completely accepted as I am. I am never alone and receive help in so many different ways, whenever I ask for it."*

★ ★ ★

✥ TAURUS ✥

TAURUS'S ELEMENTAL ARCHANGEL ★ URIEL

♉

Element of Earth
The northern quarter of the Earth
The Summer season
The colours white, burnished gold and all earth tones
The crystals tiger's eye and rutilated quartz
The astrological signs of Taurus, Virgo and Capricorn

Uriel, whose name means 'Fire of God' or 'God is light', is the archangel who brought alchemy * to humankind. He is linked with lightning, thunder and sudden happenings. Uriel may be depicted carrying a scroll that contains revelations about your true path in life. Uriel is dynamic, and his gifts are stamina, action, dynamism and dispelling fears. He is said to be the brightest archangel, a pure pillar of Fire, he can bring warmth to the winter and melt the snows with his flaming sword. Uriel is the archangel of alchemy and vision, overseeing healing, magic, nature and manifestation. This being is known as the tallest of the archangels with eyes that can see into and across eternity. Uriel is often depicted with one bare foot and the other with a shoe, and he carries an olive bough, signifying peace. He is also frequently shown with a thick book of wisdom in his left hand. Uriel oversees the work of all nature spirits - working with Uriel will open you to the fairy kingdoms - and works to assist humanity by awakening to them and working in harmony with them. Inspiring us to work with angels, Devas and higher spiritual essences, to perfect our vision of Divine realms, and to refine our mystical nature by burning away our deep-seated desire for comfort and blind ignorance, Uriel is the gatekeeper to the Garden of Eden, the gates of which we can only pass through once we have mastered the wisdom we are given to find our own path to enlightenment. He also aids with intellectual understanding, conversations, ideas, insights and epiphanies, studying, school, and tests, writing and speaking. Uriel illuminates troublesome situations and helps you to think clearly and find answers to anything that is bothering you. He is the Angel who awakens claircognisance and reveals whichever next step you should take. Stimulating physical desires, call on Uriel if you are feeling desperate, depleted or rejected and he will help to restore your vitality and get you back on your feet. In essence, Uriel is considered the guardian of the emotions, of love and of the heart. Uriel is served by Ghob, King of the Gnomes, seen traditionally as a gnome or goblin who is squat, heavy and dense.

* Alchemy is the sacred art of transmuting base metal into gold by reducing it to the primal black matter and then, by chemico-magical processes, striving to extract and refine spiritual as well as actual gold, the key to finding the way back to Paradise or Source.

URIEL'S MESSAGE FOR TAURUS ★ "I am your special being of Divine Light. I offer you, Taurus, the Divine gifts of emotional healing and unfoldment. You, the powerful manifestor and creator, are in an ever-evolving and unfolding state of creating and deep healing, which enables you to open yourself up to even greater love, beauty and creativity. I will help you to release any anger or deep-seated resentment or hurt from your heart, mind and spirit so that this release may clear your Path for infinite goodness to come into your experience. When love is achieved, all abundance will effortlessly flow into your experience. Affirm to yourself: *'Every time I honour my emotionally powerful inner self, I discover more and more about my true soul purpose. I slowly release pain and anger that block my path towards my authentic destiny which has already gathered together all the resources and energies I am needing and is now just waiting for me to catch up and expand into it. I deserve to realise my inner and outer dreams effortlessly, with joy, grace and my gentle willpower. I will achieve states of vast abundance by invoking the assistance of my special angel, Uriel.'* I am always here to envelope you with my powerful embrace. All you need to do is call on me and I will be your omnipresent All-Provider."

TAURUS'S ZODIAC ARCHANGEL ★ SANDALPHON

Sandalphon's name means 'brother', and like Metatron, he was once a human prophet (Elijah) who ascended into the realm of the Archangels. He, like his twin brother Metatron, is depicted as lofty and majestic, making an imposing figure. He is the Angel of music, voice and serenity. Sandalphon is an androgynous angel, depicted as a beautiful young man. He is concerned with the spirit behind Earthly manifestations and is guardian and protector of the Earth. He specialises in receiving and delivering prayers between the Highest Order of the Universe and humans and provides guidance and support for musicians. He can be called upon for anything relating to music or spiritual confusion. Sandalphon stimulates awareness of the Earth's needs, blessings and gifts. Bringing a sense of grounding, practicality and responsibility, Sandalphon can help you be more aware of your bodily power and assist in treating your physical body as a temple.

HALO COLOUR ★ Turquoise
CANDLE COLOUR ★ Deep green or brown
CRYSTAL ★ Jade, brown jasper or turquoise

Sandalphon's Message for Taurus ★ *"Let the Divine energy of music carry you, inspire you, move you, and radiate from your centre. Sound vibration is supremely healing and as you vibrate to its Divine frequency, its light embraces, supports and envelopes you. As a supreme* *protector of the Earth and its inhabitants, I will also keep you grounded as you wander the ethereal realms in search of your highest Self."*

OTHER SPECIAL ANGELS FOR TAURUS ★ Asmodel, Chamuel, Anael (Haniel) & Ariel

ASMODEL ★ Asmodel is one of the regents of the sign of Taurus and the month of April. He can be invoked in matters involving love and romance. Practicality, persistence, reliablity, peace, patience, and wisdom are other gifts that are bestowed by Asmodel, who some believe is a fallen angel. He is also said to work with fairies and magic.

ANAEL ★ The chief of both the order of principalities and virtues, Anael is also lord of Venus and ruler of the third heaven. He is also known as Haniel. He is the angel of sexuality and creativity, his colour is dark red and he can be invoked using the crystal garnet. He can therefore be invoked for any matters concerning romance, love, affection, sexuality, peace, harmony and inner peace. Anael can also be called upon to overcome shyness, gain confidence, and by those engaged in creative pursuits, and endeavours to create beauty wherever he goes.

Anael's Message for Taurus ★ *"Regularly affirm to yourself: 'I wholeheartedly enjoy the sensual aspects of my body since they link me to my creativity and to the sacred power of kundalini and the ultimate life-force.'"*

ARIEL ★ Ariel is an Angel of trust, courage, manifestation and abundance. Her colour is pink and she can be invoked using the crystal rose quartz. Ariel's name means 'lion or lioness of God' and she is known as the archangel of the Earth, working tirelessly on behalf of the planet. She oversees the elemental kingdom and helps one become better acquainted with the fairies. She also helps in the healing of animals and is mentioned in the Key of Solomon the King. She is believed to help Raphael cure illness in humans, animals, and plants, as well as assisting one in connecting with nature, all creatures, and nature spirits, manifesting one's earthly material needs, and guidance for a career or avocation in environmental or welfare crusades.

Ariel's Message for Taurus ★ *"I bless you with the courage to face your deepest fears because you know that in truth they cannot harm you. With every moment you are trusting more and more and dare to jump into the unknown. In doing so you open yourself up to flowing, infinite channels of abundance and prosperity."*

TAURUS'S INDIVIDUAL BIRTH GUARDIAN ANGELS

This is a personal guardian angel - not necessarily a zodiac essence - that was appointed to you at birth. You can connect with your birth guardian angel through employing many methods. Find one which works for you and know and trust that your angel has heard you and is answering you in any number of ways. Some methods that you can use to communicate with, connect to, and request help from your special guardian have already been outlined in the introduction to this chapter.

Summon your Birth Angel using one of your birthstones and a piece of rutile quartz, lighting a white candle, and by saying the following affirmation: *"My birth angel is by my side throughout my entire life, and never leaves my side. At every turn I am surrounded and embraced by my guardian angel's special energy and loving powers, and he/she watches over me, protects me, guides me, gently directs me towards my most authentic Path, and helps me to achieve my life purpose. I am always loved and completely accepted as I am. I am never alone and receive help in so many different ways, whenever I ask for it."*

✫   ✫   ✫

GEMINI

GEMINI'S ELEMENTAL ARCHANGEL ★ RAPHAEL

♊

Element of Air
The eastern quarter of the Earth
The Spring season
The colour blue (or blue and gold)
The astrological signs of Gemini, Libra and Aquarius

Raphael, meaning 'Healing power of God' or 'The Divine has healed', is the archangel of healing, the young, and safe travels. His eyes penetrate the entire Universe and see all that is wrong; he misses nothing. Raphael is the Divine healer, bringing healing in all its forms to those who need it. He leads the guardian angels, takes care of travellers, supports those in the health professions, and bestows knowledge, wisdom and therapeutic skill. Soothing and calming, he can help you to heal yourself and to feel a connection and oneness with nature. This being works to stimulate energies for overall life and success. Raphael awakens a sense of beauty, wonder and creativity which stimulates higher mental faculties. As the supreme healer in the angelic realm, his chief role is to support, heal and guide in all matters of health, working to soothe people's minds, bodies and spirits so they can enjoy overall peace and wellbeing. He also helps animals and guides Earthly healers and lightworkers in their education and practice. Overall, he is in charge of physical health and wellness. Raphael has as his servant Paralda, King of the Sylphs, who appears to clairvoyant vision as a tenuous form made of blue mist always moving and changing shape. Raphael can be invoked using a caduceus and is regarded as the Keeper of the Holy Grail.

RAPHAEL'S MESSAGE FOR GEMINI ★ "I am your special being of Divine Light. I offer you, Gemini, the Divine gift of mental creativity. You, the powerful Twins, heal others with your aura of supreme child-like wonder and curiosity. I will endow upon you the strength to carry on when you are feeling depleted or overcome. To keep your channels open to my Divine healing, affirm to yourself regularly: *'I am looking after myself well and always take care to get enough sleep, to nourish my body with healthy food, to meditate regularly, and to exercise often. The fitter I am the easier I find it to increase my vibration and have a strong, magnetic and powerful aura. When my magnetism increases, so too does evidence of vast abundance in all areas of my experience. I deserve to realise my inner and outer dreams effortlessly, and I will achieve my wildest dreams and ideals by invoking the assistance of my special angel, Raphael.'* You can summon me using your ruling planet Mercury's symbols, the caduceus, and its gemstone emerald. I am always here to envelope you with my powerful embrace and to assist you in enhancing your innate talents and creativity. All you need to do is call on me and I will be your omnipresent All-Provider."

GEMINI'S ZODIAC ARCHANGEL ★ METATRON

Metatron is the king of the angelic host and angel of the covenant. Once the prophet Enoch, he is the knower of secrets and the transmitter of mysteries between angels and humanity, overseer and keeper of the Akashic records, the books of life of all beings.

Paul Hougham

Metatron, whose name means 'angel of the Presence', is the Angel of the New Age, priorities and focus. He has been called the bright twin to Sandalphon's (preceding sign Taurus's archangel) darkness. He is said to be the supreme angel of death, an enormous being of brilliant hues and light, the most elevated of all angels. Often depicted with a scroll of knowledge in his outstretched hand, his is the light of revelation. Metatron is the supernal teacher of Divine intelligence; whose two specialties are sacred geometry and esoteric healing work. He also specialises in healing with the Universal energies, including time management and 'time warping'. Metatron assists highly sensitive people, especially young ones who are sometimes referred to as 'Indigos' or 'Crystals', as well as both living and crossed-over children. The tallest and youngest of the archangels, Metatron is thought to be one of the two angels who once walked upon the Earth as a human (as the prophet Enoch) and then ascended into Heaven and was transformed into the Angel of Fire, with thirty-six wings. In the Kabbalah, he is the chief angel of the Tree of Life, where he guides humans at the beginning of their spiritual journey. Versatile and bestowing the gift of spiritual illumination to those who are receptive, Metatron may blind those who are not ready to receive this blessing, so he must be approached with an open mind and heart. He enables you to de-clutter your life, so you are able to move forward and be freer to develop.

HALO COLOUR ★ Violet and green
CANDLE COLOUR ★ White
CRYSTALS ★ Herkimer diamond or watermelon tourmaline

Metatron's Message for Gemini ★ *"You are supremely and Divinely always aware of your natural gifts and share them at every opportunity possible. Your natural light shines through and illuminates others. Call upon me as your Tower of Inspirational Fire, to serve as your Divine Spark."*

OTHER SPECIAL ANGELS FOR GEMINI ★ Ambriel & Zadkiel

AMBRIEL ★ Ambriel is the ruling angel of Gemini and the month of May. He can be invoked for any matters involving communication. He also assists people who are seeking new jobs or searching for more opportunities and responsibility.

Ambriel's Message for Gemini ★ *"Opportunities knock all the time at your door, Gemini, but you need to actually answer the door to allow them in. To invite them into your life, you have to be ever alert to all the possibilities that are ever-present in your experience. Look out for signs of my presence, and once you begin to notice them, I will bless you with more and more opportunities designed to enhance your growth and overall success."*

ZADKIEL ★ Zadkiel is known as the Angel of Divine justice, mercy, compassion and forgiveness. Zadkiel's name means 'righteousness of God' and he helps one to remember things. Because of his association with Jupiter, Zadkiel also bestows abundance, benevolence, tolerance, prosperity, happiness, and good fortune. He can be invoked for help with legal or financial problems. Zadkiel teaches us to trust in the Universe. Labelled 'the holy one', he brings mercy, compassion, and kindness and aids meditation, brings psychic protection and boosts the immune system. He advocates teaching, the learning of new ideas, and helps students remember facts and figures for tests. As a Divine healer of painful memories, Zadkiel removes emotions and obstacles that are holding you back, so that you are able to see the bigger picture. He also assists you in remembering your Divine spiritual origin and missions, and in choosing the healing path of forgiveness.

Zadkiel's Message for Gemini ★ *"Affirmation: I forgive because it sets me free and heals myself as well as others. When I forgive, I unlock the chains that bind me, and in doing so, I have opened up the channels for vast abundance to fill up any space created by this loving act of release, acceptance and flow."*

GEMINI'S INDIVIDUAL BIRTH GUARDIAN ANGELS

This is a personal guardian angel - not necessarily a zodiac essence - that was appointed to you at birth. You can connect with your birth guardian angel through employing many methods. Find one which works for you and know and trust that your angel has heard you and is answering you in any number of ways. Some methods that you can use to communicate with, connect to, and request help from your special guardian have already been outlined in the introduction to this chapter.

Summon your Birth Angel using one of your birthstones and a piece of rutile quartz, lighting a white candle, and by saying the following affirmation: *"My birth angel is by my side throughout my entire life, and never leaves my side. At every turn I am surrounded and embraced by my guardian angel's special energy and loving powers, and he/she watches over me, protects me, guides me, gently directs me towards my most authentic Path, and helps me to achieve my life purpose. I am always loved and completely accepted as I am. I am never alone and receive help in so many different ways, whenever I ask for it."*

★ ★ ★

～ CANCER ～

CANCER'S ELEMENTAL ARCHANGEL ★ GABRIEL

♋

Element of Water
The Western quarter of the Earth
The Winter season
The colours emerald, silver and sea green
The crystals opal, fluorite and moonstone
The astrological signs of Cancer, Scorpio and Pisces

Gabriel, meaning "Strength of God" or "The Divine is my strength," is known as the messenger and can help us to find our true soul's purpose. As archangel of the Moon and ruler of dreams, Gabriel is chief archangel of the night and the alter ego of Michael, the Sun archangel. Some consider Gabriel a feminine energy. The archangel of life, hope, truth, astral travel, unconscious wisdom, illumination and love, he inspires and motivates artists and communicators, and delivers important prophetic messages to people. Gabriel is the Divine messenger angel of all Earthly messengers such as journalists, teachers and writers, and as such delivers important and clear messages, as well as helping those who are Earthly messengers, such as teachers, writers, actors and artists. Gabriel guards the sacred places of the world and the sacred waters of life. He provides intuitive teaching, guidance, mystical experiences, inspiration and enlightenment of spiritual duties, including awakening within us a greater understanding of dreams and connection to our inner child. He can be called upon when you are feeling alone, afraid or vulnerable. Gabriel is said to be the angel who chooses the souls to be born and cares for them in the womb. He assists with all aspects of parenting, including conception, adoption, birth, and early childhood. Gabriel is also an angel of death, but a gentle one, bringing release from sorrow and pain. Gabriel's servant is Nicksa, King of the Undines, who is seen as an ever-changing shape, fluid with a greenish blue aura splashed with silver and grey. His halo colour is copper, as is his special mineral.

GABRIEL'S MESSAGE FOR CANCER ★ "I am your special being of Divine Light. I offer you, Cancer, the Divine gifts of empathy, illumination, and deep emotional healing. You, the powerful celestial Crab, nurture and support others with your glowing aura of supreme vulnerability and loving attention. I will protect you in all of your emotional crusades and endeavours and endow upon you the strength to carry on when you are feeling depleted or overcome, as well as to face your deepest insecurities and any fears which may plague you. Keep reminding yourself: you are a Child of the Universe, no less than the trees and the stars. If you call upon me, I will provide you with hope and release from past traumas. Affirm to yourself: '*I listen to my inner child and recognise and honour his or her needs. In doing this I* *recognise how I may heal with grace, lightness, creativity, pure love and joy. The yearnings and expressions of my inner child offer me Divine clues and signs of my true soul purpose in life. I need only to tap into his or her power and bring him or her to the surface for expression, healing and ascendance. I will achieve all my goals by invoking the assistance of my special angel, Gabriel.'*. I am always here to envelope you with my powerful embrace. All you need to do is call on me and I will be your omnipresent All-Provider."

CANCER'S ZODIAC ARCHANGEL ★ GABRIEL

Please see previous information under the heading *'Archangel Gabriel's Associations'*.

CANDLE COLOUR ★ Orange-gold
CRYSTALS ★ Moonstone or beryl

OTHER SPECIAL ANGELS FOR CANCER ★ Muriel, Haniel & Sandalphon

MURIEL ★ One of the regents of the choir of dominions, Muriel is responsible for the sign of Cancer and looks after the month of June. Muriel can teach us that helping others is the surest way to happiness, and her angelic responsibilities are to tend to the plants and animals of the Earth. She governs over empaths and helps to restore and maintain peace and harmony. Muriel can be summoned whenever your emotions need to be kept under control.

Muriel's Message for Cancer ★ *"I shower my unconditional love and compassion upon you at all times, Cancer, for you are the precious Ones that I oversee. Call upon me when you are needing emotional support and help for those times that you may fall. As your special angel, I never allow you to fall all the way, for I will always pick you up before you hit rock bottom. I am here, and you are loved with a deep understanding. You may sense me when you smell something fragrant that evokes a beautiful memory, for my name means 'God's perfume'. Be ever alert to your senses and you will pick up on my presence."*

HANIEL ★ Haniel's name means 'grace of God'. Otherwise known as Anael, he is the Angel of grace, femininity, sensitivity, Moon energies and intuition. Haniel is a protective angel, bringing determination and the energy to understand your life's mission and true purpose. Call upon this angel whenever you wish to add grace, beauty, harmony, serenity and pleasure to your life or to a situation. Awakening and trusting your spiritual gifts of intuition and clairvoyance; releasing the old; support and healing for women's physical and emotional issues. In the female form, this archangel has a loving, nurturing, motherly presence and helps us to honour our natural cycles. Archangel Haniel can assist you with communication, soothes panic, and helps you to overcome deeply ingrained negativity and to receive communication from the higher planes. Haniel's gift is the development of pure individuality, independent of the expectations and pressures of others.

HALO COLOUR ★ Pale blue
CANDLE COLOUR ★ Turquoise
CRYSTALS ★ Turquoise or moonstone

Haniel's Message for Cancer ★ *"Affirm to yourself: 'It is safe for me to see. I am clairvoyant to a high degree and I am the master of this skill. What I envision and what is my rightful path begin to merge when I accept and live through this natural gift and share it with others. I am tuned in to my Third Eye and attuned to the Divine channels of the entire Universe, which bestow upon me the vast abundance I so desire so that I may then experience and share infinitely more and more."*

SANDALPHON ★ Sandalphon's name means 'brother', and like Metatron, he was once a human prophet (Elijah) who ascended into the realm of the Archangels. He is the Angel of music, voice and serenity. Sandalphon is an androgynous angel, depicted as a beautiful young man. He is concerned with the spirit behind Earthly manifestations and is guardian and protector of the Earth. He specialises in receiving and delivering prayers between the Highest Order of the Universe and humans and provides guidance and support for musicians. He can be called upon for anything relating to music or spiritual confusion. Sandalphon stimulates awareness of the Earth's needs, blessings and gifts. Bringing a sense of grounding, practicality and responsibility, Sandalphon can help you be more aware of your bodily power and assist in treating your physical body as a temple.

HALO COLOUR ★ Turquoise
CANDLE COLOUR ★ Deep green or brown
CRYSTALS ★ Jade, brown jasper or turquoise

Sandalphon's Message for Cancer ★ *"Cancer, as a ruling angel and supreme protector of the Earth and its inhabitants, I offer my protection, support and guidance to you when you are seeking spiritual clarity about your life's Path. As a Master of Music, I can help you to heal and discover through sound and mantras * as you seek this Path: Let the Divine energy of music and mantras calm you, inspire you and bring you to a place of deep serenity and spiritual knowing. Sound vibration is supremely healing and with my Divine guidance, you can vibrate and resonate to its deep frequency; its light embraces, envelopes, and moves you closer to that Divine self who resides inside of you."*

* Mantras are sounds or words that are repeated to aid concentration in meditation. These sacred syllables, when charged with the spiritual attention of an enlightened being, have the power to attract the attention to the point where it can contact the Light and Sound that pervade the Universe.

CANCER'S INDIVIDUAL BIRTH GUARDIAN ANGELS

This is a personal guardian angel - not necessarily a zodiac essence - that was appointed to you at birth. You can connect with your birth guardian angel through employing many methods. Find one which works for you and know and trust that your angel has heard you and is answering you in any number of ways. Some methods that you can use to communicate with, connect to, and request help from your special guardian have already been outlined in the introduction to this chapter.

Summon your Birth Angel using one of your birthstones and a piece of rutile quartz, lighting a white candle, and by saying the following affirmation: *"My birth angel is by my side throughout my entire life, and never leaves my side. At every turn I am surrounded and embraced by my guardian angel's special energy and loving powers, and he/she watches over me, protects me, guides me, gently directs me towards my most authentic Path, and helps me to achieve my life purpose. I am always loved and completely accepted as I am. I am never alone and receive help in so many different ways, whenever I ask for it."*

☙ LEO ☙

LEO'S ELEMENTAL ARCHANGEL ★ MICHAEL

♌

Element of Fire
The southern quarter of the Earth
The Autumn season
The colour red
The astrological signs of Aries, Leo and Sagittarius

Michael, meaning "Who is like God or the Divine," is the leader of all the archangels and is in charge of courage, truth, strength and integrity. He protects us physically, emotionally and psychically. Michael helps us to follow our truth without compromising our integrity and helps us find our true natures, so we can be faithful to who we really are. Michael encourages us to fight for just and noble causes; he gives us the courage and strength to stand up for what is right, especially when persecuted. Overall, Michael is the archangel of protection, peace, safety, clarity, balance, and moving forward. This being works to bring patience and a safeguard against any psychic imbalances or dangers, and if your problem is a very powerful adversary, you can summon his help. Known as the Saint of protection, he is the angelic being who is dedicated to releasing the world from fear. Most images of him show him holding a sword made of fire and light, a powerful symbol of his ability to cut through fear and liberate us from it. In this way, Michael helps us to tear down the old and build the new. If we specially ask for it, he bestows upon us the courage to follow our Truth and live by the light of our Divine purpose. His halo colours are royal purple, royal blue, and gold.

MICHAEL'S MESSAGE FOR LEO ★ "I am your special being of Divine Light. I offer you, Leo, the Divine gift of strength. You, the powerful Lion, have the courage to carry others with your glowing aura of supreme confidence and unwavering loyalty. I will protect you in all of your mighty crusades and endeavours and endow upon you the courage to carry on when you are feeling depleted or overcome. Affirm to yourself regularly: *'The aspirations and longings of my soul are way-showers of my true soul purpose. I deserve to realise my inner and outer dreams effortlessly, with joy, enthusiasm, and willpower, and I will achieve my wildest ambitions and dreams by invoking the assistance of my special angel, Michael.'* I am always here to envelope you with my powerful embrace. All you need to do is call on me and I will be your omnipresent All-Provider."

LEO'S ZODIAC ARCHANGELS ★ MICHAEL * & RAZIEL

* Please see previous information under the heading '*Archangel Michael's Associations*'.

RAZIEL ★ Raziel means 'secret of God' and he is the keeper of secrets and lord of the mysteries of life. He is said to stand very near to God, thus hearing all Divine conversations about Universal secrets and mysteries. Thus, he is the Angel of spiritual secrets and the Akashic Chronicle. He awakens the spirit so that it can comprehend things which cannot be understood by the intellect. Raziel has a special understanding the secrets of the Universe and assists with remembering and healing from our past lives and understanding esoteric wisdom. Raziel can be called upon whenever we wish to understand esoteric material, or to partake in alchemy, past-life or manifestation work. The insights of Raziel run deep and can be life-changing and difficult to express or explain to others, but ultimately these insights can bring about profound transformation. Raziel's gifts include self-awareness, release of obsessions, inner peace and harmony, and the clearing away of mental chatter to make way for true knowing. He can help original thinkers develop their ideas and can be contacted whenever you need answers to imponderable questions.

HALO COLOUR ★ Rainbow colours
CANDLE COLOUR ★ Bright yellow, sapphire blue
CRYSTALS ★ Amber, topaz, sapphire, clear quartz or mountain crystal

Raziel's Message for Leo ★ *"I deliver to you messages of magic, insight, spirit and mystery, in many forms, but it is up to you to recognise my messages and to de-code them yourself. Through my guidance and overseeing of you, Leo, you are gently led into profound understandings of your life's purpose and learning that is needed for your highest spiritual unfoldment. I will unravel your mysteries and secrets, if you wish me to. Listen to my answers, which I will leave a subtle trail of everywhere around you. They shall come to you in the forms of symbols, signs, omens and words. If you can successfully decipher them, all will be well."*

OTHER SPECIAL ANGELS FOR LEO ★ Verchiel

VERCHIEL ★ Verchiel rules over the sign of Leo and the month of July, and brings the gift of nobility, learning and a generous spirit. He is also the governor of Leo's ruler the Sun and provides the gift of clarity to those who can express gratitude for their treasures. He is known as the angel of affection. Verchiel bestows happiness, replenishes energy, and encourages play.

Verchiel's Message for Leo ★ *"I help you open up to and remain open to all opportunities to be generous to yourself and others. If you are thankful for all the blessings that grace your life, such as shelter, nourishing food and any money you give and receive, I will provide even more of those things! My guidance helps you to be accepting, affectionate, loving, joyful, and vital so that you may fulfill your Divine task of spreading generosity."*

LEO'S INDIVIDUAL BIRTH GUARDIAN ANGELS

This is a personal guardian angel - not necessarily a zodiac essence - that was appointed to you at birth. You can connect with your birth guardian angel through employing many methods. Find one which works for you and know and trust that your angel has heard you and is answering you in any number of ways. Some methods that you can use to communicate with, connect to, and request help from your special guardian have already been outlined in the introduction to this chapter.

Summon your Birth Angel using one of your birthstones and a piece of rutile quartz, lighting a white candle, and by saying the following affirmation: *"My birth angel is by my side throughout my entire life, and never leaves my side. At every turn I am surrounded and embraced by my guardian angel's special energy and loving powers, and he/she watches over me, protects me, guides me, gently directs me towards my most authentic Path, and helps me to achieve my life purpose. I am always loved and completely accepted as I am. I am never alone and receive help in so many different ways, whenever I ask for it."*

☆ ☆ ☆

༃ VIRGO ༃

VIRGO'S ELEMENTAL ARCHANGEL ★ URIEL

♍

Element of Earth
The northern quarter of the Earth
The Summer season
The colours white, burnished gold and all earth tones
The crystals tiger's eye and rutilated quartz
The astrological signs of Taurus, Virgo and Capricorn

Uriel, whose name means 'Fire of God' or 'God is light', is the archangel who brought alchemy * to humankind. He is linked with lightning, thunder and sudden happenings. Uriel may be depicted carrying a scroll that contains revelations about your true path in life. Uriel is dynamic, and his gifts are stamina, action, dynamism and dispelling fears. He is said to be the brightest archangel, a pure pillar of Fire, he can bring warmth to the winter and melt the snows with his flaming sword. Uriel is the archangel of alchemy and vision, overseeing healing, magic, nature and manifestation. This being is known as the tallest of the archangels with eyes that can see into and across eternity. Uriel is often depicted with one bare foot and the other with a shoe, and he carries an olive bough, signifying peace. He is also frequently shown with a thick book of wisdom in his left hand. Uriel oversees the work of all nature spirits - working with Uriel will open you to the fairy kingdoms - and works to assist humanity by awakening to them and working in harmony with them. Inspiring us to work with angels, Devas and higher spiritual essences, to perfect our vision of Divine realms, and to refine our mystical nature by burning away our deep-seated desire for comfort and blind ignorance, Uriel is the gatekeeper to the Garden of Eden, the gates of which we can only pass through once we have mastered the wisdom we are given to find our own path to enlightenment. He also aids with intellectual understanding, conversations, ideas, insights and epiphanies, studying, school, and tests, writing and speaking. Uriel illuminates troublesome situations and helps you to think clearly and find answers to anything that is bothering you. He is the Angel who awakens claircognisance and reveals whichever next step you should take. Stimulating physical desires, call on Uriel if you are feeling desperate, rundown or rejected and he will help to restore your vitality and get you back on your feet. In essence, Uriel is considered the guardian of the emotions, of love and of the heart. Uriel is served by Ghob, King of the Gnomes, seen traditionally as a gnome or goblin who is squat, heavy and dense.

* Alchemy is the sacred art of transmuting base metal into gold by reducing it to the primal black matter and then, by chemico-magical processes, striving to extract and refine spiritual as well as actual gold, the key to finding the way back to Paradise or Source.

URIEL'S MESSAGE FOR VIRGO ★ "I am your special being of Divine Light. I offer you, Virgo, the Divine gift of clarity. You, the beautiful celestial Maiden, have the wisdom, mental direction and discernment to create the life of your dreams. I will provide you with the insights, epiphanies and revelations that you need in order to get back to your true authentic Path, if you will just call on me to do so. Your mind is of supreme stock, and I will lovingly protect it on your behalf, in all of your creative crusades, learning, teaching and overall endeavours, and endow upon you the grace to carry on when you are feeling depleted or overcome. Affirm to yourself regularly: *'I receive the exact knowledge that I need at any given time in order to realise my soul's highest purpose and potential. Through recognising the signs, symbols, and wisdom inherent in my everyday experiences, I am shown the way towards achieving my long-held dreams and goals. I can speed this process up at any time by invoking the assistance of my special angel, Uriel'.* I am always here to envelope you with my powerful embrace. All you need to do is call on me and I will be your omnipresent All-Provider."

VIRGO'S ZODIAC ARCHANGEL ★ RAPHAEL

Raphael is the Divine healer, bringing healing in all its forms to those who need it. He leads the guardian angels, takes care of travellers, supports those in the healing professions, and bestows knowledge, wisdom and therapeutic skill. Soothing and calming, he can help you to heal yourself and to feel a connection and oneness with nature. Raphael can be invoked using a caduceus.

HALO COLOUR ★ Emerald green
CANDLE COLOUR ★ Vibrant green
CRYSTALS ★ Emerald or green tourmaline

Raphael's Message for Virgo ★ *"I offer you the gift of Divine self-healing. Use my presence and energy to heal and bless both yourself and others and know that your natural kindness is itself an act of profound healing. Your emotions are your greatest teacher, and if you can learn to live from your heart instead of your intellect, you will find great peace, power, contentment and self-mastery. Remember, your happiness is your gift to the world. Protect it, nurture it, love it. Healing yourself first and foremost will ultimately set you free."*

OTHER SPECIAL ANGELS FOR VIRGO ★ Hamaliel & Metatron

HAMALIEL ★ One of the rulers of August and the sign of Virgo, Hamaliel can be invoked for any matters involving logic and attention to detail.

Hamaliel's Message for Virgo ★ *"In a world that largely focuses on extroversion and squeaky wheels that get the oil, I help open up the channels for you to receive the rewards you are entitled to through the use of your gentle, inner workings that extend outward to help others. I gently nudge others to recognise your talents, especially at times when you are not confident enough to blow your own trumpet. Virgo, I offer you the self-confidence, fortitude and discrimination to carry out your plans to live the life of your dreams. Your clever discernment and profound wisdom does not go unnoticed."*

METATRON ★ Metatron, whose name means 'angel of the Presence', is the Angel of the New Age, priorities and focus. He has been called the bright twin to Sandalphon's darkness. He is said to be the supreme angel of death, an enormous being of brilliant hues and light, the most elevated of all angels. Often depicted with a scroll of knowledge in his outstretched hand, his is the light of revelation. Metatron is the supernal teacher of Divine intelligence; whose two specialties are sacred geometry and esoteric healing work. He also specialises in healing with the Universal energies, including time management and 'time warping'. Metatron assists highly sensitive people. In the Kabbalah, he is the chief angel of the Tree of Life, where he guides humans at the beginning of their spiritual journey. Versatile and bestowing the gift of spiritual illumination to those who are receptive, Metatron may blind those who are not ready to receive this blessing, so he must be approached with an open mind and heart. He enables you to de-clutter your life so you are able to move forward and be freer to develop.

Metatron's Message for Virgo ★ *"If you are ready to begin your spiritual journey of Divine ascension, I am here to guide you to that place. If you are already advanced along the Path, I protect and embrace you as you learn. Once you have reached the greatest heights and depths of your spiritual evolution, I will stand by you eternally as you continue to illuminate others with your healing light. At all times, you can call upon me as your Tower of Inspirational Fire, and I will serve as your Divine Spark."*

VIRGO'S INDIVIDUAL BIRTH GUARDIAN ANGELS

This is a personal guardian angel - not necessarily a zodiac essence - that was appointed to you at birth. You can connect with your birth guardian angel through employing many methods. Find one which works for you and know and trust that your angel has heard you and is answering you in any number of ways. Some methods that you can use to communicate with, connect to, and request help from your special guardian have already been outlined in the introduction to this chapter.

Summon your Birth Angel using one of your birthstones and a piece of rutile quartz, lighting a white candle, and by saying the following affirmation: *"My birth angel is by my side throughout my entire life, and never leaves my side. At every turn I am surrounded and embraced by my guardian angel's special energy and loving powers, and he/she watches over me, protects me, guides me, gently directs me towards my most authentic Path, and helps me to achieve my life purpose. I am always loved and completely accepted as I am. I am never alone and receive help in so many different ways, whenever I ask for it."*

★   ★   ★

☙ LIBRA ❧

LIBRA'S ELEMENTAL ARCHANGEL ★ RAPHAEL

♎

Element of Air
The eastern quarter of the Earth
The Spring season
The colour blue (or blue and gold)
The astrological signs of Gemini, Libra and Aquarius

Raphael, meaning 'Healing power of God' or 'The Divine has healed', is the archangel of healing, the young, and safe travels. His eyes penetrate the entire Universe and see all that is wrong; he misses nothing. Raphael is the Divine healer, bringing healing in all its forms to those who need it. He leads the guardian angels, takes care of travellers, supports those in the health professions, and bestows knowledge, wisdom and therapeutic skill. Soothing and calming, he can help you to heal yourself and to feel a connection and oneness with nature. This being works to stimulate energies for overall life and success. Raphael awakens a sense of beauty, wonder and creativity which stimulates higher mental faculties. As the supreme healer in the angelic realm, his chief role is to support, heal and guide in all matters of health, working to soothe people's minds, bodies and spirits so they can enjoy overall peace and well-being. He also helps animals and guides Earthly healers and lightworkers in their education and practice. Overall, he is in charge of physical health and wellness. Raphael has as his servant Paralda, King of the Sylphs, who appears to clairvoyant vision as a tenuous form made of blue mist always moving and changing shape. Raphael can be invoked using a caduceus and is regarded as the Keeper of the Holy Grail.

RAPHAEL'S MESSAGE FOR LIBRA ★ "I am your special being of Divine Light. I offer you, Libra, the Divine gift of grace through healing. You, the beautiful set of finely balanced celestial Scales, have the courage to carry others with your glowing aura of supreme elegance, sociability and eloquence. I will protect you in all of your quests for beauty, peace and healing of yourself and others. I will endow upon you the wisdom to carry on when you are feeling depleted or overcome. Affirm to yourself: *'Admiring beauty and surrounding myself with aesthetically pleasing things, is a self-healing act of deep courage. Libra is the sustaining, nourishing, quintessential lover of all things beautiful and pleasant, and in embracing the luxuries of life, I am consciously choosing a Path of love and harmony, which lead to serenity and bliss that I can pass on to others. To choose unlimited abundance for myself in the form of beautiful things, people and surroundings, is a profound act of courage and healing. I can call upon Archangel Raphael at any time to provide me with Divine assistance on this quest.'* I am always here to envelope you with my loving embrace. All you need to do is call on me and I will be your omnipresent All-Provider."

LIBRA'S ZODIAC ARCHANGELS ★ CHAMUEL & JOPHIEL

CHAMUEL ★ Chamuel's name means 'he who sees God', and he is the ruler of Mars, the head of the choir of dominions and one of the seven great archangels. He is known as the Angel of self-Love, self-confidence, opening the heart, global peace, and of finding things and places. Chamuel encourages both universal and personal peace and helps you to find whatever it is you are seeking. Because he helps us to locate important components of our lives, he can be called upon to find new love, friendships, careers, or indeed any lost item or 'missing' soul fragments. He can be called upon for any matters involving tolerance, understanding, forgiveness and love. He rights wrongs, soothes troubled minds, and provides justice. You can call on him whenever you need additional strength, or are in conflict with someone else, as he provides courage, persistence and determination. Chamuel is also the relationship balancer and healer, enabling the heart to open and encouraging you to value yourself and realise what you have to offer. Chamuel brings comfort if a relationship is in distress, giving you the gift of insight that you still have much to offer and your love has not been wasted. He can also connect you with your soul mate.

HALO COLOUR ★ Pale green
CANDLE COLOUR ★ Soft pink
CRYSTALS ★ Rose quartz or fluorite

Chamuel's Message for Libra ★ *"I serve to remind you that love is everything, for love is all there is, and everything is born from this power and emanates from its core. With love, the whole Universe is yours."*

JOPHIEL ★ Jophiel's name means 'beauty of God'. He is the bringer of sunshine, wisdom and joy. He carries the flame of intuition, and his blessings include creativity and inspiration. He is the dispeller of clouds of doubt and thereby increases self-esteem, courage, vitality and strength.

CANDLE COLOUR ★ Gold
CRYSTAL ★ Citrine

OTHER SPECIAL ANGELS FOR LIBRA ★ Uriel, Haniel, Zuriel & Anael (Haniel)

URIEL ★ Uriel, whose name means 'Fire of God' or 'God is light', is the archangel who brought alchemy * to humankind. He is linked with lightning, thunder and sudden happenings. Uriel may be depicted carrying a scroll that contains revelations about your true path in life. Uriel is dynamic, and his gifts are stamina, action, dynamism and dispelling fears. He is said to be the brightest archangel, a pure pillar of Fire, he can bring warmth to the winter and melt the snows with his flaming sword. Uriel is the archangel of alchemy and vision, overseeing healing, magic, nature and manifestation. This being is known as the tallest of the archangels with eyes that can see into and across eternity. Uriel is often depicted with one bare foot and the other with a shoe, and he carries an olive bough, signifying peace. He is also frequently shown with a thick book of wisdom in his left hand. Uriel oversees the work of all nature spirits - working with Uriel will open you to the fairy kingdoms - and works to assist humanity by awakening to them and working in harmony with them. Inspiring us to work with angels, Devas and higher spiritual essences, to perfect our vision of Divine realms, and to refine our mystical nature by burning away our deep-seated desire for comfort and blind ignorance, Uriel is the gatekeeper to the Garden of Eden, the gates of which we can only pass through once we have mastered the wisdom we are given to find our own path to enlightenment. He also aids with intellectual understanding, conversations, ideas, insights and epiphanies, studying, school, and tests, writing and speaking. Uriel illuminates troublesome situations and helps you to think clearly and find answers to anything that is bothering you. He is the Angel who awakens claircognisance and reveals whichever next step you should take. Stimulating physical desires, call on Uriel if you are feeling desperate, depleted or rejected and he will help to restore your vitality and get you back on your feet. In essence, Uriel is considered the guardian of the emotions, of love and of the heart.

Uriel's Message for Libra ★ *"Using my powers and blessings, open your heart to others and refuse to ever close. Yours is energy of the heart, and you possess a unique mastery over all romantic and relationship matters, provided your centre is open and flowing. Know that love is the answer to and healer of everything. Trust its inherent wisdom and connect with others through its power. 'Do not feel lonely. The entire Universe is inside you', counselled Rumi, a fellow Libran. Affirm this to yourself regularly."*

ANAEL ★ Also known as Haniel, Anael is the chief of both the order of principalities and virtues. Anael is also lord of Venus and ruler of the third heaven. He is the angel of sexuality and creativity, his colour is dark red and he can be invoked using the crystal garnet. He can therefore be invoked for any matters concerning romance, love, affection, sexuality, peace, harmony and inner peace. He can also be called upon to overcome shyness, gain confidence, and by those engaged in creative pursuits, and endeavours to create beauty wherever he goes.

Anael's Message for Libra ★ *"Libra, you need to regularly affirm to yourself: 'I wholeheartedly enjoy the sensual aspects of my body since they link me to my creativity and to the sacred power of kundalini and the ultimate life-force. I am connected and plugged in to my creative powers at all times.'"*

LIBRA'S INDIVIDUAL BIRTH GUARDIAN ANGELS

This is a personal guardian angel - not necessarily a zodiac essence - that was appointed to you at birth. You can connect with your birth guardian angel through employing many methods. Find one which works for you and know and trust that your angel has heard you and is answering you in any number of ways. Some methods that you can use to communicate with, connect to, and request help from your special guardian have already been outlined in the introduction to this chapter.

Summon your Birth Angel using one of your birthstones and a piece of rutile quartz, lighting a white candle, and by saying the following affirmation: *"My birth angel is by my side throughout my entire life, and never leaves my side. At every turn I am surrounded and embraced by my guardian angel's special energy and loving powers, and he/she watches over me, protects me, guides me, gently directs me towards my most authentic Path, and helps me to achieve my life purpose. I am always loved and completely accepted as I am. I am never alone and receive help in so many different ways, whenever I ask for it."*

★ ★ ★

～ SCORPIO ～

SCORPIO'S ELEMENTAL ARCHANGEL ★ GABRIEL

♏

Element of Water
The Western quarter of the Earth
The Winter season
The colours emerald, silver and sea green
The crystals opal, fluorite and moonstone
The astrological signs of Cancer, Scorpio and Pisces

Gabriel, meaning "Strength of God" or "The Divine is my strength," is known as the messenger and can help us to find our true soul's purpose. As archangel of the Moon and ruler of dreams, Gabriel is chief archangel of the night and the alter ego of Michael, the Sun archangel. Some consider Gabriel a feminine energy. The archangel of life, hope, truth, astral travel, unconscious wisdom, illumination and love, he inspires and motivates artists and communicators, and delivers important prophetic messages to people. Gabriel is the Divine messenger angel of all Earthly messengers such as journalists, teachers and writers, and as such delivers important and clear messages, as well as helping those who are Earthly messengers, such as teachers, writers, actors and artists. Gabriel guards the sacred places of the world and the sacred waters of life. He provides intuitive teaching, guidance, mystical experiences, inspiration and enlightenment of spiritual duties, including awakening within us a greater understanding of dreams and connection to our inner child. He can be called upon when you are feeling alone, afraid or vulnerable. Gabriel is said to be the angel who chooses the souls to be born and cares for them in the womb. He assists with all aspects of parenting, including conception, adoption, birth, and early childhood. Gabriel is also an angel of death, but a gentle one, bringing release from sorrow and pain. Gabriel's servant is Nicksa, King of the Undines, who is seen as an ever-changing shape, fluid with a greenish blue aura splashed with silver and grey. His halo colour is copper, as is his special mineral.

GABRIEL'S MESSAGE FOR SCORPIO ★ "I am your special being of Divine Light. I offer you, Scorpio, the Divine gifts of prophecy, transformation and rebirth through living your Truth. You, the powerful Scorpion, have the courage to confront your unconscious self and to bring it to the surface for profound emotional healing - of yourself and others. Each time you bring an aspect of your shadow side to the light, you are being born anew and illuminated. This allows you to better use your gifts of prophecy and innate insight to assist others on their journeys also. I will protect you in all of your transformative crusades of the spirit, which you conduct with unequalled willpower, courage and conviction. I will open up the channels of your emotional strength to enable you to carry on when you are feeling depleted or overcome. Affirm to yourself: '*I have an important life purpose involving communication through prophecy and the creative arts. My insecurities will not hold me back, for my fears are unfounded. By facing my shadowy self, I overcome all inner blocks to being the emotionally charged creator that I am.*' I am always here to envelope you with my powerfully loving embrace. All you need to do is call on me and I will be your omnipresent All-Provider."

SCORPIO'S ZODIAC ARCHANGELS ★ RAZIEL & JEREMIEL

RAZIEL ★ Raziel means 'secret of God' and he is the keeper of secrets and lord of the mysteries of life. He is said to stand very near to God, thus hearing all Divine conversations about Universal secrets and mysteries. Thus, he is the Angel of spiritual secrets and the Akashic Chronicle. He awakens the spirit so that it can comprehend things which cannot be understood by the intellect. Raziel has a special understanding the secrets of the Universe and assists with remembering and healing from our past lives and understanding esoteric wisdom. Raziel can be called upon whenever we wish to understand esoteric material, or to partake in alchemy, past-life or manifestation work. The insights of Raziel run deep and can be life-changing and difficult to express or explain to others, but ultimately these insights can bring about profound transformation. Raziel's gifts include self-awareness, release of obsessions, inner peace and harmony, and the clearing away of mental chatter to make way for true knowing. He can help original thinkers develop their ideas and can be contacted whenever you need answers to imponderable questions.

HALO COLOUR ★ Rainbow colours
CANDLE COLOUR ★ Bright yellow, sapphire blue
CRYSTALS ★ Amber, topaz, sapphire, clear quartz or mountain crystal

Raziel's Message for Scorpio ★ "*With my help, your traumas and karmic blockages are gradually dissolving within the shortest possible amount of time, in a way that is gentle and comfortable for you. Once the Path is cleared of the emotional clutter that has blocked it for so long, you can then ascend to the level of accessing the realm of the Akashic Records of your life. Your Divine purpose is awaiting you to discover it.*"

JEREMIEL ★ Jeremiel's name means 'Mercy of God', and he is the archangel of truth, who goes into shadows seeking to unravel the mysteries. He is also the angel of overcoming difficulties and letting go of attachments to the past. Jeremiel assists with developing and understanding spiritual visions and clairvoyance and helps you to conduct a life review so you can make adjustments with respect to how you wish to live. He inspires one to devote oneself to spiritual servitude and can also help us to access and attain Divine wisdom. Jeremiel can be called upon if you feel stuck spiritually and helps you to recapture the enthusiasm and zest for your Divine mission and Path. Archangel Jeremiel is also good to call upon for issues with forgiveness and to provide comfort for emotional healing.

HALO COLOUR ★ Dark purple
CANDLE COLOUR ★ Violet
CRYSTAL ★ Amethyst

Jeremiel's Message for Scorpio ★ *"You gratefully and graciously accept your past since it has made you into the special person that you are today. In doing so you release the anchor that has held you back and re-connect yourself with the insights that you have gained in the course of time. From now on you are the director and supreme master of your life."*

OTHER SPECIAL ANGELS FOR SCORPIO ★ Barbiel, Chamuel & Azrael

CHAMUEL ★ Chamuel's name means 'he who sees God', and he is the ruler of Mars, the head of the choir of dominions and one of the seven great archangels. He is known as the Angel of self-Love, self-confidence, opening the heart, global peace, and of finding things and places. Chamuel encourages both universal and personal peace and helps you to find whatever it is you are seeking. Because he helps us to locate important components of our lives, he can be called upon to find new love, friendships, careers, or indeed any lost item or 'missing' soul fragments. He can be called upon for any matters involving tolerance, understanding, forgiveness and love. He rights wrongs, soothes troubled minds, and provides justice. You can call on him whenever you need additional strength, or are in conflict with someone else, as he provides courage, persistence and determination. Chamuel is also the relationship balancer and healer, enabling the heart to open and encouraging you to value yourself and realise what you have to offer. Chamuel brings comfort if a relationship is in distress, giving you the gift of insight that you still have much to offer and your love has not been wasted. He can also connect you with your soul mate.

Chamuel's Message for Scorpio ★ *"Call upon me when you are ready to find your soul mate. As the Divine light being of relationships, I choose the right places, times and circumstances in which you may chance upon your twin flame. I serve to remind you that love is everything, for love is all there is, and everything is born from this power and emanates from its core. With love, the whole Universe is yours. But before any love can be extended outward and drawn toward you, it must have first been cultivated within. Self-love is therefore your most important lesson."*

AZRAEL ★ Azrael is the Angel of comfort, who helps to accompany the dying into the light. His name means 'whom God helps', and Azrael is sometimes called the Angel of Death because he meets people at the time of their passing over or transitioning from life to death and escorts them to the Other Side. He assists in the healing of the bereaved, helping souls cross over, and aiding grief workers. Azrael can be called upon to help newly passed-over or dying loved ones, as he helps them feel loved and comfortable. The enigmatic necromancer (diviner through the spirits of the dead) Leilah Wendell, in her books *Encounters with Death, My Name is Melancholy,* and the *Necromantic Ritual Book,* beckons us into the shadowy angels of Azrael, the Angel of Death, for she acknowledged that it is he who is appointed the task of heralding death and collecting souls for their radiant ascent into heaven or their fiery descent into hell. As such, he is our most ardent lover, a final companion of the journey of life who clutches us tenderly in his grip. He often takes the form that we are most able to relate to: as a winged angel, a grim reaper, or even hordes of black birds. In his most transcendent and Divine form, Azrael represents the very substance and flow of the Death Current itself, so he should be called upon at early dawn or descending dusk to best summon the energies of his vast powers.

"After you depart this life, God shall demand a reckoning of your deeds,
That in his ledger are recorded.
Those that are rebellious, shall be summoned.
Azrael, the angel of death, will hover over them,
And trapped in a blind alley they will know not any escape.
... Falsehood must be destroyed;
Truth in the end shall prevail."

Adi Granth, Ramkali-ki-Var

Azrael's Message for Scorpio ★ *"Let go now, or fall. You need to let go of your tight grip on possessions and even life itself. Nothing ever dies in the true sense of the word; everything, including you, is eternal and part of the spiral of the Grand Plan. Death is an ending and a new beginning in the form of a birth simultaneously. We are all essentially and Divinely immortal and unending, much like the spiral which extends ever outward and ever inward at the same time. The best thing you can offer me, when your time has come, is your open hand ... and let me lead you home."*

SCORPIO'S INDIVIDUAL BIRTH GUARDIAN ANGELS

This is a personal guardian angel - not necessarily a zodiac essence - that was appointed to you at birth. You can connect with your birth guardian angel through employing many methods. Find one which works for you and know and trust that your angel has heard you and is answering you in any number of ways. Some methods that you can use to communicate with, connect to, and request help from your special guardian have already been outlined in the introduction to this chapter.

Summon your Birth Angel using one of your birthstones and a piece of rutile quartz, lighting a white candle, and by saying the following affirmation: *"My birth angel is by my side throughout my entire life, and never leaves my side. At every turn I am surrounded and embraced by my guardian angel's special energy and loving powers, and he/she watches over me, protects me, guides me, gently directs me towards my most authentic Path, and helps me to achieve my life purpose. I am always loved and completely accepted as I am. I am never alone and receive help in so many different ways, whenever I ask for it."*

★　★　★

SAGITTARIUS

SAGITTARIUS'S ELEMENTAL ARCHANGEL ★ MICHAEL

♐

Element of Fire
The southern quarter of the Earth
The Autumn season
The colour red
The astrological signs of Aries, Leo and Sagittarius

Michael, meaning "Who is like God or the Divine," is the leader of all the archangels and is in charge of courage, truth, strength and integrity. He protects us physically, emotionally and psychically. Michael helps us to follow our truth without compromising our integrity and helps us find our true natures so we can be faithful to who we really are. Michael encourages us to fight for just and noble causes; he gives us the courage and strength to stand up for what is right, especially when persecuted. Overall, Michael is the archangel of protection, peace, safety, clarity, balance, and moving forward. This being works to bring patience and a safeguard against any psychic imbalances or dangers, and if your problem is a very powerful adversary, you can summon his help. Known as the Saint of protection, he is the angelic being who is dedicated to releasing the world from fear. Most images of him show him holding a sword made of fire and light, a powerful symbol of his ability to cut through fear and liberate us from it. In this way, Michael helps us to tear down the old and build the new. If we specially ask for it, he bestows upon us the courage to follow our Truth and live by the light of our Divine purpose. His halo colours are royal purple, royal blue, and gold.

MICHAEL'S MESSAGE FOR SAGITTARIUS ★ "I am your special being of Divine Light. I offer you, Sagittarius, the Divine gift of integrity through living your highest Truth. You, the powerful celestial Centaur, have the courage to teach others with your glowing aura of supreme sociability, wisdom, knowledge and charm. I will protect you in all of your crusades of the mind and spirit, which you conduct with strength and conviction. I will endow upon you the wisdom to carry on when you are feeling depleted or overcome. Affirm to yourself: *'Acquiring knowledge and passing it onto others is a healing act that requires deep courage. I am consciously choosing a Path of freedom and enlightenment, that I can then share with others so that all good things may expand into experiences of vast, unlimited abundance. I can call upon Archangel Michael to provide Divine assistance at any or all stages of the journey, to help me on this quest.'* I am always here to envelope you with my powerful, protective embrace. All you need to do is call on me and I will be your omnipresent All-Provider."

SAGITTARIUS'S ZODIAC ARCHANGELS ★ ZADKIEL & RAGUEL

ZADKIEL ★ Zadkiel is the ruler of Jupiter, regent of Sagittarius, and the Angel of Divine justice, compassion and forgiveness. Zadkiel's name means 'righteousness of God' and he helps one to remember things. Because of his association with Jupiter, Zadkiel bestows abundance, benevolence, mercy, tolerance, prosperity, happiness, and good fortune. He can be invoked for help with legal or financial problems. Zadkiel teaches us to trust in the Universe. Labelled 'the holy one', he brings mercy, compassion, and kindness and aids meditation, brings psychic protection and boosts the immune system. He advocates teaching, the learning of new ideas, and helps students remember facts and figures for tests. As a Divine healer of painful memories, Zadkiel removes emotions and obstacles that are holding you back, so that you are able to see the bigger picture. He also assists you in remembering your Divine spiritual origin and missions, and in choosing the healing path of forgiveness.

HALO COLOUR ★ Deep indigo
CANDLE COLOUR ★ Violet
CRYSTALS ★ Amethyst or lapis lazuli

Zadkiel's Message for Sagittarius ★ *"Affirmation: I forgive because it sets me free and heals myself as well as others. When I forgive, I unlock the chains that bind me, and in doing so, I have opened up the channels for vast abundance to fill up any space created by this loving act of release, acceptance and flow."*

RAGUEL ★ Raguel's name means 'friend of God', and as Angel of clairsentience and harmony in relationships, he is the great soother of frayed relationships. Raguel can be called upon for healing arguments and misunderstandings, for bringing harmony and justice to situations, and to help attract wonderful new friends or to champion the underdog.

HALO COLOUR ★ Pale blue
CANDLE COLOUR ★ Pale Blue
CRYSTAL ★ Aquamarine

Raguel's Message for Sagittarius ★ *"Affirmation: 'My body and my heart chakra are my best oracular instruments. I am clairsentient to a high degree and I am the master of this gift, sharing it with others accordingly. It is safe for me to heal.' Use the crystal aquamarine for any self-healing purposes."*

OTHER SPECIAL ANGELS FOR SAGITTARIUS ★ Advachiel & Adnachiel

ADNACHIEL ★ The angel of independence who looks after anyone involved in pioneering or adventurous activities. He also looks after and governs Sagittarians and the month of November.

Adnachiel's Message for Sagittarius ★ *"As one of your special overseeing angels, I bestow upon you the gifts of optimism, independence, balance, harmony, and peace in all the desires of your heart. I allow you the freedom to choose the path of adventure, which you so longingly strive towards at all times, and I have the power, if called upon, to turn your wildest dreams into reality. There is no job too big or too small for me."*

SAGITTARIUS'S INDIVIDUAL BIRTH GUARDIAN ANGELS

This is a personal guardian angel - not necessarily a zodiac essence - that was appointed to you at birth. You can connect with your birth guardian angel through employing many methods. Find one which works for you and know and trust that your angel has heard you and is answering you in any number of ways. Some methods that you can use to communicate with, connect to, and request help from your special guardian have already been outlined in the introduction to this chapter.

Summon your Birth Angel using one of your birthstones and a piece of rutile quartz, lighting a white candle, and by saying the following affirmation: *"My birth angel is by my side throughout my entire life, and never leaves my side. At every turn I am surrounded and embraced by my guardian angel's special energy and loving powers, and he/she watches over me, protects me, guides me, gently directs me towards my most authentic Path, and helps me to achieve my life purpose. I am always loved and completely accepted as I am. I am never alone and receive help in so many different ways, whenever I ask for it."*

✥ CAPRICORN ✥

CAPRICORN'S ELEMENTAL ARCHANGEL ★ URIEL

♑

Element of Earth
The northern quarter of the Earth
The Summer season
The colours white, burnished gold and all earth tones
The crystals tiger's eye and rutilated quartz
The astrological signs of Taurus, Virgo and Capricorn

Uriel, whose name means 'Fire of God' or 'God is light', is the archangel who brought alchemy * to humankind. He is linked with lightning, thunder and sudden happenings. Uriel may be depicted carrying a scroll that contains revelations about your true path in life. Uriel is dynamic, and his gifts are stamina, action, dynamism and dispelling fears. He is said to be the brightest archangel, a pure pillar of Fire, he can bring warmth to the winter and melt the snows with his flaming sword. Uriel is the archangel of alchemy and vision, overseeing healing, magic, nature and manifestation. This being is known as the tallest of the archangels with eyes that can see into and across eternity. Uriel is often depicted with one bare foot and the other with a shoe, and he carries an olive bough, signifying peace. He is also frequently shown with a thick book of wisdom in his left hand. Uriel oversees the work of all nature spirits - working with Uriel will open you to the fairy kingdoms - and works to assist humanity by awakening to them and working in harmony with them. Inspiring us to work with angels, Devas and higher spiritual essences, to perfect our vision of Divine realms, and to refine our mystical nature by burning away our deep-seated desire for comfort and blind ignorance, Uriel is the gatekeeper to the Garden of Eden, the gates of which we can only pass through once we have mastered the wisdom we are given to find our own path to enlightenment. He also aids with intellectual understanding, conversations, ideas, insights and epiphanies, studying, school, and tests, writing and speaking. Uriel illuminates troublesome situations and helps you to think clearly and find answers to anything that is bothering you. He is the Angel who awakens claircognisance and reveals whichever next step you should take. Stimulating physical desires, call on Uriel if you are feeling desperate, depleted or rejected and he will help to restore your vitality and get you back on your feet. In essence, Uriel is considered the guardian of the emotions, of love and of the heart. Uriel is served by Ghob, King of the Gnomes, seen traditionally as a gnome or goblin who is squat, heavy and dense.

* Alchemy is the sacred art of transmuting base metal into gold by reducing it to the primal black matter and then, by chemico-magical processes, striving to extract and refine spiritual as well as actual gold, the key to finding the way back to Paradise or Source.

URIEL'S MESSAGE FOR CAPRICORN ★ "I am your special being of Divine Light. I offer you, Capricorn, the Divine gift of wisdom. You, the powerful celestial Goat, have the courage to live your truth, walk your walk and follow your authentic Path to the exclusion of all else. This allows you to better use your gifts of discernment and steady determination to assist others on their journeys also. I will guide you in all of your crusades of the mind, body and spirit, and open up the channels of abundance and prosperity to flow into your experience as a reward for following your deepest truths. I will provide you with the courage to carry on when you are feeling depleted or overcome by obstacles along the way. I, Uriel, am always here to envelope you with my powerfully loving and illuminating embrace. All you need to do is call on me and I will be your omnipresent All-Provider. Affirm to yourself: *'The yearnings of my soul when I sit in stillness, are signs of my true soul purpose, showing me the way towards enlightenment and freedom. I listen to them and gently act upon them, with deep and wild faith and intuition. This is pure wisdom and is the Path I desire most to follow. In following my inner way-pointers, I set a fine example for others to follow and encourage them to live their most authentic and fulfilling lives too. I deserve to realise my inner and outer dreams effortlessly, and I am perfectly capable of achieving my wildest ambitions and desires by invoking the assistance of my special angel, Uriel.'*"

CAPRICORN'S ZODIAC ARCHANGELS ★ CASSIEL & AZRAEL

CASSIEL ★ Cassiel is the lord of Saturn and the sign of Capricorn. He is also ruler of the seventh heaven. He helps people understand patience and encourages them to overcome longstanding obstacles and problems. He provides serenity and teaches temperance. Cassiel is associated with karma and helps people understand the law of cause and effect. Because of his association with Saturn, he works slowly. As it takes Saturn nearly 30 years to orbit the Sun, Cassiel can take many years to resolve a problem, but he can be sped up by combining his energies with Raphael's.

Cassiel's Message for Capricorn ★ "*As one of your special overseeing angels, I bestow on you the courage and capacity to conquer any blocks that lay across your Path, as well as the patience and the wisdom to endure them when you must. Nothing lasts forever, and I ensure that your suffering is never prolonged or unnecessary. However, you need to know that although I may not give you what you have asked for straight away, my blessings spend time in the ripening phase before I will pass them onto you - always at exactly the right time for you. Trust in the Divine and trust in me, one of its precious winged children.*"

AZRAEL ★ Azrael is the healer, who is concerned with transitions, mortality and finality. Azrael is the Angel of comfort, who helps to accompany the dying into the light. Azrael is sometimes called the Angel of Death because he meets people at the time of their passing over or transitioning from life to death and escorts them to the Other Side. Azrael can be called upon to help newly crossed-over or dying loved ones, as he helps them feel loved and comfortable. He often takes the form that we are most able to relate to: as a winged angel, a grim reaper, or even hordes of black birds. In his most transcendent and Divine form, Azrael represents the very substance and flow of the Death Current itself, so he should be called upon at early dawn or descending dusk to best summon the energies of his vast powers.

CANDLE COLOUR ★ White
CRYSTAL ★ Yellow Calcite

Azrael's Message for Capricorn ★ *"As a Divine healer, I offer you deep comfort whenever you are feeling sorrow, loss, or grief. Call upon me when you need to know that you are loved, you are embraced, you are protected. Allow me to carry you in times of trouble. Remember that feelings of loss can sometimes linger, but love is the only energy that is pure, infinite, and eternal."*

OTHER SPECIAL ANGELS FOR CAPRICORN ★ Asariel, Casujoiah & Orifiel

ASARIEL ★ Asariel is the Divine angel of unconditional love, emotions, dreams, creativity and intuition. This angel is the patron of the waters, lakes, wells, springs, and oceans of the world. He looks after people who are involved in clairvoyance and mediumship.

Azariel's Message for Capricorn ★ *"You are a light being, whose unconditional love has the potential to light up the whole Universe. Tap into the power of your emotions using my guidance, and you will perceive whole new worlds."*

CASUJOIAH ★ Casujoiah is the Angel of the sign of Capricorn and the month of December.

ORIFIEL ★ Orifiel is a Throne, and one of a number of angels with dominion over Saturn.

CAPRICORN'S INDIVIDUAL BIRTH GUARDIAN ANGELS

This is a personal guardian angel - not necessarily a zodiac essence - that was appointed to you at birth. You can connect with your birth guardian angel through employing many methods. Find one which works for you and know and trust that your angel has heard you and is answering you in any number of ways. Some methods that you can use to communicate with, connect to, and request help from your special guardian have already been outlined in the introduction to this chapter.

Summon your Birth Angel using one of your birthstones and a piece of rutile quartz, lighting a white candle, and by saying the following affirmation: *"My birth angel is by my side throughout my entire life, and never leaves my side. At every turn I am surrounded and embraced by my guardian angel's special energy and loving powers, and he/she watches over me, protects me, guides me, gently directs me towards my most authentic Path, and helps me to achieve my life purpose. I am always loved and completely accepted as I am. I am never alone and receive help in so many different ways, whenever I ask for it."*

✯   ✯   ✯

ॐ AQUARIUS ॐ

AQUARIUS'S ELEMENTAL ARCHANGEL ★ RAPHAEL

♒

Element of Air
The eastern quarter of the Earth
The Spring season
The colour blue (or blue and gold)
The astrological signs of Gemini, Libra and Aquarius

Raphael, meaning 'Healing power of God' or 'The Divine has healed', is the archangel of healing, the young, and safe travels. His eyes penetrate the entire Universe and see all that is wrong; he misses nothing. Raphael is the Divine healer, bringing healing in all its forms to those who need it. He leads the guardian angels, takes care of travellers, supports those in the health professions, and bestows knowledge, wisdom and therapeutic skill. Soothing and calming, he can help you to heal yourself and to feel a connection and oneness with nature. This being works to stimulate energies for overall life and success. Raphael awakens a sense of beauty, wonder and creativity which stimulates higher mental faculties. As the supreme healer in the angelic realm, his chief role is to support, heal and guide in all matters of health, working to soothe people's minds, bodies and spirits so they can enjoy overall peace and well-being. He also helps animals and guides Earthly healers and lightworkers in their education and practice. Overall, he is in charge of physical health and wellness. Raphael has as his servant Paralda, King of the Sylphs, who appears to clairvoyant vision as a tenuous form made of blue mist always moving and changing shape. Raphael can be invoked using a caduceus and is regarded as the Keeper of the Holy Grail.

RAPHAEL'S MESSAGE FOR AQUARIUS ★ "I am your special being of Divine Light. I offer you, Aquarius, the Divine gift of healing through your spreading the magic of your pure genius. You, the powerful Water Bearer, have the courage of your convictions and the willpower of your personal truths, to conduct energetic healing of yourself and others on a grand scale. I will protect you in all of your individual and collective crusades, and I will open up the channels of your emotional strength to enable you to carry on when you are feeling depleted or overcome. Affirm to yourself: *'Looking after your mental health is to choose a deeply self-healing Path. Nourishing and nurturing your creative spirit allows your mind's health to flourish and radiate, attracting to you all that you desire. You are the supreme genius, and can access your mind's power at any time, which leads to deep ongoing health, healing and well-being. Healing of the self and others through the sharing of your mental gifts, is an act of profound courage, deep transformation and ever-unfolding personal evolution. Tap into your mind's greatness and the Universe will provide you with all that you've asked for.'* I am always here to envelope you with my powerfully loving embrace. All you need to do is call on me and I will be your omnipresent All-Provider."

AQUARIUS'S ZODIAC ARCHANGEL ★ URIEL

Uriel, whose name means 'Fire of God' or 'God is light', is the archangel who brought alchemy * to humankind. He is linked with lightning, thunder and sudden happenings. Uriel may be depicted carrying a scroll that contains revelations about your true path in life. Uriel is dynamic, and his gifts are stamina, action, dynamism and dispelling fears. He is said to be the brightest archangel, a pure pillar of Fire, he can bring warmth to the winter and melt the snows with his flaming sword. Uriel is the archangel of alchemy and vision, overseeing healing, magic, nature and manifestation. This being is known as the tallest of the archangels with eyes that can see into and across eternity. Uriel is often depicted with one bare foot and the other with a shoe, and he carries an olive bough, signifying peace. He is also frequently shown with a thick book of wisdom in his left hand. Uriel oversees the work of all nature spirits - working with Uriel will open you to the fairy kingdoms - and works to assist humanity by awakening to them and working in harmony with them. Inspiring us to work with angels, Devas and higher spiritual essences, to perfect our vision of Divine realms, and to refine our mystical nature by burning away our deep-seated desire for comfort and blind ignorance, Uriel is the gatekeeper to the Garden of Eden, the gates of which we can only pass through once we have mastered the wisdom we are given to find our own path to enlightenment. He also aids with intellectual understanding, conversations, ideas, insights and epiphanies, studying, school, and tests, writing and speaking. Uriel illuminates troublesome situations and helps you to think clearly and find answers to anything that is bothering you. He is the Angel who awakens claircognisance and reveals whichever next step you should take. Stimulating physical desires, call on Uriel if you are feeling desperate, depleted or rejected and he will help to restore your vitality and get you back on your feet. In essence, Uriel is considered the guardian of the emotions, of love and of the heart.

HALO COLOUR ★ Yellow
CANDLE COLOUR ★ Ruby red
CRYSTALS ★ Carnelian, amber or red jasper

Uriel's Message for Aquarius ★ *"I bless you, Aquarius, with the gift of Divine and cosmic intelligence. You are intricately linked to the stellar forces and use these to guide you in your quest for deep inner truths, which you may then share with the world. This allows for self-healing and collective healing, and dispels all fears on all levels, so that you may go forth with great wisdom that has the potential to illuminate the entire Universe. Indeed, as fellow Air sign Rumi gently counsels: 'Do not feel lonely. The entire Universe is inside you'. Affirm this to yourself regularly."*

* Alchemy is the sacred art of transmuting base metal into gold by reducing it to the primal black matter and then, by chemico-magical processes, striving to extract and refine spiritual as well as actual gold, the key to finding the way back to Paradise or Source.

OTHER SPECIAL ANGELS FOR AQUARIUS ★ Cambiel, Ausiel, Cassiel & Gabriel

AUSIEL★ Ausiel is the angel of Aquarius and the month of January.

CASSIEL ★ Cassiel is the lord of Saturn, your ancient traditional ruler. He is also ruler of the seventh heaven. He helps people understand patience and encourages them to overcome longstanding obstacles and problems. He provides serenity and teaches temperance. Cassiel is associated with karma and helps people understand the law of cause and effect. Because of his association with Saturn, he works slowly. As it takes Saturn nearly 30 years to orbit the Sun, Cassiel can take many years to resolve a problem, but he can be sped up by combining his energies with Raphael's.

Cassiel's Message for Aquarius ★ *"As I guide you in cultivating patience and calm, I bestow on you the courage and capacity to conquer any obstacles that may block your Path, as well as the wisdom to endure them when you must. Nothing lasts forever, and I ensure that your suffering is never prolonged or unnecessary. However, you need to know that although I may not give you what you have asked for straight away, my blessings spend time in the ripening phase before I will pass them onto you - always at exactly the right time for you. Trust in the Divine and trust in me, your overseeing bringer of light."*

GABRIEL ★ Gabriel's name means 'God is my strength' and she is the messenger angel of all Earthly message-bringers such as journalists, teachers and writers, as well as being the Angel of the Inner Child and all children. She delivers important and clear messages and specialises in helping those who are messengers (teachers, artists, card readers, writers, actors), as well as assisting with all aspects of parenting, including conception, adoption, birth, and early childhood.

Gabriel's Message for Aquarius ★ *"You listen to your inner child and recognise and honour his or her needs. In doing this you recognise how you may heal with grace, lightness, creativity, pure love and joy. Keep reminding yourself: you are a Child of the Universe, no less than the trees and the stars. You are loved. You are whole. You are healed."*

AQUARIUS'S INDIVIDUAL BIRTH GUARDIAN ANGELS

This is a personal guardian angel - not necessarily a zodiac essence - that was appointed to you at birth. You can connect with your birth guardian angel through employing many methods. Find one which works for you and know and trust that your angel has heard you and is answering you in any number of ways. Some methods that you can use to communicate with, connect to, and request help from your special guardian have already been outlined in the introduction to this chapter.

Summon your Birth Angel using one of your birthstones and a piece of rutile quartz, lighting a white candle, and by saying the following affirmation: *"My birth angel is by my side throughout my entire life, and never leaves my side. At every turn I am surrounded and embraced by my guardian angel's special energy and loving powers, and he/she watches over me, protects me, guides me, gently directs me towards my most authentic Path, and helps me to achieve my life purpose. I am always loved and completely accepted as I am. I am never alone and receive help in so many different ways, whenever I ask for it."*

★ ★ ★

PISCES

PISCES'S ELEMENTAL ARCHANGEL ★ GABRIEL

♓

Element of Water
The Western quarter of the Earth
The Winter season
The colours emerald, silver and sea green
The crystals opal, fluorite and moonstone
The astrological signs of Cancer, Scorpio and Pisces

Gabriel, meaning "Strength of God" or "The Divine is my strength," is known as the messenger and can help us to find our true soul's purpose. As archangel of the Moon and ruler of dreams, Gabriel is chief archangel of the night and the alter ego of Michael, the Sun archangel. Some consider Gabriel a feminine energy. The archangel of life, hope, truth, astral travel, unconscious wisdom, illumination and love, he inspires and motivates artists and communicators, and delivers important prophetic messages to people. Gabriel is the Divine messenger angel of all Earthly messengers such as journalists, teachers and writers, and as such delivers important and clear messages, as well as helping those who are Earthly messengers, such as teachers, writers, actors and artists. Gabriel guards the sacred places of the world and the sacred waters of life. He provides intuitive teaching, guidance, mystical experiences, inspiration and enlightenment of spiritual duties, including awakening within us a greater understanding of dreams and connection to our inner child. He can be called upon when you are feeling alone, afraid or vulnerable. Gabriel is said to be the angel who chooses the souls to be born and cares for them in the womb. He assists with all aspects of parenting, including conception, adoption, birth, and early childhood. Gabriel is also an angel of death, but a gentle one, bringing release from sorrow and pain. Gabriel's servant is Nicksa, King of the Undines, who is seen as an ever-changing shape, fluid with a greenish blue aura splashed with silver and grey. His halo colour is copper, as is his special mineral.

GABRIEL'S MESSAGE FOR PISCES ★ "I am your special being of Divine Light. I offer you, Pisces, the Divine gift of spiritual connection. You, the mystical celestial Fish, have all the tools of magic and spirit at your disposal at all times, and I am the supreme provider of them. Call upon me to access the higher realms and for the courage to live your higher purpose and truth. I will psychically protect you in all of your healing, spiritual, and Divine endeavours, during which you assist both yourself and others, and I will open up the channels of your emotional strength to enable you to carry on when you are feeling depleted or overcome. Affirm to yourself: *'The yearnings and dreams of my soul are signs of my true spiritual purpose, and I listen to them with deep, untamed intuition. Allowing my spirit to move me where I need to* *be is an act of profound self-healing and courage, which I can then help empower others with. I deserve to realise my inner and outer dreams effortlessly, with joy, grace and gentle willpower, and I will achieve these desires by invoking the assistance of my special angel, Gabriel.'* I am always here to envelope you with my powerfully loving embrace. All you need to do is call on me and I will be your omnipresent All-Provider."

PISCES'S ZODIAC ARCHANGELS ★ TZAPHKIEL & SANDALPHON

TZAPHKIEL ★ Tzaphkiel is understood as a feminine presence and is close to Sophia, the 'mind of God'. She is the angel of understanding and compassion. Tzaphkiel is a capable nurturer and encourages mystical states, altered consciousness and the blessings of an open heart. She reveals other realities and the mysteries of the Universe and Source. Tzaphkiel can help you release the thoughts, feelings or pressures that emanate from others, as well as releasing tension and bringing deep emotional healing.

CANDLE COLOUR ★ Lilac
CRYSTALS ★ Labradorite or purple fluorite

Tzaphkiel's Message for Pisces ★ *"I am your Divine feminine guide, who innately incorporates the Divine masculine where it is needed also. Whether you are male, or female makes no difference to my healing powers whatsoever, as all life forms contain the polarities of both masculine and feminine, light and dark, yin and yang, and only when these two seeming opposites are reconciled, balanced and integrated, may you experience peace, healing, flow, harmony and purity. Call me forth when you need help in bringing the two together in a meaningful whole."*

SANDALPHON ★ Sandalphon's name means 'brother', and like Metatron, he was once a human prophet (Elijah) who ascended into the realm of the Archangels. He is the Angel of music, voice and serenity. Sandalphon is an androgynous angel, depicted as a beautiful young man. He is concerned with the spirit behind Earthly manifestations and is guardian and protector of the Earth. He specialises in receiving and delivering prayers between the Highest Order of the Universe and humans and provides guidance and support for musicians. He can be called upon for anything relating to music or spiritual confusion. Sandalphon stimulates awareness of the Earth's needs, blessings and gifts. Bringing a sense of grounding, practicality and responsibility, Sandalphon can help you be more aware of your bodily power and assist in treating your physical body as a temple.

HALO COLOUR ★ Turquoise
CANDLE COLOUR ★ Deep green or brown
CRYSTALS ★ Jade, brown jasper or turquoise

Sandalphon's Message for Pisces ★ *"Healing through sound and mantras *: Let the Divine energy of music and mantras calm you, inspire you and bring you to a place of deep* serenity. Sound vibration is supremely healing and with Sandalphon's guidance, you vibrate to its Divine frequency; its light embraces, envelopes, and heals you. I can also be summoned to help you to gain spiritual knowledge and undertake special personal missions."

* Mantras are sounds or words that are repeated to aid concentration in meditation. These sacred syllables, when charged with the spiritual attention of an enlightened being, have the power to attract the attention to the point where it can contact the Light and Sound that pervade the Universe.

OTHER SPECIAL ANGELS FOR PISCES ★ Barchiel, Zadkiel & Asariel

BARCHIEL ★ Barchiel is one of the seven great Archangels, an Angel with dominion over lightning, the sign of Pisces and the month of February.

ZADKIEL ★ Zadkiel is the ruler of Jupiter, Pisces's traditional ruler, and is the Angel of Divine justice, mercy, compassion and forgiveness. Zadkiel's name means 'righteousness of God' and he helps one to remember things. Because of his association with Jupiter, Zadkiel also bestows gifts of abundance, benevolence, tolerance, prosperity, happiness, and good fortune. He can be invoked for help with legal or financial problems. Zadkiel teaches us to trust in the Universe. Labelled 'the holy one', he brings mercy, compassion, and kindness, aids meditation, and brings psychic protection. He advocates teaching, the learning of new ideas, and helps students remember facts and figures for tests. As a Divine healer of painful memories, Zadkiel removes emotions and obstacles that are holding you back, so that you are able to see the bigger picture. He also assists you in remembering your Divine spiritual origin and missions, and in choosing the healing path of forgiveness.

Zadkiel's Message for Pisces ★ *"I assist you with manifesting good fortune using the benevolent rays of your ancient ruler Jupiter. To summon my powers and bring forth abundance and prosperity in your experiences, use the crystal amethyst. I will help you to clear the channels for vast abundance to flow into your life. You need only ask and I will come to your aid."*

ASARIEL ★ Asariel is the lord of Neptune and the Divine angel of unconditional love, emotions, dreams, creativity, and intuition. This angel is the patron of the waters, lakes, wells, springs, and oceans of the world. He looks after people who are involved in clairvoyance and mediumship.

Asariel's Message for Pisces ★ *"As I have dominion over the waters of the Universe, as well as the waters of within, I see to it that abundance flows to you through this channel. As a supreme Water healer, I speak to you through intuition, creative urges, dreams, spirituality, emotions, mystic insights, prophecies, and the breathings of your inner soul. Call upon me and be receptive to receiving my answers, through the medium of dreams, wishes, fantasies, and inspiring* *ideas. When you receive or perceive a sign from the Divine, in whatever form it may take, it is most certainly me delivering a message to you."*

PISCES'S INDIVIDUAL BIRTH GUARDIAN ANGELS

This is a personal guardian angel - not necessarily a zodiac essence - that was appointed to you at birth. You can connect with your birth guardian angel through employing many methods. Find one which works for you and know and trust that your angel has heard you and is answering you in any number of ways. Some methods that you can use to communicate with, connect to, and request help from your special guardian have already been outlined in the introduction to this chapter.

Summon your Birth Angel using one of your birthstones and a piece of rutile quartz, lighting a white candle, and by saying the following affirmation: *"My birth angel is by my side throughout my entire life, and never leaves my side. At every turn I am surrounded and embraced by my guardian angel's special energy and loving powers, and he/she watches over me, protects me, guides me, gently directs me towards my most authentic Path, and helps me to achieve my life purpose. I am always loved and completely accepted as I am. I am never alone and receive help in so many different ways, whenever I ask for it."*

Tarot Messages

ABOUT TAROT

The Tarot offers a spiritual philosophy to a Western generation looking for meaning. Meaning is healing. To live without meaning is soul-destroying. The Tarot affirms our worth. It affirms the value of our journey. It affirms our place in relation to a greater whole ... (The Tarot) is a whole way of responding that includes the imagination and touches our sense of connection to everything. This is the seed of heart thinking. This is the seed of living holistically. This is the seed of a way of life that heals.

Naomi Ozaniec

The Tarot deck is a set of cards used for divination and fortune telling. It has a long history and has assumed an air of mystery over the centuries. The Tarot is one of the easiest gateways to the Great Mysteries of Life. It is beautiful beyond any written doctrine because it is wordless.

The deck consists of seventy-eight cards in total and is divided into two subsections: The Major Arcana (22 cards) and the Minor Arcana (56 cards). The Major Arcana comprises 22 trump, or key, cards; the Minor Arcana comprises the remaining 56 cards, which are often called pips. The Major Arcana contains the most familiar imagery of the Tarot, such as Death, the Hanged Man, The Star, and The Devil.

The Tarot represents a pictorial symbolic map of the inner world and provides us with a particular opportunity to reflect upon whether there is a deeper spiritual dimension to our existence. The pictures on the 78 Tarot cards are worth more than a thousand words - they can actually paint a picture of you. The Tarot's symbolism encompasses everything from ancient cave paintings, to magical belief systems, to Jungian archetypes, and examining them can create a unique metaphor for the story of your life, where you're heading on your wondrous journey, and indeed at what stage you are at presently.

The precise origin of Tarot cards is obscure, but one popular theory is that the deck dates back to Ancient Egypt and that the god Thoth * was its creator. Tarot and playing cards may have had their beginning as long ago as Ancient Egypt (although the earliest complete sets of Tarot cards to have survived are all Italian and appear to date to some time between 1420 and 1450), since scholars have reportedly recognised the Major Arcana as Egyptian hieroglyphic books *. Other scholars, however, report uncanny similarities between playing cards and early Eastern games and deities. Further, it is not known with certainty whether the Major Arcana cards, with their emblematic designs, and the Minor Arcana cards in their familiar four suits, were devised separately and at a later date combined into one pack by an innovative genius, or if they were created as a 78-card deck from the beginning.

As well as no one really knowing where the Tarot originated, nor does anyone really know how and why it works, but what we do know is that if we can 'tune in' to the images, archetypes and symbolism of the cards, we can gain access to a deeper understanding of ourselves and the people and events in our lives.

The Tarot deck most widely used today is known as the Rider-Waite, or Universal Waite, deck and was first published in 1910 by the Rider Company. The designs were drawn by the artist Pamela Colman Smith at the instigation of Arthur Edward Waite, a prominent member of the secret esoteric society the Hermetic Order of the Golden Dawn, a movement founded in England in 1886. Within the society the Tarot was identified as giving access to the secrets of the Universe. Arthur Waite, born 2 October 1957 in New York, was an author, mystic, magician, alchemist and occultist who was active in both Rosicrucianism and Freemasonry. Waite had been influenced by a nineteenth century philosopher, Eliphas Levi, who had stated in a book written in the 1850s, that 'an imprisoned person with no other book than the Tarot, if he knew how to use it, could in a few years acquire Universal knowledge'. A grandiose statement perhaps, but probably not far from the truth.

The Major Arcana reflects major turning points in our lives: our commitments, milestones, rites of passage, triumphs and tragedies, while the Minor Arcana deals more with the day-to-day aspects and smaller intricacies of life. The Tarot, rather than telling the future outright, seems to help the seeker make choices and examine more closely what is going on in their life at the time of the reading; therefore, it helps to point to a route through difficult or trying circumstances. The Tarot is ambiguous, allowing much room for interpretation, yet can be surprisingly accurate. The best Tarot readers understand that no card has any one meaning, but rather is a metaphor for a variety of interpretations. Ultimately, Tarot cards are a tool to unlock your imagination, and how you read the cards is up to you. But as a tool for understanding ourselves and for plugging in to a great universal wisdom, the vivid imagery, archetypal impressions and other symbolism contained in the Tarot remind us that we should seek the answers to our questions not just through reason and external study, but through deeply felt inner experience. After all, we are who we are, and the very essence of ourselves invariably always offers us the answers to our own questions; the Tarot just provides a brighter light to illuminate our Path. Indeed, with practice, you can learn to become your very own fortune teller, your own diviner, your own Magician, your own wizard, your own *oracle*!

* Thoth, or Tehuti, is an ancient Egyptian god, depicted in some vignettes as the dog-headed baboon but mostly as an ibis-headed man. Thoth is the Greek Hermes, the god of medicine, learning, truth, magic, libraries and books, keeper of the Akashic records, lord of karma, and time lord. Thoth's symbols are the white feather and the caduceus, his colour is amethyst and the ibis is sacred to him.

THE TAROT & ASTROLOGY

Tarot and astrology are inextricably linked. All the cards of the Major Arcana, which comprises 22 of the Tarot's 78 cards, are 'ruled by' or connected with either one of the twelve zodiac signs, one of the planets or luminaries, or one of the four elements.

The 22 Major Arcana cards contain the richest symbolism of all the cards in the Tarot deck, each carrying a myriad of messages for the reader to decipher. The symbolism contained within these images represents the archetypal aspects of your character. It also describes the Path your soul takes through each stage of life, revealing clues through which you can explore different parts of yourself. Each of the cards also represents an aspect of universal human experience and has a name that either directly conveys the meaning of the card, such as Strength or Justice, or depicts individuals that represent these human archetypes, such as The Hermit or The Empress. The illustrations on each card contain one or more figures and tuning into a card's imagery enables you to grasp its meaning intuitively. Consider the demeanour of the characters, if anything is obscured or veiled, whether it is day or night, daybreak or nightfall, the background, any symbols, the buildings, the colours, the animals, the vegetation, the weather and the season. Every card has its own story to impart, and through entering that story you can gain deeper insights into the full picture of your journey so far, as well as lighting up your Path ahead.

The following are the cards which correspond to each zodiac sign. (Please note that these may differ between various schools of thought. These are my interpretations and correspondences only, but they do align with the general consensus among most Tarot scholars.)

ARIES ★ No. 4 ~ The Emperor
TAURUS ★ No. 5 ~ The Hierophant
GEMINI ★ No. 6 ~ The Lovers
CANCER ★ No. 7 ~ The Chariot
LEO ★ No. 8 ~ Strength
VIRGO ★ No. 9 ~ The Hermit
LIBRA ★ No. 11 ~ Justice
SCORPIO ★ No. 13 ~ Death
SAGITTARIUS ★ No. 14 ~ Temperance
CAPRICORN ★ No. 15 ~ The Devil
AQUARIUS ★ No. 17 ~ The Star
PISCES ★ No. 18 ~ The Moon

Additionally, because every Major Arcana card has a link with at least one zodiac sign, element or planet; each sign will have at least two Tarot cards to which it essentially vibrates. These cards will have special meaning for your particular sign, planetary influence and elemental forces, and can carry powerful messages and lessons for you to reflect upon. They are as follows:

ARIES ★ The Emperor, The Tower & Judgement
TAURUS ★ The Hierophant, The Empress & The World
GEMINI ★ The Lovers, The Magician & The Fool
CANCER ★ The Chariot & The High Priestess
LEO ★ Strength, The Sun & Judgement
VIRGO ★ The Hermit, The Magician & The World
LIBRA ★ Justice, The Empress & The Fool
SCORPIO ★ Death, Judgement, The Tower & The High Priestess
SAGITTARIUS ★ Temperance, Wheel of Fortune & Judgement
CAPRICORN ★ The Devil & The World
AQUARIUS ★ The Star, The Fool & The World
PISCES ★ The Moon, The Hanged Man, Wheel of Fortune & The High Priestess

TAROT MESSAGES FOR ARIES

★ THE EMPEROR ★

Ruled by Aries

Number ★ 4

Keywords ★ Discipline, Authority, Structure, Influence, Power

Meditation ★ "I light the way for others through my natural leadership, resoluteness, iron will, strength, authority, holding true to my beliefs and having the courage of my convictions. Influence, power and dynamism are my way of life, and I am a willing and able guide and supreme example to anyone seeking my counsel."

MESSAGE FOR ARIES FROM THE EMPEROR ★ "Where the fire of the preceding female Empress card is shamanistic, healing and sensual, the fire of The Emperor is warlike, ascetic and domineering. In astrological terms The Magician's fire is Arien: "I Am," while The Emperor's fire is Leonine: "I Will." Fiery nonetheless, hence its connection with you, Aries, the impulsive, independent, strong-willed, authoritative born leader of the zodiac! In essence, the Emperor is the Grand Architect of the Universe. He symbolises the intellect - the creative, powerful building tool of the human mind - having detached itself from nature, the heart and the emotions, and makes it function in an autonomous, orderly, detached yet completely immaculate manner. The Emperor, through his stern rulership and overseeing of others, is keen to make his ideas and plans solid and tangible. He signifies that although your dreams are valid and sound, they still need guidelines, foundations, and structure so that they can manifest effectively. It therefore is important to create a detailed plan for how you wish to proceed and maintain firm and authoritative control over how that plan is implemented; it is imperative that you cultivate logic, discipline and organisation. You feel a need to protect what you have gained and develop strength of character through setting firm boundaries and recognising that there are rules for playing the game of life. Aries, the Emperor teaches you - and you are rapidly learning - to start to take control of your own Path. The Emperor, however, has climbed the mountain and even claimed it as his own, but doing this has reduced the number of options available to him, therefore rendering his life rather lonely. He has been a pioneer and a leader, becoming the master of his material world, and with his great reasoning abilities he has triumphed over emotion and passion. As a true patriarch, he lacks female intuition, but no such 'weakness' would be acknowledged by him for fear he may lose footing or authority. Dedicated, disciplined and stable, he has no difficulty in getting others to carry out his orders. Ambitious, he will begin innovative projects that are not always as staid and conservative as he himself appears. If old patterns must be broken, he will consider his options as he wishes to be perceived as benevolent and thoughtful as well as infallible. Though sometimes bossy and domineering, he will always remain responsible, reliable, solid, and, ultimately, charismatic. So, you need to see the whole picture clearly before you act, as if you stood atop The Emperor's mountain. Most of all, what is needed here is a return to the consciousness represented by The Empress card - the goddess of archaic, gentle wisdom and compassionate understanding. The childlike wisdom of The Fool - the first Tarot card - can also help loosen up The Emperor's firm grip on his need to control his world. But despite his firm austerity and discipline over your life, the Emperor has his part to play, and we do need him to show us that we do need to build a strong foundation under our castles in the air sooner or later."

★ THE TOWER ★

Ruled by Mars

Number ★ 16

Keywords ★ Collapse, Upheaval, Awakening, Rebuilding

Meditation ★ "I trust that whatever disaster or unexpected events befall me, they occur for my ultimate higher good. I understand that all adverse happenings, without exception, allow me a chance to rebuild."

MESSAGE FOR ARIES FROM THE TOWER ★ "A sturdy tower erected on a hill is struck by lightning and explosively blown apart. The castellated top of the tower is lifted by the blast, fire strikes deep within, and flames roar from the narrow windows as two figures fall from their ruined refuge. The security afforded by this strong, old structure, has been reduced to ruin by the forces of natural law. Flames erupt, and smoke fills the air, sparks and debris fall on either side; there has been a dramatic reversal of fortune. Future plans have been aborted. The Tower represents the shock that shatters your illusions, removes the rug from beneath your feet, and clears away the refuse. Aries, a sudden catastrophe may break down all your previous conceptions about yourself or others. You sometimes feel as if there is no firm foundation upon which to rest your life as the veils of illusion are torn away. This forces you to face painful truths, but also liberates you from the past and provides sudden insights. The Tower tears down your world but in doing so provides a new focus. And once the storm settles, you are free! Lightning has struck, but enlightenment is sure to follow. This card indicates the needs to find fresh ways to do things, as the old have become rigid and imprisoning. We often live our lives as we have been conditioned to, never examining closely whether our lifestyle really suits us, until this complacency comes crashing down around us and forces us to re-consider and revaluate. The lightning that strikes The Tower on the card represents the new visions and possibilities which await us, and which will soon be brought to our attention through an upheaval or crisis. The change may be something that happens to you, an event or situation that transforms you. You may suddenly just know your marriage is over, your job is ending, or the time has come for a move. You may have a sudden lucid understanding of your own destructive behaviours or addictions and the need for an immediate and radical overhaul. These insights may be momentary, like a lightning bolt, but the effects are far-reaching and enduring. If possible, open yourself right up to the power inherent in The Tower card. The time has come to spread your wings and be born anew!"

★ JUDGEMENT ★

Ruled by Pluto & the Element of Fire

Number ★ 20

Keywords ★ Evaluation, Self-assessment, Opportunities, New Directions

Meditation ★ "I stand at the Oracle of Judgement. In its innate wisdom and pure truths, I trust that it will light the way ahead by allowing for my redemption, renewal and rebirth."

MESSAGE FOR ARIES FROM JUDGEMENT ★ "The Judgement card is the respected mentor, who leads the way to a fresh perspective on life and leaves you feeling elated. Its main divinatory meanings are atonement, judgement, improvement, evaluation and finally, rebirth. In the symbolism of the Tarot, Judgement is not concerned with eternal damnation or heavenly bliss based upon this 'judgement' of your life experience so far, from birth onward; it is not a time for punishment and retribution, but a time of being called to account for past actions and experiences. After facing one's 'moment of truth', one can see oneself with more clarity and acceptance, and is then able to see others in the same way. This acceptance is an understanding of the human condition, human beauty, and embraces imperfections and Divine wisdom alongside each other. Our past, having been reflected upon, ensures that a positive resolution will be reinforced. With atonement and repentance, real advancement can occur. Therefore, Judgement is less about guilt and more about self-knowledge. On a spiritual wavelength, this card implies that one particular phase of your soul's journey is ending, and you will shortly assess what you learned and how you dealt with the passing situation, summing up your performance and its value to you. Judgement is telling you that at this point in your life it is time to assess and evaluate yourself, and perhaps address any underlying issues which up until now may have been ignored. To do this, you need simply to become more self-aware. Judgement emphasises that in undertaking this self-examination, you should be fair on yourself and focus on your positive character traits. It is telling you that once you have done this, like the symbolic people on the card, you will be ripe and ready to move in a new direction and onto a higher, more worthwhile plane of existence! You're either near the end of a project or at a crossroads, but either way, you are on the threshold of making an important change in your life. From deep within the core of your being comes this call announcing that it is time to make an important change. You must concern yourself with finding meaning and purpose, evaluating past deeds and becoming more aware of who you are and who you wish to become."

TAROT MESSAGES FOR TAURUS

★ THE HIEROPHANT ★

Ruled by Taurus

Number ★ 5

Keywords ★ Advice, Wisdom, Questing, Enlightenment

Meditation ★ "I seek to do the right thing, to uphold tradition, and choose the high moral ground on all issues. I impart my knowledge, wisdom and spiritual lessons to others through both my gentle example and wise counsel, and in doing so spread a message of peace and compassion."

MESSAGE FOR TAURUS FROM THE HIEROPHANT ★ "The Hierophant represents spiritual wisdom and is the mediator between heaven and Earth. He is a great teacher, always compassionate and fair. A sympathetic ruler, he listens and is merciful. He has breadth of vision and is able to encompass and understand all facets of human needs and desires. Taurus, the Hierophant indicates there is a search for meaning underway in your life. Seek out mentors, experts and like-minded friends. The Hierophant is a conservative, patient man who appreciates stability and tradition. He is quietly persevering and offers a chance to examine spirituality as a means for understanding life's changes. To be mentored is both a privilege and an enriching experience. The Hierophant imparts the message that you should not only seek out a mentor, but also develop your own wisdom and insights so that you might then be able to act as a Hierophant to others. As The Hierophant sets you thinking about the deeper meaning of life, you are beginning to question the purpose of your existence, and this leads you to explore your spiritual nature. A guide or mentor helps to set you on this Path, and you discover a rich connection with a source of all-embracing love. In any case, The Hierophant urges us to listen to our conscience and uphold our moral responsibilities. We all gain from a guide. At the heart of this is a spiritual mentor. The Hierophant acts as this teacher. There is a need to return to your spiritual roots, make a confession or explore forgotten traditions. We consult The Hierophant about the great questions of the soul which sometimes torture the mind; we ask for his benediction. The Hierophant can be regarded as the spiritual master representing the higher powers and forces, who through his role and his presence, reminds us that we are mortal, fallible, and that we must put our trust in him as much as in ourselves. The Hierophant has three stages of grace - faith, hope and charity - of which he is a symbol. He is a man to whom you can confide, and a good advisor, who will offer enlightened support, help and backing. But The Hierophant insists that if you seek his guidance, that you follow his example and adhere to the rules, thereby setting a good example for others. He also encourages you to walk the Path that you choose for yourself, because he knows that learning through experience - after being taught by example - is the best way."

★ THE EMPRESS ★

Ruled by Venus

Number ★ 3

Keywords ★ Nurturance, Fertility, Security, Abundance, Emotional Wealth

Meditation ★ "I am the lover, the provider, the nurturer and the carer, who bestows myself and others with a free and steady flow of feminine gifts. Abundance, fertility, plenitude and natural Earthly wisdom are my way of life."

MESSAGE FOR TAURUS FROM THE EMPRESS ★ "The Empress represents the Great Mother, in all her simplicity and purity. She promises abundance, birth, growth, harmony, community, and relationship. The Empress's Hebrew name is Daleth and means 'door'. As the Qabbalist's Great Mother, she is the doorway through which all forms of life must pass in order to become manifest, hence her deep associations with fertility and creation. As such, she represents the Earth from which all life is born, and to which it returns at the end of its cycle. The Empress in her contemporary 'seductress' pose symbolises the unconscious knowledge contemporary women share of the ancient mysteries and female reverence, of healing and transformation, that live on in our much-diminished but ever-pure Divinity. The Empress feels her connection to the Earth. She knows - has always known - the mystery of procreation, the potential for growing and nurturing life, the sacred act of birthing, and the communal life close to the soil - a time when people did not make war, but spent their leisure time making love and art. The Empress is a sensual, practical woman who appreciates good, wholesome, hearty food, nature and a pleasantly simple life. She is nurturing and generous and teaches that you need to foster your dreams and desires. If the card preceding this, The High Priestess, holds the secrets of life, then The Empress is what gives that life soul and emotion, for she represents the understanding and the power of that life. The Empress's potency lies primarily in feelings, as she is able to exploit both the riches of the heart and the psyche. The Empress, the archetypal fertile Earth Mother, can help bring daydreams to fruition in a world where logic and intuition should dwell together as heaven and Earth do. As such, The Empress is telling you to give birth to your dreams, to nurture yourself and others, spend time in nature, and indulge in creative and artistic endeavours. She suggests a possible pregnancy, a harmonious home environment and progress with your plans. She encourages you to enjoy material comforts and sensual fulfillment but to be wary of overindulgence. Enjoy the beautiful things in life, knowing that you deserve to be exquisitely and Divinely provided for. The realisation that life is inherently a creative process motivates you to explore what brings you harmony. The upsurge of energy and passion that arises with this awakening, attracts cooperation in others, as well as abundance into your experience. The Empress helps you to understand that growth occurs only when you nurture your dreams. Have an open and sympathetic heart and your wishes will be provided for. Exert your power with a loving hand and then creativity, productivity, heaven and Earth will all exist for you on the same plane. Taurus, The Empress brings out your artistic side, opens up your love of beauty, and heightens your aesthetic appreciation. She represents 'prosperity thinking' and the power of positive imagination and instils the faith that your hopes *will* come to fruition, finances *will* improve, green leaves *will* sprout, shows you examples and symbols that fertility *will* abound, and you *will* begin to feel more confident as you reap the rewards of your efforts. Finally, it is interesting to note that the words 'material' and 'matter' originate from the Latin word for mother, *mater*. You can ask this Great Earth Mother for what you need, for she is the unerring All-Provider."

★ THE WORLD/UNIVERSE ★

Ruled by Saturn & the Element of Earth

Number ★ 21

Keywords ★ Completion, Attainment, Fulfilment, Success

Meditation ★ "I have completed one journey and will now rebirth myself to begin a brand new one. I welcome every chance to grow and learn, and I truly never stop evolving."

MESSAGE FOR TAURUS FROM THE WORLD ★ "A statue of a woman has come to life and is dancing, looking back at a leaf she holds in her outstretched hand. Just as the Earth, Divine Mother of us all, evolved from the stars and materialised into reality, so have our physical selves been created out of the same essence so that we may dance the dance of life just as She dances through the cosmos. This dream-like journey is one of going deep within and finding our essential harmony with All There Is. When we arrive at the knowledge of who we really are we gain The World. Taurus, you have arrived at the beginning of the Path to Enlightenment or could be considerably advanced along it by now. The World card suggests a job well done - you have happily completed something of great significance. Enjoy these feelings of wholeness and completion as your amazing accomplishments have been well-earned. You're now ready to move onto something new. You have grown spiritually and have evolved to a whole new level in your understanding of the Universe and your place in it. As well as this, you have attained complete clarity, cosmic awareness, significant enlightenment, an expanded consciousness and above all, the true freedom that accompanies all this. The World imparts the message that each one of us carries a world inside of us, which is neither unattainable, illusory or utopian. It is simply what we are. All the elements are gathered here so that our conscience may awaken, and our future will unfold as it is meant to before us. Form a circle with a group of friends, imaginary or real. Slowly move around it, dancing and swaying and chanting. Complete the circle twenty-two times. As you do so, close your eyes and visualise the Earth in the centre of your circle, bathed in white light, receiving the love, wisdom and healing energy from your group. Know that we are all blessed with the sacred duty of being the caretakers of our Mother Earth - and of finding our own unique place within it."

☆ ☆ ☆

TAROT MESSAGES FOR GEMINI

★ THE LOVERS ★

Ruled by Gemini

Number ★ 6

Keywords ★ Choices, Options, Complementary Opposites, Decisions

Meditation ★ "I have the right and the power to make my own decisions as I stand at the many forks in the roads of life, and I know all these choices will be correct and for my higher good."

MESSAGE FOR GEMINI FROM THE LOVERS ★ "The Lovers can represent both virtue and vice - the basic alternatives. This card obviously refers to strong emotions, and choices of the heart which cannot be made by logic alone. Traditionally an image of duality and choice, The Lovers represent the yin and yang forces of the Universe and their natural attraction to each other. Love, or the coming together of these complementary forces, can occur on many levels. In its deeper, more esoteric form, the image refers to the merging of these opposite qualities within a being, which leads to wholeness. With The Lovers as your primary guiding card, being a lover is on your mind often. Feeling the pull of this magnetic force, you face a choice. If the question is something to the tune of, "Are we going to be lovers or not?" and you feel passionate excitement about this query, then you can be assured you will soon be taking a journey to a deeper place, but to do so, you are asked to trust, to risk and to face the unknown. The yielding required of you as you leap into space together is a surrender to the Divine force of love itself, and the resultant energy is transpersonal - that is, it transcends both your own and the other person's characters. Either way, trust is of the essence. It also indicates a time to make an important decision about your life, for any conclusions you reach now will significantly influence your future, making it all the more important to weigh up your options carefully and thoroughly consider all angles. You come to understand that your relationships with others are an outer expression of your desire for inner connection, and that loving another person helps you to discover new aspects of yourself, and so to grow. With The Lovers, you learn more about yourself through another, and it follows on that your relationships reflect your own inner balance. The Lovers are telling you to be happy and enjoy your relationships. However, you must be prepared to make compromises and sacrifices if it is to work successfully. They warn you not to fall in love with love itself: it is the other person who matters, and it is important that you know the others' true character. The second meaning of The Lovers concerns choice: at some stage on your spiritual journey, you will have to make a difficult decision and usually this will involve certain amount of sacrifice. You may be torn between what you think you should do and what you really want to do. The Lovers card can also be interpreted as representing a choice between two allurements of some kind, no always love. However, because this card is about unity as well as choice, the inner and outer Paths must be brought together in harmony and integrated into the self. The Winged God of Love, Cupid, who is aiming his arrow at the male figure in the card, indicates through wearing a blindfold that he cannot help the man make the decision; rather, that the man must face the task of reconciling the opposites alone. How he does this will have a significant impact on his future Path and a ripple effect on those around him, therefore the needs of others will need to be considered. Knowing all this, The Lovers represents a person's deep motivations, desires, wishes, and their ability to select one Path."

★ THE MAGICIAN ★

Ruled by Mercury

Number ★ 1

Keywords ★ Initiative, Will, Mindpower, Independence

Meditation ★ "I have the willpower, magical tools and initiative to create my own experiences. I am spiritually, mentally, emotionally, psychically and physically equipped to exercise my unique brand of personal power to manipulate the inner and outer worlds to suit my needs, for the ultimate benefit of all. I will use this power wisely."

MESSAGE FOR GEMINI FROM THE MAGICIAN ★ "The Magician is telling you that you are ready! You are swiftly coming to realise that you can bring about desired effects through using specific tools that are at your disposal. This gives you a special sense of power and enables you to choose a specific goal or path and work towards it. Even though your methods and motives may focus on self-interest and grandiosity, you have the resources or the ability to manifest them. The Magician is an effective, powerful man with a strong focus upon goals. He makes plans and then fulfils them. He is a skilled and clever character, who performs occult rituals, pouring energy from his extended hand which erupts into a pillar of living fire. The Magician wears a pointed hat, the apex of which alludes to the ability to draw down cosmic forces. On the table (or altar) before him lie a Pentacle, Cup, Sword and Wand; each is a token of his use of and mastery over the four elements. The Magician offers a choice of directions and the opportunity to take one of them; the Cup represents the realm of feeling and relationships; the Sword is connected with the mind and the logical, rational world; the Wand symbolises creativity and imagination; and the Pentacle is associated with the material, the body and the physical world. Opportunities are available in each, or all, of these areas. Through embracing these magical opportunities, you are undertaking or achieving something new, and are starting a period in your life where you can exert your free spirit and willpower. If your willpower is consciously and assertively directed, you can now accomplish all that you visualise. The Magician impels you to go forward into the world and use your skill and intelligence to produce highly potent results. Gemini, The Magician lights the way ahead of you for fresh beginnings, the start of a new phase or cycle, and a directed sense of purpose."

★ THE FOOL ★

Ruled by Uranus & the Element of Air

Number ★ Zero (or 22 in some decks)

Keywords ★ Beginnings, Innocence, Exploration

Meditation ★ "I have the courage to step forward; I am not afraid of the unknown. I am Divinely protected."

MESSAGE FOR GEMINI FROM THE FOOL ★ "Wide-eyed and innocent as a newborn child, The Fool has descended from the celestial realms, eager to begin his mystical journey on the Path towards enlightenment. All is new to him and he has not yet learned to fear. Living from moment to moment, going forward without plan nor care, unaware of potential perils and joyful, in his luggage he carries the memories, instincts and experiences of past lives, waiting to be utilised afresh this time around. He carries a wand symbolising the pure faith of his actions, upon which sits a head that looks backwards, representing The Fool's past as he moves ever-forward. The Fool, who is young in years, is the true spiritual guide, and this card's presence suggests that you are entering a new and exciting phase of your life. It is therefore important that you believe in yourself and realise that the benevolent and ever-expansive Universe wishes you to succeed. But he is also telling you to listen to your wiser self, and to think carefully before making any move, reminding you that a thoughtless action will inhibit your progress. Develop a sense of purpose and don't allow yourself to become hesitant or indecisive. You must prepare the ground very thoroughly and make certain that you see every aspect of your present situation clearly and with a calm, resolute mind. Now is the time for faith, belief and commitment to your deepest dreams. Step into - and up to - the challenge. Throw caution to the wind and let it carry you where it will. Do not over-analyse things; this is a time for innocence and faith; take any necessary steps forward with confidence and hope. As the whimsical and wide-eyed adventurer, The Fool gives you the distinct and exquisite feeling that sometimes taking a leap of faith is the only mode of transportation you have available to you. Make the jump!"

★ ★ ★

TAROT MESSAGES FOR CANCER

★ THE CHARIOT ★

Ruled by Cancer

Number ★ 7

Keywords ★ Victory, Willpower, Control, Progress

Meditation ★ "I practice self-restraint, control and gentle influence to obtain any desire or goal I wish to. I understand intuitively that I must exercise balance, discretion, discipline and sound management in my life's journey if I am to arrive at my destination victoriously."

MESSAGE FOR CANCER FROM THE CHARIOT ★ "The Chariot is a card of movement, travel and transport. It depicts a victorious young man, standing upright in a chariot that has four columns and a luxuriant canopy, sets out on an adventure, or returns triumphant from battle. His chariot is drawn by two horses or sphinxes, who offer him wisdom, but may also represent his sexual drive and spirituality. He is powerful, demonstrated by his crown, and he appears positive in outlook. The Chariot is representative of achievement, popularity, control, and celebration. You may feel that your particular chariot is being drawn by two very different horses because doubt, uncertainty, struggles and conflicts plague your journey. However, the outcome will be worthwhile. The ability to relate to another increases your sense of inner strength and guidance, allowing you to make decisions to consciously initiate changes in your life. In order to triumph, you must take the reins of control and not let go. Enlist the help of outside forces in your quest and know that right now there is no time or place for emotions, just single-minded concentration on your goal. This need for control shifts into the knowledge that by being focused and true to your objectives, you can shape the course of your life rather than drift along aimlessly. You are quite right to feel strong and optimistic and should accept any challenge that is offered. The Chariot encourages you to expand your horizons through study and adventure, for whatever your age you are young at heart! You can now focus your will and work towards your goals. The time is ripe for travel, intellectual journeys and fulfilling your potential. The Chariot card is saying congratulations, as you have successfully balanced a challenging situation and it is now time to bask in the joy of this accomplishment. It is important to exercise determination, kind but firm self-control, and the willingness to go the distance. The Chariot represents the perseverance not to give up when emotional issues threaten your stability. You have garnered approval, respect and admiration from those around you for your ability to see both sides, make decisions and take action. Stay grounded and calm and above all, be clear about what you're ultimately trying to achieve."

★ THE HIGH PRIESTESS ★

Ruled by the Moon & the Element of Water

Number ★ 2

Keywords ★ Intuition, Wisdom, Knowledge, Mystery

Meditation ★ "I possess a wealth of arcane wisdom, knowledge, secrets and mysteries, which I choose to share with discretion and discernment to those who are ready and willing to receive it. I trust my intuition when selecting these Chosen Ones."

MESSAGE FOR CANCER FROM THE HIGH PRIESTESS ★ "The High Priestess is a private, all-seeing and spiritual woman with hidden depths and a deep, albeit veiled, compassion for others. In the card, she is seated upon a cube-shaped stone throne, which signifies her great depth and dimension as well as her connection with the Wisdom of the Ages ~ all the knowledge that ever was, is and will be. Passive, humble and silent, she represents a vessel of memory and holy female wisdom. Her powers are so great that they are almost beyond actions, her timeless secrets communicated through an inner voice, and only those wise enough to retreat into silence and undertake thoughtful study will know them. The High Priestess embodies the highest spiritual values, representing an open door to the sacred realms of mysticism and magic. She is telling you to learn from emotional situations. The answers you seek lie in your emotions and feelings, so trust your intuition and the power of your natural psychic abilities. The High Priestess tells you that within your subconscious mind lies the means to find your path home. Also, by paying special attention to your dreams and any intuitive messages you receive, you will be accurately guided by them. Being a Water sign, your intuition generally functions more strongly than your intellect. Stay open to your emotions and your feelings in order to come into contact with what you already know. Study spiritual topics, and remember that silence and solitude can be golden, as they yield the answers you seek. Selective in your desire for knowledge, you aspire to know and hold the key to life's mysteries, the essential, primordial principles and secrets that are the unique and sacred nature of life on Earth. Silent, secretive, clairvoyant and enlightened, The High Priestess can guide you through the dark wood of ignorance, indicating that reason alone cannot guide you. Her message to you is to go quietly within yourself to become aware of your eternal connection to All That Is, and the strength you gain from this knowledge will bring profound insights. If you are in the process of trying to answer an important question about your life, The High Priestess invites you to relax and listen to your inner voice. Take a deep breath, and imagine an open, illuminated space in the centre of your chest where all wisdom resides, and let the answer come to you. The High Priestess imparts a simple yet meaningful message: Look for the answers to questions within your heart. Trust your insights, intuition and gut feelings, and act on your hunches."

★ ★ ★

TAROT MESSAGES FOR LEO

★ STRENGTH ★

Ruled by Leo

Number ★ 8 (or 11 in some decks)

Keywords ★ Gentle Force, Courage, Inner Fortitude, Power

Meditation ★ "I have the courage, resolve and spiritual fortitude to overcome all."

MESSAGE FOR LEO FROM STRENGTH ★ "Strength signifies a courageous person, endowed with a tranquil strength, a resolute temperament and sound self-control. The lady depicted in most decks has tamed the animal's wild nature with her spiritual touch. She has no need of physical strength, for by love she has conquered. Strength gives you the message that you're stronger than you realise and that you can definitely handle your current challenges. However, instead of using force and barging through obstacles, you're better off with an approach of compassion, gentleness and firm kindness, as the strength that your setbacks call for can only come from the softness of a spiritual core. You need to release harsh judgements and practice forgiveness and patience, and your strength and effectiveness will increase. You need to believe in yourself and your ability to grow from your trials. Strength can conversely mean that you are experiencing yourself as ready and able to get what you want in life. Grounded and centered in your experience of energy, you know from your *heart* what you need. There is indeed magic afoot in your life at all times, and if you haven't already accessed it, it is available to you. When working with this card, try wishing for what you have always wanted - now is the time it may manifest; in any case, the energy is there for you to harness and utilise to your great advantage. Look upon your current situations as opportunities from which to learn and grow so that you can apply the knowledge gained with a superbly magical touch. In the face of fear, act calmly and with love and you will gain the true strength of an integrated body and spirit. Through gentleness you will accomplish what force cannot. Strength promises victory to those who know how to direct their natural gifts and willpower into the right channels, and who persevere in their efforts with unflagging energy and focus. It is through the power of inner peace and love that the character featured on this card is able to tame the ferocious beast and can open his mouth with sheer will but little physical effort. Indeed, the strength of her soul and the force of her love will tame the lion more effectively than any violence, aggression or savagery. She represents the overcoming of difficulties and weaknesses of character through steady persistence. The lion symbolises power and positive energy, and the human figure harnesses that power. Drawing this card will always make you the master of yourself and/or the situation in which you find yourself. It tells you that, if you handle circumstances in a positive, concentrated and gentle manner, you will achieve your deepest desires."

★ THE SUN ★

Ruled by the Sun

Number ★ 19

Keywords ★ Success, Joy, Vitality, Radiance

Meditation ★ "I express immense gratitude for the sheer joy of being alive. My heart is open and my soul streams out in an uninhibited flow of endless luminosity, love, generosity, radiance and spirit. I am pure happiness."

MESSAGE FOR LEO FROM THE SUN ★ "Two almost naked children, perhaps the celestial Castor and Pollux, the Gemini of the zodiac, are standing in front of a wall with the Sun above casting down radiant rays, falling like drops of gold around them. Some decks show a beaming Sun gazing down on a single naked child riding a white horse. The child holds up a banner, and behind him is a wall, over which sunflowers, the ultimate symbol of the Sun, can be seen. Whatever its imagery, The Sun symbolises the Divine, wise child, who reminds you how to frolic. This motif is an appeal to us to re-realise the passionate simplicity of the unfettered child, serving as a potent reminder to laugh, play and *love* more. The Sun card reminds us of times when we were or are at our happiest and brings us back to basics. In idyllic scenes from childhood, everything is open and always flooded with the Sun's rays. This card allows you to freely open your heart to the world and simply to feel good. There are no boundaries and no secrets. The Sun represents rebirth - the emergence of the butterfly out of the cocoon, the soul's appearance in all its radiance. The Sun card indicates that now is a marvellous time for all who bask under its rays, especially Leos. Any endeavours undertaken or beginning at this time will be blessed with abundance and success. This is a time for shining in every sense of the word; keep your thoughts positive and turned to the Sun, and your brilliant ideas will turn out magnificently. The spiritual and personal work you've been doing is yielding results and is bringing astounding changes to your life. Indeed, you are well on your way to spiritual enlightenment, as well as the perfect gifts of powerful physical and emotional health. Quite simply, The Sun urges you to give in to satisfaction, contentment, spontaneous and pure feelings, and to be yourself. The presence of The Sun provides you with a feelings relief, clarity, success and abundance. The Sun is a very lucky omen, and perhaps the happiest, most positive card in the Tarot. Success abounds for you!"

★ JUDGEMENT ★

Ruled by Pluto & the Element of Fire

Number ★ 20

Keywords ★ Evaluation, Self-assessment, Opportunities, New Directions

Meditation ★ "I stand at the Oracle of Judgement. In its innate wisdom and pure truths, I trust that it will light the way ahead by allowing for my redemption, renewal and rebirth."

MESSAGE FOR LEO FROM JUDGEMENT ★ "The Judgement card is the respected mentor, who leads the way to a fresh perspective on life and leaves you feeling elated. Its main divinatory meanings are atonement, judgement, improvement, evaluation and finally, rebirth. In the symbolism of the Tarot, Judgement is not concerned with eternal damnation or heavenly bliss based upon this 'judgement' of your life experience so far, from birth onward; it is not a time for punishment and retribution, but a time of being called to account for past actions and experiences. After facing one's 'moment of truth', one can see oneself with more clarity and acceptance, and is then able to see others in the same way. This acceptance is an understanding of the human condition, human beauty, and embraces imperfections and Divine wisdom alongside each other. Our past, having been reflected upon, ensures that a positive resolution will be reinforced. With atonement and repentance, real advancement can occur. Therefore, Judgement is less about guilt and more about self-knowledge. On a spiritual wavelength, this card implies that one particular phase of your soul's journey is ending, and you will shortly assess what you learned and how you dealt with the passing situation, summing up your performance and its value to you. Judgement is telling you that at this point in your life it is time to assess and evaluate yourself, and perhaps address any underlying issues which up until now may have been ignored. To do this, you need simply to become more self-aware. Judgement emphasises that in undertaking this self-examination, you should be fair on yourself and focus on your positive character traits. It is telling you that once you have done this, like the symbolic people on the card, you will be ripe and ready to move in a new direction and onto a higher, more worthwhile plane of existence! You're either near the end of a project or at a crossroads, but either way, you are on the threshold of making an important change in your life. From deep within the core of your being comes this call announcing that it is time to make an important change. You must concern yourself with finding meaning and purpose, evaluating past deeds and becoming more aware of who you are and who you wish to become."

TAROT MESSAGES FOR VIRGO

★ THE HERMIT ★

Ruled by Virgo

Number ★ 9

Keywords ★ Withdrawal, Retreat, Solitude, Contemplation, Inner Journeying

Meditation ★ "I embrace my inner self through solitude. I will find the answers I seek through quiet, gentle retreat and thoughtful introspection, and endeavour to share the insights with others when I re-emerge restored, enlightened and transformed."

MESSAGE FOR VIRGO FROM THE HERMIT ★ "Carrying his luminous but strangely lit lantern, The Hermit walks the enlightened Path of wisdom. He walks alone and at night, where both his robe and the dark conceal him, for his teachings are only for those who seek him out. The Hermit's symbolism shows you how to attune to your inner wisdom. He represents a turning away from the external world to focus inwardly. In spite of his reclusiveness, he carries a lantern to light the Path ahead, which may be symbolic of his quest for knowledge, and also that introspection is not all about darkness - in fact, one requires the darker recesses of the soul to be illuminated during the 'search'. The Hermit is the wise, Solitary One, a seeker who knows how to call down the power of the Moon, to converse with spirits and work magical spells. The Hermit is telling you that you need to spend some quiet time in meditation. This is a time to reflect, in order to reassess your direction and your commitments. You would benefit from some time alone, listening to your inner voice. Be silent and experience the joy that comes from seeking the truth and Path of your own heart. This card is compelling you to learn to feel comfortable in your own company. It indicates a time of spiritual awakening, enlightenment, wisdom-seeking, and journeying to the inner depths. But it also suggests that perhaps it is time for you to seek out a spiritual guide, teacher, healer or mentor for yourself before undertaking the arduous task of questioning the inner workings of your soul. Virgo, you have an innate desire for quiet introspection, to assimilate the changes taking place within. Through this, you understand that by listening to your inner spirit you can acquire wisdom. Others recognise this and seek out your advice, after which you find yourself drawn out into the world again. The Hermit encourages you to increase your knowledge of the world through study and experience. He suggests that sometimes you need to withdraw and re-consider your true self. Like the accomplished shamans and wise women everywhere, The Hermit contains both the male and the female, the active and the receptive, and the Sun and Moon within. He has learned the power of energy retention and transmutation and can now choose how to spend or store those energies. He knows that plunging down into the unconscious is a vital part of the soul's search for meaning. The time out he embarks upon is both healing and rejuvenating. Like a caterpillar, he seeks transformation. And like the caterpillar, he spins fibres around himself and later emerges as something new and different. But the awakening can evoke pain: indeed, turning away from the world to discover whether you are really alive is undoubtedly painful, but it is in this conscious acceptance of loneliness that a natural process of healing occurs. And through this inner listening, The Hermit - and his cosmic student, Virgo - often becomes a teacher, a way-shower to others."

★ THE MAGICIAN ★

Ruled by Mercury

Number ★ 1

Keywords ★ Initiative, Will, Mindpower, Independence

Meditation ★ "I have the willpower, magical tools and initiative to create my own experiences. I am spiritually, mentally, emotionally, psychically and physically equipped to exercise my unique brand of personal power to manipulate the inner and outer worlds to suit my needs, for the ultimate benefit of all. I will use this power wisely."

MESSAGE FOR VIRGO FROM THE MAGICIAN ★ "The Magician is telling you that you are ready! You are swiftly coming to realise that you can bring about desired effects through using specific tools that are at your disposal. This gives you a special sense of power and enables you to choose a specific goal or path and work towards it. Even though your methods and motives may focus on self-interest and grandiosity, you have the resources or the ability to manifest them. The Magician is an effective, powerful man with a strong focus upon goals. He makes plans and then fulfils them. He is a skilled and clever character, who performs occult rituals, pouring energy from his extended hand which erupts into a pillar of living fire. The Magician wears a pointed hat, the apex of which alludes to the ability to draw down cosmic forces. On the table (or altar) before him lie a Pentacle, Cup, Sword and Wand; each is a token of his use of and mastery over the four elements. The Magician offers a choice of directions and the opportunity to take one of them; the Cup represents the realm of feeling and relationships; the Sword is connected with the mind and the logical, rational world; the Wand symbolises creativity and imagination; and the Pentacle is associated with the material, the body and the physical world. Opportunities are available in each, or all, of these areas. Through embracing these magical opportunities, you are undertaking or achieving something new, and are starting a period in your life where you can exert your free spirit and willpower. If your willpower is consciously and assertively directed, you can now accomplish all that you visualise. The Magician impels you to go forward into the world and use your skill and intelligence to produce highly potent results. Virgo, The Magician lights the way ahead of you for fresh beginnings, the start of a new phase or cycle, and a directed sense of purpose."

★ THE WORLD/UNIVERSE ★

Ruled by Saturn & the Element of Earth

Number ★ 21

Keywords ★ Completion, Attainment, Fulfilment, Success

Meditation ★ "I have completed one journey and will now rebirth myself to begin a brand new one. I welcome every chance to grow and learn, and I truly never stop evolving."

MESSAGE FOR VIRGO FROM THE WORLD ★ "A statue of a woman has come to life and is dancing, looking back at a leaf she holds in her outstretched hand. Just as the Earth, Divine Mother of us all, evolved from the stars and materialised into reality, so have our physical selves been created out of the same essence so that we may dance the dance of life just as She dances through the cosmos. This dream-like journey is one of going deep within and finding our essential harmony with All There Is. When we arrive at the knowledge of who we really are we gain The World. Virgo, you have arrived at the beginning of the Path to Enlightenment or could be considerably advanced along it by now. The World card suggests a job well done - you have happily completed something of great significance. Enjoy these feelings of wholeness and completion as your amazing accomplishments have been well-earned. You're now ready to move onto something new. You have grown spiritually and have evolved to a whole new level in your understanding of the Universe and your place in it. As well as this, you have attained complete clarity, cosmic awareness, significant enlightenment, an expanded consciousness and above all, the true freedom that accompanies all this. The World imparts the message that each one of us carries a world inside of us, which is neither unattainable, illusory or utopian. It is simply what we are. All the elements are gathered here so that our conscience may awaken, and our future will unfold as it is meant to before us. Form a circle with a group of friends, imaginary or real. Slowly move around it, dancing and swaying and chanting. Complete the circle twenty-two times. As you do so, close your eyes and visualise the Earth in the centre of your circle, bathed in white light, receiving the love, wisdom and healing energy from your group. Know that we are all blessed with the sacred duty of being the caretakers of our Mother Earth - and of finding our own unique place within it."

TAROT MESSAGES FOR LIBRA

★ JUSTICE ★

Ruled by Libra

Number ★ 11 (or 8 in some decks)

Keywords ★ Fairness, Morality, Balance, Karma

Meditation ★ "I rely upon the Divine unseen force of Justice to prevail in all situations. I seek not to control but to balance. I hold true and deep to the belief that what goes around comes around; I trust that Karma will serve the natural justice that I, in my human Earthly form, cannot."

MESSAGE FOR LIBRA FROM JUSTICE ★ "Justice is a detached, but fair, mediator who helps to resolve inner and outer conflicts through the courage of her convictions. The crowned figure of Justice is often seated between pillars representing mercy and punishment. In her hands she holds the balance and sword. Her face is resolute and firm in conviction and in most images, she wears no blindfold, so she sees all the facts. The Justice card evokes in us the Universal understanding of virtue that can be traced to Philo's four cardinal traits: wisdom, temperance, courage and justice. Justice represents the laws of nature, as well as the relentless workings of fate - through the slow, regular turning of the Wheel of Karma. Libra, this card understands and advises you that you must remain in harmony with this Universal order and maintain your connection with it through blessings and rituals. If harmony does not prevail, then your life will not progress smoothly and all around you cannot prosper. Errors must be recognised and order must be restored in order for karmic forces to adjust to and overcome any adverse conditions. This is Justice's task - to maintain and restore order and equilibrium, therefore ensuring karmic balance. Justice guides you towards wise and carefully considered decisions, ones made with fairness and objectivity. It suggests that you have a decision to make, and also that a decision has been or will be made in your favour. Justice always implies the need to find or recover a balance between opposing forces or contradictory elements in your life. She advises that although the *human* judicial system may be fooled, Divine justice can never be escaped. You are coming to consciousness about your place in the Universal scheme of things. There are special ways you can feel karma working in your life; perhaps you have a newfound sense of yourself as powerful and moving through life with purpose. Maybe some conflict in your life has come to a resolution, or things have worked out after a period of deep disharmony. Whatever the case, things are setting themselves right again and you can feel your own peace returning. You understand that what is happening is a result of past actions that are having karmic results. But you also have to realise that even if things aren't working out so well, or if you are off-balance, that nature works in calm, quiet ways, sometimes giving us what we *need* rather than what we *want*. The Justice card belongs to Libra, the cardinal Air sign of social fairness and equality, symbolised by the Scales. Libra, being ruled by Venus (goddess of love) considers everything in terms of others. Libra loves beauty and harmony and wants to bring her surroundings to a state of peaceful co-existence. In this way, Libra is Nemesis, the cords of retribution and just rewards, that draw the human race together, and urges to connect each of us with the All - after all, a blessing on one of Earth's children blesses all, just as a curse on one hurts all. Justice advises to be practical, rigorous, stern but fair, kind, patient, objective, honest, and sympathetic to those weaker than yourself. Of course, it is always possible to appeal against what has been judged. But, once the sword has fallen, a page has been turned. Ultimately, Justice is implacable; in the search for truth, Justice will always prevail. Have faith that karma will triumph and leave the punishment of those you think have done the wrong thing in its wise and capable hands."

★ THE EMPRESS ★

Ruled by Venus

Number ★ 3

Keywords ★ Nurturance, Fertility, Security, Abundance, Emotional Wealth

Meditation ★ "I am the lover, the provider, the nurturer and the carer, who bestows myself and others with a free and steady flow of feminine gifts. Abundance, fertility, plenitude and natural Earthly wisdom are my way of life."

MESSAGE FOR LIBRA FROM THE EMPRESS ★ "The Empress represents the Great Mother, in all her simplicity and purity. She promises abundance, birth, growth, harmony, community, and relationship. The Empress's Hebrew name is Daleth and means 'door'. As the Qabbalist's Great Mother, she is the doorway through which all forms of life must pass in order to become manifest, hence her deep associations with fertility and creation. As such, she represents the Earth from which all life is born, and to which it returns at the end of its cycle. The Empress in her contemporary 'seductress' pose symbolises the unconscious knowledge contemporary women share of the ancient mysteries and female reverence, of healing and transformation, that live on in our much-diminished but ever-pure Divinity. The Empress feels her connection to the Earth. She knows - has always known - the mystery of procreation, the potential for growing and nurturing life, the sacred act of birthing, and the communal life close to the soil - a time when people did not make war, but spent their leisure time making love and art. The Empress is a sensual, practical woman who appreciates good, wholesome, hearty food, nature and a pleasantly simple life. She is nurturing and generous and teaches that you need to foster your dreams and desires. If the card preceding this, The High Priestess, holds the secrets of life, then The Empress is what gives that life soul and emotion, for she represents the understanding and the power of that life. The Empress's potency lies primarily in feelings, as she is able to exploit both the riches of the heart and the psyche. The Empress, the archetypal fertile Earth Mother, can help bring daydreams to fruition in a world where logic and intuition should dwell together as heaven and Earth do. As such, The Empress is telling you to give birth to your dreams, to nurture yourself and others, spend time in nature, and indulge in creative and artistic endeavours. She suggests a possible pregnancy, a harmonious home environment and progress with your plans. She encourages you to enjoy material comforts and sensual fulfillment but to be wary of overindulgence. Enjoy the beautiful things in life, knowing that you deserve to be exquisitely and Divinely provided for. The realisation that life is inherently a creative process motivates you to explore what brings you harmony. The upsurge of energy and passion that arises with this awakening, attracts cooperation in others, as well as abundance into your experience. The Empress helps you to understand that growth occurs only when you nurture your dreams. Have an open and sympathetic heart and your wishes will be provided for. Exert your power with a loving hand and then creativity, productivity, heaven and Earth will all exist for you on the same plane. Libra, The Empress brings out your artistic side, opens up your love of beauty, and heightens your aesthetic appreciation. She represents 'prosperity thinking' and the power of positive imagination and instills the faith that your hopes *will* come to fruition, finances *will* improve, green leaves *will* sprout, shows you examples and symbols that fertility *will* abound, and you *will* begin to feel more confident as you reap the rewards of your efforts. Finally, it is interesting to note that the words 'material' and 'matter' originate from the Latin word for mother, *mater*. You can ask this Great Earth Mother for what you need, for she is the unerring All-Provider."

★ THE FOOL ★

Ruled by Uranus & the Element of Air

Number ★ Zero (or 22 in some decks)

Keywords ★ Beginnings, Innocence, Exploration

Meditation ★ "I have the courage to step forward; I am not afraid of the unknown. I am Divinely protected."

MESSAGE FOR LIBRA FROM THE FOOL ★ "Wide-eyed and innocent as a newborn child, The Fool has descended from the celestial realms, eager to begin his mystical journey on the Path towards enlightenment. All is new to him and he has not yet learned to fear. Living from moment to moment, going forward without plan nor care, unaware of potential perils and joyful, in his luggage he carries the memories, instincts and experiences of past lives, waiting to be utilised afresh this time around. He carries a wand symbolising the pure faith of his actions, upon which sits a head that looks backwards, representing The Fool's past as he moves ever-forward. The Fool, who is young in years, is the true spiritual guide, and this card's presence suggests that you are entering a new and exciting phase of your life. It is therefore important that you believe in yourself and realise that the benevolent and ever-expansive Universe wishes you to succeed. But he is also telling you to listen to your wiser self, and to think carefully before making any move, reminding you that a thoughtless action will inhibit your progress. Develop a sense of purpose and don't allow yourself to become hesitant or indecisive. You must prepare the ground very thoroughly and make certain that you see every aspect of your present situation clearly and with a calm, resolute mind. Now is the time for faith, belief and commitment to your deepest dreams. Step into - and up to - the challenge. Throw caution to the wind and let it carry you where it will. Do not over-analyse things; this is a time for innocence and faith; take any necessary steps forward with confidence and hope. As the whimsical and wide-eyed adventurer, The Fool gives you the distinct and exquisite feeling that sometimes taking a leap of faith is the only mode of transportation you have available to you. Make the jump!"

TAROT MESSAGES FOR SCORPIO

★ DEATH ★

Ruled by Scorpio

Number ★ 13

Keywords ★ Change, Renewal, Transformation, Endings, Beginnings

Meditation ★ "All that has gone before, including my mistakes, is preparation for a better Path ahead. This new life or way of being, will be exactly the right one for me. Death will show me the way. I surrender to it with the enlightened knowledge that it is for my higher good and am letting go of all that is no longer needed."

MESSAGE FOR SCORPIO FROM DEATH ★ "Here we have two symbols which both have a sinister reputation: death and the number thirteen. On no account should this card be regarded as a portent of literal, physical death. Like all the other Major Arcana cards, it is merely a *symbol* of death - essentially, that of an ending or a change. The skeletal form of the figure in the Death card is a reminder that death exists within life. In the skeleton, we see that the superficial has been pared away; all the desires of the flesh have been banished. He wishes not to be feared, for he symbolises the ultimate rebirth or regeneration that occurs with any death or ending; when transition occurs, new growth arises. An act of release can make it possible to move forward again. Though death can involve profound change, it can also be seen as a form of purging, of liberation. You must destroy old patterns to reveal a new, uncluttered, rewarding Path. Endings are usually painful, but ultimately, your fear of Death must be recognised and faced before it is allowed to interfere further with your enjoyment of life. The Death card signifies the end of a phase or situation. This will be a time for spiritual transformation, a time to move on! Shake off the old and welcome in the new! The Death card signifies relief or sadness, but there is no benefit in remaining in this situation or feeling. It is a card pointing to inevitable positive changes, confronting your fears, relationship transitions and eventual spiritual evolution. You are beginning to realise how much you have been weighed down by past mental and emotional baggage. Unhealthy relationships and old habits need to be consciously discarded and this is usually an uncomfortable and unpleasant process, but leaves you feeling free to be more truly and fully yourself. And although change is a necessary part of life, few of us welcome it with an open heart. For most, letting go of the unfamiliar can be sad and harrowing. If you are having trouble dealing with change, be assured that a sense of liberation will swiftly follow and replace any sorrow or pain - in essence, you will undergo a spiritual rebirth and awakening once you allow for this very necessary release."

★ JUDGEMENT ★

Ruled by Pluto & the Element of Fire

Number ★ 20

Keywords ★ Evaluation, Self-assessment, Opportunities, New Directions

Meditation ★ "I stand at the Oracle of Judgement. In its innate wisdom and pure truths, I trust that it will light the way ahead by allowing for my redemption, renewal and rebirth."

MESSAGE FOR SCORPIO FROM JUDGEMENT ★ "The Judgement card is the respected mentor, who leads the way to a fresh perspective on life and leaves you feeling elated. Its main divinatory meanings are atonement, judgement, improvement, evaluation and finally, rebirth. In the symbolism of the Tarot, Judgement is not concerned with eternal damnation or heavenly bliss based upon this 'judgement' of your life experience so far, from birth onward; it is not a time for punishment and retribution, but a time of being called to account for past actions and experiences. After facing one's 'moment of truth', one can see oneself with more clarity and acceptance, and is then able to see others in the same way. This acceptance is an understanding of the human condition, human beauty, and embraces imperfections and Divine wisdom alongside each other. Our past, having been reflected upon, ensures that a positive resolution will be reinforced. With atonement and repentance, real advancement can occur. Therefore, Judgement is less about guilt and more about self-knowledge. On a spiritual wavelength, this card implies that one particular phase of your soul's journey is ending, and you will shortly assess what you learned and how you dealt with the passing situation, summing up your performance and its value to you. Judgement is telling you that at this point in your life it is time to assess and evaluate yourself, and perhaps address any underlying issues which up until now may have been ignored. To do this, you need simply to become more self-aware. Judgement emphasises that in undertaking this self-examination, you should be fair on yourself and focus on your positive character traits. It is telling you that once you have done this, like the symbolic people on the card, you will be ripe and ready to move in a new direction and onto a higher, more worthwhile plane of existence! You're either near the end of a project or at a crossroads, but either way, you are on the threshold of making an important change in your life. From deep within the core of your being comes this call announcing that it is time to make an important change. You must concern yourself with finding meaning and purpose, evaluating past deeds and becoming more aware of who you are and who you wish to become."

★ THE TOWER ★

Ruled by Mars

Number ★ 16

Keywords ★ Collapse, Upheaval, Awakening, Rebuilding

Meditation ★ "I trust that whatever disaster or unexpected events befall me, they occur for my ultimate higher good. I understand that all adverse happenings, without exception, allow me a chance to rebuild."

MESSAGE FOR SCORPIO FROM THE TOWER ★ "A sturdy tower erected on a hill is struck by lightning and explosively blown apart. The castellated top of the tower is lifted by the blast, fire strikes deep within, and flames roar from the narrow windows as two figures fall from their ruined refuge. The security afforded by this strong, old structure, has been reduced to ruin by the forces of natural law. Flames erupt and smoke fills the air, sparks and debris fall on either side; there has been a dramatic reversal of fortune. Future plans have been aborted. The Tower represents the shock that shatters your illusions, removes the rug from beneath your feet, and clears away the refuse. Scorpio, a sudden catastrophe may break down all your previous conceptions about yourself or others. You sometimes feel as if there is no firm foundation upon which to rest your life as the veils of illusion are torn away. This forces you to face painful truths, but also liberates you from the past and provides sudden insights. The Tower tears down your world but in doing so provides a new focus. And once the storm settles, you are free! Lightning has struck, but enlightenment is sure to follow. This card indicates the needs to find fresh ways to do things, as the old have become rigid and imprisoning. We often live our lives as we have been conditioned to, never examining closely whether our lifestyle really suits us, until this complacency comes crashing down around us and forces us to re-consider and revaluate. The lightning that strikes The Tower on the card represents the new visions and possibilities which await us, and which will soon be brought to our attention through an upheaval or crisis. The change may be something that happens to you, an event or situation that transforms you. You may suddenly just know your marriage is over, your job is ending, or the time has come for a move. You may have a sudden lucid understanding of your own destructive behaviours or addictions and the need for an immediate and radical overhaul. These insights may be momentary, like a lightning bolt, but the effects are far-reaching and enduring. If possible, open yourself right up to the power inherent in The Tower card. The time has come to spread your wings!"

★ THE HIGH PRIESTESS ★

Ruled by the Moon & the Element of Water

Number ★ 2

Keywords ★ Intuition, Wisdom, Knowledge, Mystery

Meditation ★ "I possess a wealth of arcane wisdom, knowledge, secrets and mysteries, which I choose to share with discretion and discernment to those who are ready and willing to receive it. I trust my intuition when selecting these Chosen Ones."

MESSAGE FOR SCORPIO FROM THE HIGH PRIESTESS ★ "The High Priestess is a private, all-seeing and spiritual woman with hidden depths and a deep, albeit veiled, compassion for others. In the card, she is seated upon a cube-shaped stone throne, which signifies her great depth and dimension as well as her connection with the Wisdom of the Ages ~ all the knowledge that ever was, is and will be. Passive, humble and silent, she represents a vessel of memory and holy female wisdom. Her powers are so great that they are almost beyond actions, her timeless secrets communicated through an inner voice, and only those wise enough to retreat into silence and undertake thoughtful study will know them. The High Priestess embodies the highest spiritual values, representing an open door to the sacred realms of mysticism and magic. She is telling you to learn from emotional situations. The answers you seek lie in your emotions and feelings, so trust your intuition and the power of your natural psychic abilities. The High Priestess tells you that within your subconscious mind lies the means to find your path home. Also, by paying special attention to your dreams and any intuitive messages you receive, you will be accurately guided by them. Being a Water sign, your intuition generally functions more strongly than your intellect. Stay open to your emotions and your feelings in order to come into contact with what you already know. Study spiritual topics, and remember that silence and solitude can be golden, as they yield the answers you seek. Selective in your desire for knowledge, you aspire to know and hold the key to life's mysteries, the essential, primordial principles and secrets that are the unique and sacred nature of life on Earth. Silent, secretive, clairvoyant and enlightened, The High Priestess can guide you through the dark wood of ignorance, indicating that reason alone cannot guide you. Her message to you is to go quietly within yourself to become aware of your eternal connection to All That Is, and the strength you gain from this knowledge will bring profound insights. If you are in the process of trying to answer an important question about your life, The High Priestess invites you to relax and listen to your inner voice. Take a deep breath, and imagine an open, illuminated space in the centre of your chest where all wisdom resides, and let the answer come to you. The High Priestess imparts a simple yet meaningful message: Look for the answers to questions within your heart. Trust your insights, intuition and gut feelings, and act on your hunches."

☆ ☆ ☆

TAROT MESSAGES FOR SAGITTARIUS

★ TEMPERANCE ★

Ruled by Sagittarius

Number ★ 14

Keywords ★ Moderation, Balance, Blending

Meditation ★ "I walk the Path of moderation, temperance and gentleness, and trust that when working from my pure heart and soul, successful blendings and unions will take place and unfold naturally."

MESSAGE FOR SAGITTARIUS FROM TEMPERANCE ★ "In Tarot tradition, the Temperance card represents the empowerment of alchemy, that mystical process of blending the parts of the self until fusion is achieved and the 'philosopher's stone' is created. Alchemy is a philosophy and practice that spans both science and mysticism. First conceived as a process similar to fermentation, in which common base metals might be transmuted into gold or silver, over time the alchemical process became an analogy for psychological and physical transformation also. In ancient times, as alchemy became ever more spiritual and concerned with more abstract and philosophical concepts, eventually it was considered that the transmutation of base metals into gold was simply a metaphor for the transformation of the prime matter, in this case the human soul, into a much purer and higher state of wisdom and being. Temperance reveals the ability to maintain equilibrium even in the midst of chaotic change. The freedom to discover new aspects of yourself leads you to explore your inner space once more. You become aware that if you are balanced and centred, life flows more smoothly. Enthralling you with the sense of harmony this creates, you discover qualities that can be explored from the inside and then expressed outwardly. The natural movements of energy around and within you are in harmony and integrated; you are not fragmented or disconnected from yourself. You may even feel in a heightened state of consciousness, able to absorb much more than usual and to assimilate it naturally within your being. You may be experiencing a new sense of courage and well-being. However, we use our personal magic, there are times in everyone's life when things work out well and when everything runs smoothly. Temperance suggests that such a time is on its way to you, perhaps after a considerable period of inner conflict. Temperance, after all, is all about balance and moderation. It also signifies cooperation and compromise, keeping a moderate pace and striking equilibrium between contemplation and action. It suggests that you need to be cautious about making impulsive decisions or moves, and instead choose the 'Middle Way', the Path of moderation and balance. If you're considering making a dramatic life change, approach this change slowly and methodically. This card is also about working in concert with others and encourages you to see things from their points of view and to work in unison with them for the best results. Extending this compassion, kindness and tolerance are key to manifesting your dreams. Forgiveness will also allow for healing, which will help bring about the new beginnings you so desire. The dialogue is always open with Temperance, its presence reassuring because it tells you simply that, with time, everything becomes transformed and ultimately sorted out. Of course, it also pledges moderation, understanding, and tolerance, and it frequently appears when a transaction or negotiation is underway. Finally, by allowing this free flow of energies and currents, it presents you with new opportunities and possibilities that you may seize."

★ WHEEL OF FORTUNE ★

Ruled by Jupiter

Number ★ 10

Keywords ★ Change, Acceptance, Fate

Meditation ★ "I accept that life has its inevitable ups and downs, some over which I have control, others which I don't. At the heart of this is providence, and in providence I trust."

MESSAGE FOR SAGITTARIUS FROM WHEEL OF FORTUNE ★ "Tarot historians believe the word Tarot itself derives from the Latin word *rota*, as in 'rotation', and reflects the ancient sense of life as a moving wheel. The 'wheels within wheels' that make up the Wheel of Fortune, rotate and turn like the ever-spinning rhythms and cycles of life. The traditionally shaped wheel holds the symbolism of the Sun and the cosmos and is an enduring symbol of human endeavour and advancement. A spin of the wheel may bring unexpected luck, opportunity and good fortune, or it may cause the reverse, and present obstacles to our desires. A confrontation with some 'demon' from the past may occur with a turn of the wheel. These could be fate, part of a Divine plan, or karma, but what seem to be beginnings and endings are in fact just part of the never-ending circle of life. The Sphinx, who sits at the top of the image, in her quiet wisdom, knows that no one stays on top forever. The Wheel of Fortune signifies an important turning point for good or bad, and tells you that life is not a merry-go-round, but rather a roller coaster, encouraging you to realise that there is ultimately purpose and equilibrium in everything that happens to you. This card usually denotes a time of positive change, or a situation that suddenly moves forward, in which case fortune is on your side! It also offers a chance to step back from circumstances in order to notice life's seasons, or the natural 'turning of the wheel'. In doing this, you will know when to plant seeds and when to harvest. It is not the Wheel of Fate but the Wheel of Fortune; this nuance is important. Indeed, the very fact that the wheel is activated by a handle, suggests the notion of free will at play. In other words, you have the choice to act or not to act, to use or not to use the handle in order to activate the wheel of your destiny. In any case, this card must prompt you to become aware of your share of active, conscious or unconscious responsibilities in the situations, circumstances or events you inevitably have to confront. Sometimes it indicates that we have to remain committed in order to progress; other times it means that for the moment, we can do nothing else but allow events to take their natural course. The turning of the Wheel of Fortune carries the message that what goes around, comes around, or what goes up, must come down. All you need to do is to be open to new and unexpected opportunities, allow for receiving, and above all, take risks. It is vitally important to always expect the unexpected. Ask your own spiritual guides or gods or goddesses to deliver to you your desires and just fortunes. Meditate on the Wheel of Fortune as you ask, and finally, take the chance and turn the wheel, for you never know where it may come to rest. The Wheel of Fortune represents the ability to understand and accept things, encouraging you to embrace changes in life wholeheartedly. There will always be highs and lows. Good or bad, trust that all is happening for your higher good. Accepting this brings a calmer, more holistic perspective."

★ JUDGEMENT ★

Ruled by Pluto & the Element of Fire

Number ★ 20

Keywords ★ Evaluation, Self-assessment, Opportunities, New Directions

Meditation ★ "I stand at the Oracle of Judgement. In its innate wisdom and pure truths, I trust that it will light the way ahead by allowing for my redemption, renewal and rebirth."

MESSAGE FOR SAGITTARIUS FROM JUDGEMENT ★ "The Judgement card is the respected mentor, who leads the way to a fresh perspective on life and leaves you feeling elated. Its main divinatory meanings are atonement, judgement, improvement, evaluation and finally, rebirth. In the symbolism of the Tarot, Judgement is not concerned with eternal damnation or heavenly bliss based upon this 'judgement' of your life experience so far, from birth onward; it is not a time for punishment and retribution, but a time of being called to account for past actions and experiences. After facing one's 'moment of truth', one can see oneself with more clarity and acceptance, and is then able to see others in the same way. This acceptance is an understanding of the human condition, human beauty, and embraces imperfections and Divine wisdom alongside each other. Our past, having been reflected upon, ensures that a positive resolution will be reinforced. With atonement and repentance, real advancement can occur. Therefore, Judgement is less about guilt and more about self-knowledge. On a spiritual wavelength, this card implies that one particular phase of your soul's journey is ending, and you will shortly assess what you learned and how you dealt with the passing situation, summing up your performance and its value to you. Judgement is telling you that at this point in your life it is time to assess and evaluate yourself, and perhaps address any underlying issues which up until now may have been ignored. To do this, you need simply to become more self-aware. Judgement emphasises that in undertaking this self-examination, you should be fair on yourself and focus on your positive character traits. It is telling you that once you have done this, like the symbolic people on the card, you will be ripe and ready to move in a new direction and onto a higher, more worthwhile plane of existence! You're either near the end of a project or at a crossroads, but either way, you are on the threshold of making an important change in your life. From deep within the core of your being comes this call announcing that it is time to make an important change. You must concern yourself with finding meaning and purpose, evaluating past deeds and becoming more aware of who you are and who you wish to become."

TAROT MESSAGES FOR CAPRICORN

★ THE DEVIL ★

Ruled by Capricorn

Number ★ 15

Keywords ★ Temptation, Excesses, Entrapment, Bondage

Meditation ★ "I am confronting my shadow self, and shall not succumb to greed, temptations or obsessions that are ultimately of my own creation. I acknowledge that I crave inner peace through having the courage to meet with my dark side, and that a more spiritually enlightened Path awaits me. I am abandoning my material desires in order to seek the proper Way."

MESSAGE FOR CAPRICORN FROM THE DEVIL ★ "The Devil is the archetypal face of evil. He compels us to look deeper into ourselves to examine our motives and untamed desires. Blinded to his spiritual nature, The Devil looks down on his captors, his slitted eyes suggestive of a complete obsession with and surrender to the material world. Although the epitome of the darker side of human nature, we do need to acknowledge that within each of us resides an invisible, wild, gratification-seeking spirit, wanting expression, yearning for freedom. The Devil is a complex card full of paradoxical meanings. In Jungian terms, we could regard The Devil as the collective 'shadow' that our culture has projected onto us, a symbol of societal bondage and power. Traditionally, and particularly to the common medieval psyche, The Devil was a living force of evil and thus greatly feared. However, in modern Tarot decks, the meaning of this card is more in line with Kabbalistic thought, which sees The Devil as the 'tester' or the quality controller - indeed a negative force, but one which provides the challenges and hardships against which you have to strive in your life. For without this active, discordant force, there would be nothing to strive *against*, and therefore little chance to progress. The main idea in this card is that of bondage and this can take many forms, most of which tie you down or give you the feeling of being trapped. It can indicate enslavement to something or someone, and could be an idea, a relationship, a way of life, an unhappy job, a bad habit or a self-destructive pattern. But this card's message is that your perceived entrapment isn't real; it isn't based in reality, but rather it is based in the ego and the shadowy self that lurks deep within. Your trap is of your own making and, even though you may imagine you can't escape its constriction, there is a way out if only you can see it. You will remain enslaved to the challenging situation until you acknowledge that you are in fact your *own* imprisoner and *you* therefore hold the key to unlock your chains. Capricorn, an encounter with The Devil brings back your deepest primal fears. To overcome these, you need to change your emphasis from physical concerns, to those of the spirit. Your bondage is the result of your limited beliefs about the world and your resorting to deceit or avarice to get what you want. You have within the power to change and use your beliefs, through visualisation, new habits, actions, free will and affirmations that are in harmony with natural and cosmic laws. In essence The Devil may exist in some form in each one of us, but it can always be exorcised."

★ THE WORLD/UNIVERSE ★

Ruled by Saturn & the Element of Earth

Number ★ 21

Keywords ★ Completion, Attainment, Fulfilment, Success

Meditation ★ "I have completed one journey and will now rebirth myself to begin a brand new one. I welcome every chance to grow and learn, and I truly never stop evolving."

MESSAGE FOR CAPRICORN FROM THE WORLD ★ "A statue of a woman has come to life and is dancing, looking back at a leaf she holds in her outstretched hand. Just as the Earth, Divine Mother of us all, evolved from the stars and materialised into reality, so have our physical selves been created out of the same essence so that we may dance the dance of life just as She dances through the cosmos. This dream-like journey is one of going deep within and finding our essential harmony with All There Is. When we arrive at the knowledge of who we really are we gain The World. Capricorn, you have arrived at the beginning of the Path to Enlightenment or could be considerably advanced along it by now. The World card suggests a job well done - you have happily completed something of great significance. Enjoy these feelings of wholeness and completion as your amazing accomplishments have been well-earned. You're now ready to move onto something new. You have grown spiritually and have evolved to a whole new level in your understanding of the Universe and your place in it. As well as this, you have attained complete clarity, cosmic awareness, significant enlightenment, an expanded consciousness and above all, the true freedom that accompanies all this. The World imparts the message that each one of us carries a world inside of us, which is neither unattainable, illusory or utopian. It is simply what we are. All the elements are gathered here so that our conscience may awaken, and our future will unfold as it is meant to before us. Form a circle with a group of friends, imaginary or real. Slowly move around it, dancing and swaying and chanting. Complete the circle twenty-two times. As you do so, close your eyes and visualise the Earth in the centre of your circle, bathed in white light, receiving the love, wisdom and healing energy from your group. Know that we are all blessed with the sacred duty of being the caretakers of our Mother Earth - and of finding our own unique place within it."

☆ ☆ ☆

TAROT MESSAGES FOR AQUARIUS

★ THE STAR ★

Ruled by Aquarius

Number ★ 17

Keywords ★ Renewed Hope, Inspiration, Dreams, Optimism

Meditation ★ "The energy, hope, faith and love I intend to summon and pour forth today will light up my whole future."

MESSAGE FOR AQUARIUS FROM THE STAR ★ "The Star represents the idea that hope, courage and inspiration will bring the promise of better times to come, and that there will be peace after a storm. In The Star card, a star of hope and wonder shines in the heavens, promising spiritual illumination and enchantment. Below, with one foot on the land and the other poised magically on the surface of the stream of the unconscious, a near-naked maiden stands entranced, joyously receiving the waters of the pool, which rise up to her as she pours an endless shower of liquid from her two containers. She demonstrates that as heaven nourishes the earthly planes, the wonders of the physical world nourishes the heavens. The Star is a symbol of the cleansing and purification that occurs after the turbulence of life's upheavals calms down; it ultimately stands for the sense of wonder that heralds the restored belief that dreams can - and do - come true. Aquarius, The Star advises you to take time to recharge yourself with a period of relaxation. Enjoy being 'the star' of your own life journey. This is the time for the allowing, acceptance and enjoyment of spiritual ideas and concepts. Let your ideas pour out to nourish those around you. Allow your mind to dwell on what is pleasant in your life and avoid negativity for a time. It is important for you to express your deep creative urges by either creating or enjoying art. Also, she compels you to wish upon a star. You should become more positive in outlook, and while you may look to the stars for guidance, you should also make a practical effort to achieve your heart's desire. Avoid daydreaming and nurturing unattainable fantasies. The Star is a brilliant and positive influence, so take her advice and you will gain in self-confidence and travel far along life's wondrous, awe-filled Path. The Star's character is someone who hopes to achieve or tries to make their thoughts, ideas, plans or beliefs a reality. A combination of circumstances favouring your hopes and aims will ensure that your prospects are bright. So under the star-spangled sky above you, always remember and keep the faith that dreams *do* come true."

★ THE FOOL ★

Ruled by Uranus & the Element of Air

Number ★ Zero (or 22 in some decks)

Keywords ★ Beginnings, Innocence, Exploration

Meditation ★ "I have the courage to step forward; I am not afraid of the unknown. I am Divinely protected."

MESSAGE FOR AQUARIUS FROM THE FOOL ★ "Wide-eyed and innocent as a newborn child, The Fool has descended from the celestial realms, eager to begin his mystical journey on the Path towards enlightenment. All is new to him and he has not yet learned to fear. Living from moment to moment, going forward without plan nor care, unaware of potential perils and joyful, in his luggage he carries the memories, instincts and experiences of past lives, waiting to be utilised afresh this time around. He carries a wand symbolising the pure faith of his actions, upon which sits a head that looks backwards, representing The Fool's past as he moves ever-forward. The Fool, who is young in years, is the true spiritual guide, and this card's presence suggests that you are entering a new and exciting phase of your life. It is therefore important that you believe in yourself and realise that the benevolent and ever-expansive Universe wishes you to succeed. But he is also telling you to listen to your wiser self, and to think carefully before making any move, reminding you that a thoughtless action will inhibit your progress. Develop a sense of purpose and don't allow yourself to become hesitant or indecisive. You must prepare the ground very thoroughly and make certain that you see every aspect of your present situation clearly and with a calm, resolute mind. Now is the time for faith, belief and commitment to your deepest dreams. Step into - and up to - the challenge. Throw caution to the wind and let it carry you where it will. Do not over-analyse things; this is a time for innocence and faith; take any necessary steps forward with confidence and hope. As the whimsical and wide-eyed adventurer, The Fool gives you the distinct and exquisite feeling that sometimes taking a leap of faith is the only mode of transportation you have available to you. Make the jump!"

★ THE WORLD/UNIVERSE ★

Ruled by Saturn & the Element of Earth

Number ★ 21

Keywords ★ Completion, Attainment, Fulfilment, Success

Meditation ★ "I have completed one journey and will now rebirth myself to begin a brand new one. I welcome every chance to grow and learn, and I truly never stop evolving."

MESSAGE FOR AQUARIUS FROM THE WORLD ★ "A statue of a woman has come to life and is dancing, looking back at a leaf she holds in her outstretched hand. Just as the Earth, Divine Mother of us all, evolved from the stars and materialised into reality, so have our physical selves been created out of the same essence so that we may dance the dance of life just as She dances through the cosmos. This dream-like journey is one of going deep within and finding our essential harmony with All There Is. When we arrive at the knowledge of who we really are we gain The World. Aquarius, you have arrived at the beginning of the Path to Enlightenment or could be considerably advanced along it by now. The World card suggests a job well done - you have happily completed something of great significance. Enjoy these feelings of wholeness and completion as your amazing accomplishments have been well-earned. You're now ready to move onto something new. You have grown spiritually and have evolved to a whole new level in your understanding of the Universe and your place in it. As well as this, you have attained complete clarity, cosmic awareness, significant enlightenment, an expanded consciousness and above all, the true freedom that accompanies all this. The World imparts the message that each one of us carries a world inside of us, which is neither unattainable, illusory or utopian. It is simply what we are. All the elements are gathered here so that our conscience may awaken, and our future will unfold as it is meant to before us. Form a circle with a group of friends, imaginary or real. Slowly move around it, dancing and swaying and chanting. Complete the circle twenty-two times. As you do so, close your eyes and visualise the Earth in the centre of your circle, bathed in white light, receiving the love, wisdom and healing energy from your group. Know that we are all blessed with the sacred duty of being the caretakers of our Mother Earth - and of finding our own unique place within it."

★ ★ ★

TAROT MESSAGES FOR PISCES

★ THE MOON ★

Ruled by Pisces

Number ★ 18

Keywords ★ Hidden Depths, Betrayals, Illusions, the Subconscious

Meditation ★ "I trust my intuition; it always knows what to do. I dare to be vulnerable and to bare my soul, even if this is frightening, as doing this will enrich me beyond measure."

MESSAGE FOR PISCES FROM THE MOON ★ "Pisces, The Moon is telling you that the waters around you might look calm on the surface, but a powerful current might be brewing just beneath. The water can tell us about looking past illusion, into the vision of what is really there. Its reflective surface challenges us to look at ourselves and the image we present to the world. It also tells us that only a person of truth will have the truth shone back at them. The Moon is the intuitive clairvoyant, who opens you up to your deeper self and uncovers your hidden depths. The kingdom of darkness represents all that is concealed, buried and deep inside you. The darkness contained within the night symbolises the hidden side of your personality, the Divine part of yourself. When the symbolic dark intervenes in your life through hardships, setbacks, trials and obstacles, it tests your strength and what you thought you knew of yourself. Trials lead you to question yourself and also to search for the light - which you would not do if life was smooth, serene and going well. Everyone experiences times in their lives when they are fearful or insecure. Sometimes these fears are based on the 'seen' and that which we can recognise, while other times they stem from the unknown, irrational, hidden or illusory forces. In both cases it is important to go within and be guided by your intuition. Ask your inner self about the true source of your fears and trust its answer. The Moon card appears when we are experiencing times that open us up to our intuition and psychic abilities through increased self-awareness and the acknowledgement of past blocks that have held us back - or things which have been suppressed and need to rise to the surface. It is from our shadow selves that we must endeavour to draw regenerating energies so as not to become overcome by our emotions or ravaged by insurmountable circumstances. Its main message is to encourage you to face the unknown without being afraid, to acknowledge your anxieties, weaknesses and mistakes, and to conquer the inner darkness within you. You need to awaken to the truths about yourself that you have so far kept hidden and reawaken to your brilliant light and power. As you delve deeper into yourself, you become more reflective and aware of the messages of your subconscious mind, intuition and dreams. This leads you to explore a profound sense of connection within yourself and to see the threads of your life woven as a rich tapestry - you need only to join them all up through the use of your imagination."

THE HANGED MAN ★

Ruled by Neptune & the Element of Water

Number ★ 12

Keywords ★ Suspension, Sacrifice, New Perspectives, Faith, Surrender

Meditation ★ "I am willing to be patient and accepting as I await the next chapter of my ever-unfolding life experience, and to sacrifice things to make way for other, improved things."

MESSAGE FOR PISCES FROM THE HANGED MAN ★ "Under a calm, blue sky and above a radiant, flourishing earth, a man hangs upside down, suspended by one foot from a wooden beam. This scene is not one of torture or punishment, but part of a natural and even necessary, process. The young man's life appears to be in limbo, but his expression shows only acceptance and absolute faith at this moment of total surrender to a higher force. This enforced period of suspension may be viewed as a way of gaining new eyes and a fresh standpoint. The Hanged Man represents change, but it is usually an alternation in mental attitudes rather than physical circumstances. Sometimes you need to view things from a different perspective. The Hanged Man cuts across all our ideas of materialism, hedonism and selfishness, and tells us that new perspectives are required to conquer these potentially ravaging vices and states of being. These new viewpoints can be acquired through sacrifice and self-imposed suspension, and you are reluctantly forced to accept that it is necessary to adopt an attitude of surrender while you wait for the tide to turn. The Hanged Man signifies the ability to accept delays, and to recognise that correct timing is essential. This period may seem restrictive, but you are being forced to step back from the situation and become introspective in order to listen to your higher, stiller mind. Waiting has its place in any plan. Try not to become a martyr but do not be afraid to make sacrifices or be unwilling to adapt to changing circumstances. Sometimes if you feel powerless, stuck in a rut or blocked in some way, you must lift yourself up by your own feet and suspend yourself. Take yourself out of the frenetic game of life for a time and see what valuable lessons and insights it yields."

★ WHEEL OF FORTUNE ★

Ruled by Jupiter

Number ★ 10

Keywords ★ Change, Acceptance, Fate

Meditation ★ "I accept that life has its inevitable ups and downs, some over which I have control, others which I don't. At the heart of this is providence, and in providence I trust."

MESSAGE FOR PISCES FROM WHEEL OF FORTUNE ★ "Tarot historians believe the word Tarot itself derives from the Latin word *rota*, as in 'rotation', and reflects the ancient sense of life as a moving wheel. The 'wheels within wheels' that make up the Wheel of Fortune, rotate and turn like the ever-spinning rhythms and cycles of life. The traditionally shaped wheel holds the symbolism of the Sun and the cosmos and is an enduring symbol of human endeavour and advancement. A spin of the wheel may bring unexpected luck, opportunity and good fortune, or it may cause the reverse, and present obstacles to our desires. A confrontation with some 'demon' from the past may occur with a turn of the wheel. These could be fate, part of a Divine plan, or karma, but what seem to be beginnings and endings are in fact just part of the never-ending circle of life. The Sphinx, who sits at the top of the image, in her quiet wisdom, knows that no one stays on top forever. The Wheel of Fortune signifies an important turning point for good or bad, and tells you that life is not a merry-go-round, but rather a roller coaster, encouraging you to realise that there is ultimately purpose and equilibrium in everything that happens to you. This card usually denotes a time of positive change, or a situation that suddenly moves forward, in which case fortune is on your side! It also offers a chance to step back from circumstances in order to notice life's seasons, or the natural 'turning of the wheel'. In doing this, you will know when to plant seeds and when to harvest. It is not the Wheel of Fate but the Wheel of Fortune; this nuance is important. Indeed, the very fact that the wheel is activated by a handle, suggests the notion of free will at play. In other words, you have the choice to act or not to act, to use or not to use the handle in order to activate the wheel of your destiny. In any case, this card must prompt you to become aware of your share of active, conscious or unconscious responsibilities in the situations, circumstances or events you inevitably have to confront. Sometimes it indicates that we have to remain committed in order to progress; other times it means that for the moment, we can do nothing else but allow events to take their natural course. The turning of the Wheel of Fortune carries the message that what goes around, comes around, or what goes up, must come down. All you need to do is to be open to new and unexpected opportunities, allow for receiving, and above all, take risks. It is vitally important to always expect the unexpected. Ask your own spiritual guides or gods or goddesses to deliver to you your desires and just fortunes. Meditate on the Wheel of Fortune as you ask, and finally, take the chance and turn the wheel, for you never know where it may come to rest. The Wheel of Fortune represents the ability to understand and accept things, encouraging you to embrace changes in life wholeheartedly. There will always be highs and lows. Good or bad, trust that all is happening for your higher good. Accepting this brings a calmer, more holistic perspective."

★ THE HIGH PRIESTESS ★

Ruled by the Moon & the Element of Water

Number ★ 2

Keywords ★ Intuition, Wisdom, Knowledge, Mystery

Meditation ★ "I possess a wealth of arcane wisdom, knowledge, secrets and mysteries, which I choose to share with discretion and discernment to those who are ready and willing to receive it. I trust my intuition when selecting these Chosen Ones."

MESSAGE FOR PISCES FROM THE HIGH PRIESTESS ★ "The High Priestess is a private, all-seeing and spiritual woman with hidden depths and a deep, albeit veiled, compassion for others. In the card, she is seated upon a cube-shaped stone throne, which signifies her great depth and dimension as well as her connection with the Wisdom of the Ages ~ all the knowledge that ever was, is and will be. Passive, humble and silent, she represents a vessel of memory and holy female wisdom. Her powers are so great that they are almost beyond actions, her timeless secrets communicated through an inner voice, and only those wise enough to retreat into silence and undertake thoughtful study will know them. The High Priestess embodies the highest spiritual values, representing an open door to the sacred realms of mysticism and magic. She is telling you to learn from emotional situations. The answers you seek lie in your emotions and feelings, so trust your intuition and the power of your natural psychic abilities. The High Priestess tells you that within your subconscious mind lies the means to find your path home. Also, by paying special attention to your dreams and any intuitive messages you receive, you will be accurately guided by them. Being a Water sign, your intuition generally functions more strongly than your intellect. Stay open to your emotions and your feelings in order to come into contact with what you already know. Study spiritual topics, and remember that silence and solitude can be golden, as they yield the answers you seek. Selective in your desire for knowledge, you aspire to know and hold the key to life's mysteries, the essential, primordial principles and secrets that are the unique and sacred nature of life on Earth. Silent, secretive, clairvoyant and enlightened, The High Priestess can guide you through the dark wood of ignorance, indicating that reason alone cannot guide you. Her message to you is to go quietly within yourself to become aware of your eternal connection to All That Is, and the strength you gain from this knowledge will bring profound insights. If you are in the process of trying to answer an important question about your life,

The High Priestess invites you to relax and listen to your inner voice. Take a deep breath, and imagine an open, illuminated space in the centre of your chest where all wisdom resides, and let the answer come to you. The High Priestess imparts a simple yet meaningful message: Look for the answers to questions within your heart. Trust your insights, intuition and gut feelings, and act on your hunches."

Genie Messages

ABOUT GENIES

Genies are magically confined members of a type of being otherwise known as Ginn. Genies originated in what was once ancient Persia and is now modern Iran. If you like the idea of having your own wish-granting genie, you can find out your genie by your birth date, and once you know them by name, you can ask them for help with anything ~ as long as it is backed up by your firm belief & intentions.

GENIES BY YOUR BIRTHDATE & THEIR SYMBOL MESSAGE TO YOU

GENIE & MESSAGE FOR THOSE BORN 1 - 10 January ✯ EPIMA ~ "I will make your deepest wish come true. Call upon my assistance and then follow your heart. Use the crystal garnet to draw me out."

GENIE & MESSAGE FOR THOSE BORN 11 - 20 January ✯ HOMOTH ~ "I will make your deepest wish come true. Call upon my assistance and then follow your heart. Use a cat symbol to draw me out."

GENIE & MESSAGE FOR THOSE BORN 21 - 29 January ✯ OROASOER ~ "I will make your deepest wish come true. Call upon my assistance and then follow your heart. Use a rainbow candle flame to draw me out."

GENIE & MESSAGE FOR THOSE BORN 30 January - 8 February ✯ ASTIRO ~ "I will make your deepest wish come true. Call upon my assistance and then follow your heart. Use the crystal turquoise to draw me out."

GENIE & MESSAGE FOR THOSE BORN 9 - 18 February ✶ TEPISATRAS ~ "I will make your deepest wish come true. Call upon my assistance and then follow your heart. Use a key symbol to draw me out."

GENIE & MESSAGE FOR THOSE BORN 19 - 29 February ✶ ARCHATAPIAS ~ "I will make your deepest wish come true. Call upon my assistance and then follow your heart. Use something made of tin to draw me out."

GENIE & MESSAGE FOR THOSE BORN 1 - 10 March ✶ TNOPIBUI ~ "I will make your deepest wish come true. Call upon my assistance and then follow your heart. Use the crystal amethyst to draw me out."

GENIE & MESSAGE FOR THOSE BORN 11 - 20 March ✶ ATEMBUI ~ "I will make your deepest wish come true. Call upon my assistance and then follow your heart. Use a wolf symbol to draw me out."

GENIE & MESSAGE FOR THOSE BORN 21 - 30 March ✶ ASSICAN ~ "I will make your deepest wish come true. Call upon my assistance and then follow your heart. Use something made of iron to draw me out."

GENIE & MESSAGE FOR THOSE BORN 31 March - 9 April ✶ SENACHER ~ "I will make your deepest wish come true. Call upon my assistance and then follow your heart. Use a diamond to draw me out."

GENIE & MESSAGE FOR THOSE BORN 10 - 20 April ✶ ACENTACER ~ "I will make your deepest wish come true. Call upon my assistance and then follow your heart. Use a red candle flame to draw me out."

GENIE & MESSAGE FOR THOSE BORN 21 - 30 April ✶ ASICATH ~ "I will make your deepest wish come true. Call upon my assistance and then follow your heart. Use a green candle flame to draw me out."

GENIE & MESSAGE FOR THOSE BORN 1 - 10 May ✶ VIRAOSO ~ "I will make your deepest wish come true. Call upon my assistance and then follow your heart. Use the crystal emerald to draw me out."

GENIE & MESSAGE FOR THOSE BORN 11 - 20 May ✶ AHARAPH ~ "I will make your deepest wish come true. Call upon my assistance and then follow your heart. Use an owl symbol to draw me out."

GENIE & MESSAGE FOR THOSE BORN 21 - 31 May ✶ THESOGAR ~ "I will make your deepest wish come true. Call upon my assistance and then follow your heart. Use a yellow candle flame to draw me out."

GENIE & MESSAGE FOR THOSE BORN 1 - 10 June ✶ VERSUA ~ "I will make your deepest wish come true. Call upon my assistance and then follow your heart. Use the crystal citrine to draw me out."

GENIE & MESSAGE FOR THOSE BORN 11 - 21 June ✶ TEPISATOSOA ~ "I will make your deepest wish come true. Call upon my assistance and then follow your heart. Use a caduceus symbol to draw me out."

GENIE & MESSAGE FOR THOSE BORN 22 - 30 June ✶ SOTHIS ~ "I will make your deepest wish come true. Call upon my assistance and then follow your heart. Use an anchor symbol to draw me out."

GENIE & MESSAGE FOR THOSE BORN 1 - 10 July ✶ SYTH ~ "I will make your deepest wish come true. Call upon my assistance and then follow your heart. Use the crystal moonstone to draw me out."

GENIE & MESSAGE FOR THOSE BORN 11 - 22 July ✶ THUIMIS ~ "I will make your deepest wish come true. Call upon my assistance and then follow your heart. Use something made of silver to draw me out."

GENIE & MESSAGE FOR THOSE BORN 23 July - 2 August ✶ APHRIUMIS ~ "I will make your deepest wish come true. Call upon my assistance and then follow your heart. Use a heart symbol to draw me out."

GENIE & MESSAGE FOR THOSE BORN 3 - 11 August ✶ SITHACER ~ "I will make your deepest wish come true. Call upon my assistance and then follow your heart. Use the crystal ruby to draw me out."

GENIE & MESSAGE FOR THOSE BORN 12 - 22 August ✶ PHUONISIE ~ "I will make your deepest wish come true. Call upon my assistance and then follow your heart. Use something made of gold to draw me out."

GENIE & MESSAGE FOR THOSE BORN 23 August - 2 September ✶ THUMIS ~ "I will make your deepest wish come true. Call upon my assistance and then follow your heart. Use a silver candle flame to draw me out."

GENIE & MESSAGE FOR THOSE BORN 3 - 12 September ✶ APHUT ~ "I will make your deepest wish come true. Call upon my assistance and then follow your heart. Use the crystal peridot to draw me out."

GENIE & MESSAGE FOR THOSE BORN 13 - 22 September ✶ THOPITUS ~ "I will make your deepest wish come true. Call upon my assistance and then follow your heart. Use a caduceus symbol to draw me out."

GENIE & MESSAGE FOR THOSE BORN 23 September - 2 October ✯ SERUCUTH ~ "I will make your deepest wish come true. Call upon my assistance and then follow your heart. Use a pink candle flame to draw me out."

GENIE & MESSAGE FOR THOSE BORN 3 - 12 October ✯ ATERECHINIS ~ "I will make your deepest wish come true. Call upon my assistance and then follow your heart. Use something made of copper to draw me out."

GENIE & MESSAGE FOR THOSE BORN 13 - 22 October ✯ ARPIEN ~ "I will make your deepest wish come true. Call upon my assistance and then follow your heart. Use an opal to draw me out."

GENIE & MESSAGE FOR THOSE BORN 23 October - 2 November ✯ SENTACER ~ "I will make your deepest wish come true. Call upon my assistance and then follow your heart. Use a snake symbol to draw me out."

GENIE & MESSAGE FOR THOSE BORN 3 - 12 November ✯ TEPISEUTH ~ "I will make your deepest wish come true. Call upon my assistance and then follow your heart. Use the crystal topaz to draw me out."

GENIE & MESSAGE FOR THOSE BORN 13 - 22 November ✯ SENCINER ~ "I will make your deepest wish come true. Call upon my assistance and then follow your heart. Use a Tau symbol to draw me out."

GENIE & MESSAGE FOR THOSE BORN 23 November - 1 December ✯ EREGBUO ~ "I will make your deepest wish come true. Call upon my assistance and then follow your heart. Use a purple candle flame to draw me out."

GENIE & MESSAGE FOR THOSE BORN 2 - 11 December ✯ SAGEN ~ "I will make your deepest wish come true. Call upon my assistance and then follow your heart. Use the crystal turquoise to draw me out."

GENIE & MESSAGE FOR THOSE BORN 12 - 21 December ✯ CHENEN ~ "I will make your deepest wish come true. Call upon my assistance and then follow your heart. Use an arrowhead symbol to draw me out."

GENIE & MESSAGE FOR THOSE BORN 22 - 31 December ✯ THEMES ~ "I will make your deepest wish come true. Call upon my assistance and then follow your heart. Use a brown candle flame to draw me out."

✯   ✯   ✯

Animal Spirit Messages

ABOUT SPIRIT ANIMALS

How will you know your totems? On some level, you already do ... Think back to your favourite childhood animals. Which animals intrigued you, delighted you, comforted you most in childhood? Do certain animals or their images keep appearing in your life? What animals do you really love? When you go to the zoo, who do you *have* to visit? Conversely, which animals do you really fear or hate? (For) any extremely powerful emotion tends to indicate some sort of an alliance.

Judika Illes

Some astrological systems, such as Shamanistic * or Native American Astrology, tell us that the Sun sign we were born under has a corresponding animal totem ^, which informs us about our characteristics and act as a kind of spiritual guide or mentor throughout our life's journey. These totems are described as Solar totems, because many of them share similarities with the Solar system and the sign the Sun was passing through at the time of our birth, and therefore relate to animals and animal behaviours which also correspond to environmental conditions and seasonal changes. These animals encompass many aspects of the Solar system, from seasonal relationships, to creature instincts, to reciprocal links with the planetary vibrations, and 'clans' within nature that you are inherently closely connected with through your date of birth.

Carl Jung, a master of dream analysis and interpretation, proposed that animals symbolise our natural instincts, operating through our dreams. He theorised that certain dream symbols, among them animals, represent core emotions and concepts, archetypes that will hold true for all of us the world over, regardless of so-called 'divisions' such as sex, customs, age or culture. In *Man and His Symbols*, Jung states that primitive societies believed that each person had a bush soul and a human soul. The bush soul incarnates as a tree or animal - a totem - and when the bush soul is harmed or injured, the human soul is considered injured as well.

Some of the most important and powerful spirit guides are those belonging to the animal kingdom. Both in ancient times and in some traditional modern tribal systems, people consult with animals for their wisdom and personal power. Even though most societies today have drifted away from this connection, it has never really left us, and different creatures continue to communicate with us on both the physical and spiritual planes in an attempt to speak to our souls and spirits.

When we are plagued with limiting beliefs or negative thoughts we need to find ways to enhance and empower ourselves, and we can achieve this by connecting with certain power animals. By reflecting or even meditating on these animals, we can work with them to harness our internal courage and strength. In her book *The Complete Handbook of Quantum Healing*, which lists power animals for all manner of ailments and conditions, author Deanna M. Minich tells us, "Incorporating power animals into your healing can be therapeutic, as they provide role models or even support systems, functioning much like Earth-based angels." Shamanic teachers recommend that as we begin a quest or healing journey, we begin to notice the creatures that wander, fly, or walk across our path - acknowledge them and consider what they might be saying to you. If they pause, look at you or engage you in any way, their message may be all the more personal, profound and powerful.

As part of the teaching world, animals can bring us wisdom and survival skills, while others show us how to adapt, transcend or morph. Others still can remind us the importance of play and humour and guide us around how to overcome life's challenges. Many are known for their loyalty and ability to love unconditionally and without judgement, while some have a grounded and healthy detachment, remaining true to themselves rather than pleasing others, an important lesson in itself. Whatever the qualities of the unique animal guides for your Sun sign, all have some enlightening soul-awakening traits that can teach us much about our own true inner selves. Ultimately, your animal spirit guides, and in particular your Solar totem animal, endow you with qualities that will enhance your life and help to activate your creativity, wisdom and intuition, helping to heal the broken or return the lost pieces of your soul and reconnect you to the natural world. The goal is the eventual absorption of something of their nature and power, so that you are able to infuse your own personal power with their essence and positive qualities.

Your Solar totem animal (listed last on your lucky birds and animals list) is not the same as an animal spirit guide, which is based on metaphysical principles and is also based on your soul's mission in this embodiment - however, you can definitely make your birth Solar totem animal your spiritual guide if you wish, as you may find that its qualities, traits, symbolism and messages strongly reflect and define your own nature - or what you aspire to become, manifest or draw towards you. Your birth totem power animal comes from a place of trust and innocence and represents the essence of your creative inner child. If you spend some time meditating on your Solar totem animal, asking what lessons it can teach, and reflect deeply on its character, life and habits, you may find it connects with you on a deep spiritual level and you can make the necessary changes to your life to draw in more magic and power.

Overall, if your life is stagnant or in need of healing or an energy boost, you can request your animal spirit or spirits to come and help you change your vibration, awaken your truth and arouse your inner forces. If you are aware of your animal spirit's presence in your life every day, you can use its particular energies to support, guide and teach you. And above all, pay attention to any signs and expressions of its lessons, and remember to thank your chosen animal guide for helping you.

* Shamanism is a traditional spiritual practice of the Native American culture. A shaman, one who practices this age-old art, is an intermediary between the human world and the world of the spirits. He inherits his magical powers at birth, but spends many years as an apprentice, so that he is usually much older in age before he is able to practice and call upon his skills. People ask for a shaman's help when there is a crisis on either a personal or wider spread scale, such as famine, drought, war or illness. The shaman makes contact with the spirits by going into a trance. First, he may perform a series of rituals, which usually include drumming, singing and chanting, and when these have brought on the right conditions, he leaves his body behind to travel to the other world. There he meets with the spirits of his ancestors, who inform him what must be done to relieve the suffering of his people. If the shaman is asked to cure someone of a dis-ease, then the spirits may accompany him to find the correct medicinal herbs or treatments for his patient.

^ The Algonquin word *totem* means a person's personal guardian.

SPIRIT ANIMAL MESSAGES FOR THE ZODIAC

ARIES

ARIES'S SPIRIT ANIMAL ★ RED HAWK

The Hawk's Message ★ Strike while the iron is hot
Brings the totem gift of ★ Initiative, courage, leadership, discernment
Shares the power energies of ★ Achievement, action, opportunity, wisdom, truth
Brings forth and teaches the magic of ★ Passion, fire, confidence, persistence, observation

★ MESSAGE FOR ARIES FROM THE HAWK ★

"Aries, I am the Red-tailed Hawk and I am especially powerful as I will always be with, for life. Having direct ties to the kundalini (life force) and links to the Base chakra, I represent the seat of your primal force. With the Hawk as your power animal, you have a responsibility to recognise and work towards fulfilling your soul's destiny; and you will be especially aware of omens and spirit messages that draw you towards this. I reflect a great intensity of energy at work in your life, and you will feel these spiritual forces strongly. Hawks are the supreme flyers, protectors and visionaries of the Air, holding the key to higher levels of consciousness. So I am the power animal who has the potential to inspire your vision and awaken you to your creative life purpose. My gifts to you clear-sightedness, long-term memory, messages from the Universe, being observant, guardianship, memories from past lives, courage, illumination, seeing the bigger picture, creativity, wise use of opportunities, the 'truth', magic, focus and overcoming your problems. I am also the great communicator, giving reason to the conversations in your head, and expression to our ideas. As a natural born leader myself, I teach you initiative and to always take action while the time is ripe. I help you to soar in your ability to maintain the passion and Fire in your experiences. In Native American culture, the Hawk stands for messenger, and as such I will often show up in your life in some form if something requires your attention or focus. As with all messages received, it is important to undercover the underlying meanings, and through this you will learn to become more observant and pay attention to that which you may overlook. This could mean an untapped talent, a gift or some unexpected help for which you haven't shown gratitude, or it could even be a message from the wider Universe. As there are so many Hawk varieties, their messages can vary and can affect all and different levels of our psyches. Therefore, your personal qualities of wisdom, discernment and discrimination are important when deciphering my code. I, the Hawk, denote All That Is. I am truly a bird of the heavens, arranging circumstances and conditions necessary to prompt your spiritual growth. Aries, you may ignore the Hawk chasing you, or dodge me for a time, but you can never fully escape your ultimate destiny, for when I get hold of you in my powerful talons, you will be asked to evaluate who you really are, what you are trying to escape from, destroy your self-created illusions, and invite your inner self out to shine in the light of your Truth. After all, having me as your totem can be a bittersweet experience, for through accepting my presence in all your experiences, you will be asked to surrender anything that doesn't honour integrity in your life. From me, the powerful, all-seeing Hawk, you can certainly run, but you can never truly hide."

TAURUS

TAURUS SPIRIT ANIMAL ★ BEAVER

The Beaver's Message ★ Strength of will; your persistence will pay off
Brings the totem gift of ★ Endurance, security through abundance, freedom from attachments
Shares the power energies of ★ Resourcefulness, enduring value, inner security, strategy
Brings forth and teaches the magic of ★ Acceptance of change, perseverance, security, cunning

★ MESSAGE FOR TAURUS FROM THE BEAVER ★

"I, your spirit animal guide, Beaver, am the Master Builder and Great Creator. As expert builders, Beavers build their dams extremely strongly and securely. Because of this expertise, the skills of Beavers have been linked to ancient masonry, and often people born under this totem have past lives associated with this magical art. 'Take charge, adapt and overcome', is the Beaver's motto. Beavers get the job done with characteristic aplomb and maximum efficiency. Strategic and cunning, the mental acuity of the Beaver will ensure it wins in all endeavours, business and combative. Studying masonry can even uncover deeper, hidden insights about who you are and who you have been. My medicine brings you the wisdom of creativity, persistence and using all available resources. It teaches you to seek and use alternative ways of doing things, to achieve through completion, to understand the dynamics of group work, and not to dam the flow of your life's experiences. Without the human ego meddling in their affairs, the Beaver's group mindset strikes a balance between communication and purpose. A team-oriented mind is also essentially close to the spirit of Oneness, reminding us that we all come from the same Source and that every individual in the world, is a unique expression of this All-pervading original creative energy. This signifies that working together and appreciating the resultant coming together of minds, produces a unification that for many creations is far more effective than individual efforts. Transforming the environment, Beavers are also master engineers. My dam consists of wood held together with mud and leaves; streams are even changed into lakes by our dams. When we vacate an area, the dam gradually decomposes, leaving a fertile meadow where the dam lake once was. In this way, and throughout the building and manifesting process, I can show you the value of strength and resourcefulness, culminating in new promise and fertility. Ultimately, I can show you how to work in harmony you're your environment. Adept at teamwork, Beavers work together to construct their homes, and effectively I can demonstrate that we create and manifest things most powerfully when we integrate individual talents and skills within the group, to work together to produce a harmonious whole. As I create the many entrances and exits in my home, I teach the importance of pliability throughout each stage of creation. Often when we wish to manifest something in physical reality, we see and hold a vision of it, without understanding that the creative process doesn't end there - in fact, it begins with the vision, and during the course of bringing it into materialisation, we change and grow, and often changes and improvements are made *while* it is becoming reality. If you push these ideas aside, you may get stuck mid-creation. Instead, it is important to be flexible throughout the process, and to restructure your plan or your creation accordingly. As the great builder and manifester, I teach you that you have to act on your dreams to bring them alive, and it is now time for action. When the Beaver symbolism appears in your life, I may even be telling you that you have been neglecting your dreams - or worse, that you have failed to build a doorway for your desires to enter your life. Time to start planning and building, Taurus!"

☆ ☆ ☆

GEMINI

GEMINI'S SPIRIT ANIMAL ★ DEER

The Deer's Message ★ Be gentle in word, thought and touch
Brings the totem gift of ★ Sociability, inspiration, lively conversation, majesty, compassion
Shares the power energies of ★ A youthful outlook, unique humour, clear expression, gentleness
Brings forth and teaches the magic of ★ Grace, respectability, charm, daintiness

★ MESSAGE FOR GEMINI FROM THE DEER ★

"As well as being a Universal symbol of dainty grace, the Deer also represents unconditional love and kindness. As you spirit animal guide, Gemini, I teach you the ability to listen, to express gratitude and to understand what is necessary for your survival. My medicine brings healing through the power of love and gentleness. Treading softly and daintily, I have the ability to appear and disappear in the wink of an eye. In the Celtic tradition, the I embody two aspects - male and female. The female Deer symbolises femininity, grace and subtlety. She is believed to call us from the Faery realm, helping us to release the material trappings of civilisation, and to delve deep into the forest's treasure to explore our magical and spiritual selves. The male Deer, the Stag, is also linked to the sacredness of the magical woods, representing independence, pride and purification. It is believed the set of antlers growing from the male's head are antennae which connect it to higher energy sources. Gemini, if you come across one in the wild, try to count the number of points on their antlers, as this number is said to have numerological significance for you. The Deer teaches us to be gentle above all else, and to have compassion for, to protect and to touch the hearts and minds of wounded beings in your life, by gently nudging them in the right direction rather than forcing them to change. The love that comes from my medicine teaches you to love and accept others for who or what they are, and that true power lays in softness and compassion. Ultimately, I teach you how powerful - and empowering - it is to be of gentle demeanour, and to exercise sensitivity. As a sacred carrier of peace, I am in tune with nature and all it comprises, with an unconditional and unassuming acceptance of it. So, with me as your totem, your life is sure to abound with opportunities to express that gentle love that will open doors for you everywhere."

★ ★ ★

CANCER

CANCER'S SPIRIT ANIMAL ★ WOODPECKER

The Woodpecker's Message ★ When opportunity knocks, answer the door
Brings the totem gift of ★ Loyalty, protection, resourcefulness, discernment
Shares the power energies of ★ Progress, support, nurturance
Brings forth and teaches the magic of ★ Listening, sympathy and devotion

★ MESSAGE FOR CANCER FROM THE WOODPECKER ★

"I, the Woodpecker, am a little worker who brings you closer to the healing energies of Mother Earth and teaches you to protect your environment - before it is too late. I also represent knowledge of personal Truths, mental fortitude and inner strength. Known as the Earth's drummer, this little bird is connected with Native American drumming; drumming is the heartbeat of Mother Earth and is associated with shamanism and the ability to move into other dimensions at will. The Woodpecker represents self-discovery for those born with this totem, for as you peck into trees you uncover hidden layers of the psyche. The flight patterns of Woodpeckers are unique, and you may find that your life's path won't always conform to society's standards, and furthermore, that your own individual and unique rhythms need to be honoured and nurtured. I teach you to discover and live through your personal Truths and to move through life with inner strength and perseverance. By staying grounded and maintaining your rhythms, your goals will be more easily attained. Symbolically, I can represent opportunity, and reminds us of the old adage, 'When opportunity knocks, answer the door'. The symbolic meaning of Woodpeckers can also point to a need for creative vision and capitalising on your available resources; being opportunistic, the Woodpecker can see potential and value in everything, including dead trees. I remind you to be mindful of your words, and to be succinct in your use of them. This symbolism stems from the fact that the Woodpecker has a narrow tongue, which is extremely effectively in getting to food in tight places, and therefore teaches that you should use the narrowest (and most efficient) route to make the most profound impact; in this way, it invites you to use fewer words for a stronger effect. A keyword for the Woodpecker is progress, because she will doggedly hammer at her purpose until it bears fruit. Concepts of the determination and drive of this bird can also be understood when we consider the Woodpecker's love of the mighty Oak tree. Oak trees are symbolic of strength of character, endurance and stability. Further, the Woodpecker indicates a return to our roots, and a need to trust our basic instincts, which are both strong themes in the Cancerian's psyche. Dr. Carl Jung observed this bird as a symbol of the return to the 'womb' of creativity. This symbolism may be trying to tell you that you need to breathe new life into a project, through building your home even in an old, withering tree, for even in an apparently infertile place you can bring it to life through your imagination - and build your very own castle within. The Woodpecker's home in the tree is analogous of a fierce determination to return to and protect that which is sacred to us. As your power animal, this bird is calling you to return to your roots, back to the womb in which you gave birth to your ideas."

LEO

LEO'S SPIRIT ANIMAL ★ SALMON

The Salmon's Message ★ Inspiration and motivation through example and influence
Brings the totem gifts of ★ Focus, intuition, energy, activity, wisdom
Shares the power energies of ★ Motivation, purpose, noble crusades
Brings forth and teaches the magic of ★ Generosity, inspiration and confidence

★ MESSAGE FOR LEO FROM THE SALMON ★

"Just as the lion is the king of the jungle, I, Salmon, am king of the fish. I am the keeper of long life and a fruitful old age, representing power, deep wisdom and endurance. I teach you to count your blessings. Wholly creative, electric, focused and intuitive, the Salmon's energy is palpable. The word somersault conjures up images of children being nimble and playful, which is another lesson the Salmon teaches. The word somersault itself stems from the word salmon - *sault* - and was actually inspired by Salmons leaping out of the water as they made their important trip up raging rivers. Leo, tapping into your childlike qualities is therefore another lesson you can learn from this wondrous fish. The Salmon is also a symbol of wisdom, its wisdom including the value of returning home to regenerate, and swimming upstream through turbulent waters to gain insight and Divine messages. My aim is to overcome all obstacles that stand in my way, and to become united with All That Is. In Celtic tales and legends, the Salmon was considered the wisest and oldest of animals, dwelling in a sacred well which was the source of the River Boyne that flowed past ancient Druid temples. These salmon would feed on hazelnuts, a reputed source of wisdom. The well was shaded by nine magic hazel trees, which bore crimson nuts that gave knowledge to everything in the world. The Divine salmon who lived in the well ate the nuts and no one, not even the high gods or kings, was allowed to go near the well. Comparing my aquatic journey to your own life journey can help you gain understanding as to why the Salmon was regarded as such a wise animal. It may appear that the Salmon's up-river journey to the spawning grounds is quite literally a struggle and an 'uphill battle', similar to a human's life journey. However, the reality is very different. Difficulties *are* present, but when travelling upstream, the Salmon in fact is not fighting the current, rather it travels with the reverse current that is flowing beneath the surface. With Salmon as your power animal, significant life changes or events usually occur for you every five to seven years; the Salmon takes its long upstream journey every five to seven years, to return to the place where it was spawned, in order to spawn new life. People with this animal as their guide are tough and can persevere when others are being pulled under. Often you will choose a life that is fraught with obstacles, danger or challenges, knowing full well that within each challenge, there is a positive seed, a new beginning or an opportunity. Leo, my Salmon medicine helps you to flow with the currents beneath the surface. You must be determined, but also open to the simple flow of life, which will carry us along and support us if we allow it to. After all, the Salmon can teach you the wisdom that being light-hearted, joyful, open and innocent is not the aid to reaching the goal, but the goal itself."

★   ★   ★

VIRGO

VIRGO'S SPIRIT ANIMAL ★ BEAR

The Bear's Message ★ Embrace the power of your spirit
Brings the totem gift of ★ Fearlessness, leadership, inner power, protection, meditation
Shares the power energies of ★ Cave-dwelling (withdrawal), contemplation, protection, ferocity, strength
Brings forth and teaches the magic of ★ Dreamtime, vision quests, wildness, introspection

★ MESSAGE FOR VIRGO FROM THE BEAR ★

"I, the Bear, am a natural nurturer, protector and healer. I am usually docile, but shamans are able to summon my brute strength to help them. I am a fierce ally who symbolises protection and I am one of the most powerful spiritual guides, bringing forth the gifts of intuition, self-knowledge and spiritual wisdom. Although strong and fearless, I also teach you to be mindful of your limitations - sometimes you need to exercise caution, even in fierce and instinctive defense. Among the natives of Siberia, the northern islands of Japan, and parts of Alaska, I am considered the luckiest of animals. Linked to the pole star, I help to guide you towards your highest principles. When a steady and careful hand is needed, I am the one you can call upon. As your animal spirit guide, I give you the gift of being an ideal teacher, healer and mentor."

HERBAL BEAR MEDICINE FOR VIRGO ★ Osha is a herb which is prescribed and recommended for those who have a strong affinity or totemic connection with the Bear. According to author Dr. Rudolph Ballentine, the herb osha has a "deep connection to the bear …Osha tincture is strong-tasting and potent. But, like the bear, it is a power to be reckoned with … Its life and power is in the root … let your mind travel down along its stem under the ground to where osha lives. There you will see it like a bear, curled in its den. When you call on osha to become your plant ally, you must have your own 'warrior' energy available. You do not beg osha to come and be with you. You ask it from a place of strength and power. When osha knows you are a warrior too, it will be with you and help you. People who are struggling with their internal demons, who are trying to develop their own warrior strength - for those who fight with the darkness within - (should work with) osha. You must be willing to become a person of passion and strong feelings to work with osha. You must allow your rage and power to come out … Osha goes to the root of the matter. It is a plant that helps those who are going through destructuring. It understands the stripping-away process necessary to deep transformation. It is for those who struggle to learn the truth of the Bear."

★ ★ ★

LIBRA

LIBRA'S SPIRIT ANIMAL ★ RAVEN / CROW

The Raven's Message ★ Bearer of magic, harbinger of messages from the cosmos
Brings the totem gift of ★ Easygoing nature, flow, enthusiasm
Shares the power energies of ★ Entrepreneurship, well-received ideas, diplomacy, sociability

Brings forth and teaches the magic of ★ Romance, charm, balanced give and take in relationships

★ MESSAGE FOR LIBRA FROM THE RAVEN ★

"Raven is the primary magical ambassador from the animal kingdom. Raven and his cousin, Crow, are the shaman's allies. They teach and perform soul retrieval and transformation. Raven journeys back and forth between dimensions, the realms of life and death, spirit and flesh, and can deliver and transmit messages. Raven gives magic lessons, is a sponsor of healing emotion and teaches the futility of healing the body without also healing the spirit and emotions."

Judika Illes

"I, the Raven, or Crow, am the master magician, keeper of secrets and magic, guardian of sacred and esoteric mysteries, and holder of the power of the unknown. With me as your animal spirit guide, something special is always in the air for Libra, but you need to recognise it and ask yourself how you can use it to spiritually grow. The Raven is blessed with keen eyesight, helping you to clearly see that which lies before you. Ravens are associated with psychic powers and their feathers are sometimes used to aid clairvoyance. With me as your spiritual guide, you may well excel in the magical arts, as you are blessed with high levels of enthusiasm and a natural entrepreneurial bent. Some early cultures feared the Raven and regarded them as bad omens, as they would feed on human corpses. In fact, the Raven's mythology and mysticism have a long history enshrouding them. Shamans know the power of a sudden piercing sound that accompanies shifting consciousness, and Ravens share this knowledge and power, giving out varied sounds, which can assist you in learning how to shift your own consciousness into various dimensional realms; this is why I, the Raven, am regarded as a shape shifter with magical powers. Based upon this symbolism, people born under the Raven totem can expect many spiritual changes, epiphanies and awakenings throughout their lifetime. Some Native tribes refer to the Raven as a keeper of secrets. I am believed to be linked to the 'void', a mysterious place in which Universal secrets are kept. My black colour is linked to darkness, the place where unconscious fears can reside. In this way, I am a master magician who represents transformational energy, assisting you to release your fears by delving into your inner self and those dark places in order to illuminate them. Magic and deep healing will abound in your life with me as your totem animal. My medicine can awaken these energies in you, especially those of conjury, connecting them to your will and intentions. With Raven as your special guide, you have the ability to make great changes, for the Raven knows the mysteries of life and is the guardian of the arcane and is strongly linked with death and rebirth. It is important not to be afraid when this bird flies into your life, as he has great lessons to teach and wisdom to impart if you listen attentively and receive the information mindfully. I choose my students according to their knowledge, and I will usually stay for as long as you need me, to help transmute karma and return you to the light. Further, I will lead you into your multidimensional self and reunite you with the inter-dimensional Universe. I am a powerful animal, whose gifts to you include introspection, self-knowledge, courage, healing, magic, creation, mysteries, shape shifting, mysticism, death, rebirth, and connection with other dimensions."

★   ★   ★

SCORPIO

SCORPIO'S SPIRIT ANIMAL ★ SNAKE

The Snake's Message ★ Shed your old skin to make way for the new
Brings the totem gift of ★ Creativity, acceptance, imagination, healing
Shares the power energies of ★ Rebirth, transformation, ability to change, influence, power
Brings forth and teaches the magic of ★ Emergence of new self, expression of inner intuition

★ MESSAGE FOR SCORPIO FROM THE SNAKE ★

Snake's power is particularly multifaceted. Snake is believed to be the official repository and guardian of Earth's secrets. In addition to magic lessons, Snake can assist with all matters regarding health, fertility, knowledge and wealth. Snake can also be considered the animal equivalent of a white candle: if you don't know which animal to address, you can always approach Snake.

Judika Illes

"Among Native American tribes, the Snake embodies the powers of transmutation and creation. Representing fire, passion and energy, I teach you, Scorpio, to welcome change as an opportunity for growth, and to let go of the past. Snakes are symbols of transformation, renewal and morphosis, as they shed their old skin to reveal the new one beneath. They are also associated with water, your primal element. The Snake is powerful, unseen, and working at ground level. Snakes have been linked to magic in every spiritual tradition. Serpents make strong healing allies, helping us to shed the fears and negative beliefs that may trigger mental and physical illnesses. The Snake is a natural at all things spiritual, and most shamans are born under this Solar animal totem. Easily attuned to the ethereal realm, I make a wonderful and influential spiritual guide or leader for you. As well as being highly regarded as a potent healer, I excel at the medical professions. I can, however, be seen as mysterious and even frightening, due to my preoccupation with intangible matters and unseen dimensions. I can indeed be secretive and dark, and prone to despondence and abnormal mood swings, but in a nurturing supportive environment, will be passionate, helpful, sensitive, caring and inspiring, and help you move others to deep experiences of personal transformation and transcendence. I assist you in any shamanic wanderings and all transformative, healing processes, as these are my domain and my forte."

★ ★ ★

SAGITTARIUS

SAGITTARIUS'S SPIRIT ANIMAL ★ ELK

The Elk's Message ★ Application of the spiritual to the physical self to bring about healing
Brings the totem gift of ★ Love, heartiness, independence, strength, agility, confidence
Shares the power energies of ★ Optimism, happiness, spiritual evolution, stamina
Brings forth and teaches the magic of ★ Understanding of human nature and Spirit, trust, focus

★ MESSAGE FOR SAGITTARIUS FROM THE ELK ★

"I, The Elk, possess a unique power that comes from the Earth and the Great Mystery. My medicine helps you to know when your true soul mate appears. Regal and impressive, I will bring confidence when you are unsure or unaware of your gifts, and modesty and grace when you are. With me as your power animal, you probably feel the need for companionship and group support. I teach that you do not have to do everything by yourself, as help is always within reach if you just ask for it. Elks are indeed found in large herds and are rarely seen alone. They enjoy the company of their own kind, but also have a need for their own space. People with this totem animal need a sacred place to go now and again in order to restore and to keep their energy balanced. I, the majestic Elk, deserve and demand respect. I have a regal demeanour and a strong self-image. Having me as your totem animal means that you most probably often find yourself on life's centre stage, either in your personal or professional life. My medicine includes strength, endurance, agility, nobility and sensual passion, teaching you how to make the best use of your energy and spirit. I also impart wisdom on how to pace yourself as you work towards your dreams - by learning this, although you may not always be the first to arrive at your destination, you will at least get there without being burnt out by the journey. Alert and ever able to sense danger, even that emanating from very subtle energies, you have high energy levels and well-developed perceptive skills. I teach you to work on the way you conduct yourself, and to operate with power and pride, strength and empowerment. If you are lacking in confidence, call on me to guide you towards becoming more self-loving and impressive. After all, there are few more wondrous sights than a mature Elk, with its winter coat, standing tall, antlers reaching towards the heavens, exuding an air of command and exquisite, powerful regality - and truly standing out from the herd."

☆ ☆ ☆

CAPRICORN

CAPRICORN'S SPIRIT ANIMAL ★ GOOSE

The Goose's Message ★ The destination at the top is more important than the climb
Brings the totem gift of ★ Excellence, perseverance, setting goals and achieving them
Shares the power energies of ★ Ambition, drive, competitiveness
Brings forth and teaches the magic of ★ Unique humour, sensuality and warmth

☆ MESSAGE FOR CAPRICORN FROM THE GOOSE ☆

"I, the Goose, am often seen as a symbol of protection and am therefore associated with some of the warrior deities such as Mars or Athena. I have long been revered: the Goose was a sacred bird in the Roman temples of Juno, it was associated with the North Wind in Greek mythology, and is a Native American totem for the Winter Solstice. The Greeks associated it with Hermes the messenger and to the ancient Egyptians the Goose had direct links to the gods, believing the Goose could fly to the gods, and so they became the symbol of the soul of the pharaoh. In Eastern cultures, the Goose is an important bird associated with the Sun and masculine elements. I bring clarity to your Earthly dreams and help you to trust your intuition about which way to go and to know instinctively when it is right to change direction. While some branches of wisdom advise that we should never go back, I teach that you certainly can and sometimes should. I symbolise cooperation, the sacred circle, communication and dedication. As a potent symbol of the Sacred Circle, I remind you of the sanctity of the cycles of your life, and the time when Canadian Geese migrate highlights the passages of the Great Circle of the Year. The Goose, also being symbols of fertility and fidelity, mean that people born under this totem often have deep-rooted faith and belief that there is one special person out there just for them. Persevering, dogged and with an unlimited capacity for ambition, if you want something done and done properly, give it to a Goose, as I am determined to succeed at all costs, but I suggest that you first need to conquer your inner critic. Once you have overcome the internal struggles of striving so high, you will accomplish great things."

☆ ☆ ☆

AQUARIUS

AQUARIUS'S SPIRIT ANIMAL ★ OTTER

The Otter's Message ★ The application of spiritual knowledge, play, fun and wisdom to daily Earthly life. If you go with the natural ebbs and flows of life, you will discover joy, wonder, and simple pleasures
Brings the totem gift of ★ Perception, inventiveness, playfulness and original thinking
Shares the power energies of ★ Tolerance, courage, originality, invention and exuberance
Brings forth and teaches the magic of ★ Creativity, the attaining of wisdom, the acquisition of knowledge, and the value of play, imagination, spontaneity and joy

★ MESSAGE FOR AQUARIUS FROM THE OTTER ★

"Being a water creature, my symbolism is linked to the Divine and primal feminine, my watery habitat symbolising water as the giver and elixir of life. As your Solar totem and spirit animal guide, I can remind you of the importance of play, good-natured rough handling, frolicking, laughter, pure joy and spontaneous, spirited romps with others. Having few enemies in the wild, the otter can also impart lessons in feelings of well-being, security and fearlessness. Joyful, agile and nimble, the otter represents agility, curiosity, energy, dexterity, and creativity. Further, otters are commonly regarded as lucky animals. They feature as light-hearted tricksters in most folklore, and although their exploits are mischievous, they are generally not considered malicious or aggressive. I am also linked with the Moon, and because of this I am often used in initiation and fertility ceremonies in certain cultures. There is a belief among the North American Indians that I have been the otter has been granted special powers, so some shamans use otter-skin bags in initiation rituals. Aquarius, if you are feeling a little depleted in energy or enjoyment, try calling upon me to enliven your soul and restore your spirit. It might even stir you into dancing with life again and will almost definitely loosen you up and help to re-program the value of play. My more serious side is that I can be a little quirky and unorthodox, making me sometimes difficult to figure out. Although unconventional and misunderstood, my methods are usually very effective. I may have an odd way of doing, expressing or perceiving things, but I am ever-blessed with a brilliant imagination and intelligence, giving me an edge over all others. Through me, you Aquarius, can learn the courage to open up through play, and to surrender to the trust that your needs will always be met."

★ ★ ★

PISCES

PISCES'S SPIRIT ANIMAL ★ WOLF

The Wolf's Message ★ The idea that freedom, compassion and passion can reside harmoniously together. Birth totem Wolf individuals arrive on this plane of existence to learn the gifts of the seer. Your life path is one of love and the application of spiritual knowledge.
Brings the totem gift of ★ Compassion, benevolence, generosity, sensitivity, identity, and the 'way of the seer'
Shares the power energies of ★ Liberation, intuition, trust, deep emotions and unwavering loyalty
Brings forth and teaches the magic of ★ Illumination, psychic ability, mysticism, creativity and freedom, cooperation, leadership

★ MESSAGE FOR PISCES FROM THE WOLF ★

In many cultures, the wolf appears as a psychopomp, a figure that acts as a mediator between the ego and the unconscious, between death and transformation. Historically, we have over-identified with the dark side of the wolf. But the wolf is not just one or the other. It moves between and throughout both realms. It embodies the light and the shadow ... No one seems eager to confront and make peace with the wild wolf lurking around inside each of us, (for) it is easier to despise our projection than to do the personal work necessary to integrate our own inner dark wolf. But unless we can face and claim the dark aspects of the wolf, we are not free to enjoy the light aspects: the courage, intelligence, and fierce joy of living that the wolf also embodies. This is the wolf's challenge to us: to embrace it all.

Dr. Elizabeth Kirkhart, Jungian psychologist

"I, the Wolf, tend to embody a mythic vision of duality, possessing both masculine and feminine aspects, since the Wolf is considered both a gifted parent (the feminine) and a fierce hunter (the masculine). Also, because wolves can see well in both day and night, they are considered an animal representing both light and dark. I am ultimately associated with the dual roles of destroyer and provider. I instinctively understand that all we need is love and am perfectly capable and willing to provide it. Deeply emotional and wholly compassionate, I am the lover of the animal totem zodiac, in both the physical and philosophical sense of the word. I am also the messenger and guide to otherworldly realms, especially at the time of a Full Moon. If you call upon me at this time, you will be rewarded with my gifts. With me as your totem animal, you possess the gifts of specialised wisdom and the skill of prophecy. You tend to draw a clear line between those who belong to your 'pack' and outsiders. You are intensely loyal to your own, and it can take some time for you to accept others outside of your own circle. But once you do, your sense of loyalty to the whole community is legendary. Due to your unique inner knowing and perspective, you can offer incredible insights and contributions to others within your clan. I stand for endurance and balance and teach you to tread the fine line between independence and dependence, between the needs of others and your own personal development. If it is time for you to move on and to start or lead your own pack, I will support, counsel and guide you. Wolf energy calls you to acknowledge your primal urges and helps you to take risks in pursuit of your desires. Wolves are faithful animals offering companionship through the most difficult stages of your spiritual journey. As your Solar totem and spirit animal guide, I can remind you of the importance of leadership and that of providing your insightful wisdom to your 'pack', but also of *belonging* to it, so all can live in harmony. As Rudyard Kipling so eloquently put it: "The strength of the pack is the wolf, and the strength of the wolf is the pack." Through my special medicine, this strength is inherent within you too, Pisces."

★ ★ ★

Rune Messages

ABOUT RUNES

The wizards who used the runes for magical purposes regarded themselves as blood kin to Odin, the Nordic god who was popularly accredited with inventing the runic alphabet ... They were basically followers of the shamanistic tradition which is one of the oldest, if not the oldest, belief system in the world.

Michael Howard

Runes are the letters in a set of related alphabets known as runic alphabets, and were used among the Germanic peoples in the first or second centuries AD. The runes functioned as letters, but they were also more than just letters, each rune being a pictographic, ideographic or philosophic representation of some cosmological power or principle that is believed to pervade the whole Universe. In fact, the word rune itself derived from the proto-Germanic *runo*, which means both 'letter' and 'secret' or 'mystery'. The runes are symbols, or occult formulae, for the working Cosmic Forces as perceived by their alleged discoverer Odin, a powerful deity of the Nordic pantheon. Runes were traditionally carved onto stone, metal, bone, wood or some other similarly hard surface, which explains their sharp, angular forms, which were easier to carve onto the materials they were etched upon. The runes have endured through the centuries and today, they are used as tools of divination, prophecy and mediums from which to derive magical and esoteric meanings.

There is some rich mythology around the origins and magical uses of the runes. One of the mystical of the various Tree of Life legends is that of the Tree of Yggdrasil in Norse mythology. The main character of the story, Odin (sometimes called Woden), the Father/God of the Nordic pantheon. He is the invisible Soul of the World that animates all things and travels through the nine Nordic worlds like a breeze. He rides upon a magical steed named Sleipnir, as his deep azure cloak reaches into infinite space. A white serpent (wisdom), skilled in magic, lies at his feet at all times, and he has two familiars, ravens called Muninn, meaning 'memory', and Huginn, meaning 'thought', who represent his soul. Each day the birds fly around the world and then report back to him, telling him everything that has occurred. Not only does he stand for the mind of God, he also has many other talents, including writing, shape shifting, intellect, communication, inspiration, magic and seership. The story goes that this legendary hero wanted above all to find wisdom and acquire the gift of prophecy. To do this he was required to hang upside down on the world tree, Yggdrasil, for nine days and nights, each day and night representing one of the nine sacred worlds in Nordic lore. At the dawn of the tenth day, Odin was said to have reached down into the roots of Yggdrasil and drew out the runes, which became the magical alphabet of the Nordic peoples.

THE RUNE CALENDAR

There are twenty-four runes and their transitions through the year are calculated on the same motions of the stars as are the signs of the zodiac. Exploring the energies of the rune during its half-month will provide great insights, as the dance of the cosmos resonates most with that particular rune at that specific time. Due to crossovers, each zodiac sign has three runes which vibrate especially to its energy. Check this list for your sign's runes and then read the following more detailed rune descriptions.

ARIES	Ehwaz	30 March - 14 April
ARIES & TAURUS	Mann	14 April - 29 April
TAURUS	Lagu	29 April - 14 May
TAURUS & GEMINI	Ing	14 May - 29 May
GEMINI	Othel	29 May - 14 June
GEMINI & CANCER	Daeg	14 June - 29 June
CANCER	Fehu	29 June - 14 July
CANCER & LEO	Ur	14 July - 29 July
LEO	Thorn	29 July - 13 August
LEO & VIRGO	Ansur	13 August - 29 August
VIRGO	Rad	29 August - 13 September
VIRGO & LIBRA	Ken	13 September - 28 September
LIBRA	Geofu	28 September - 13 October
LIBRA & SCORPIO	Wynn	13 October - 28 October
SCORPIO	Hagal	28 October - 13 November
SCORPIO & SAGITTARIUS	Nied	13 November - 28 November
SAGITTARIUS	Is	28 November - 13 December
SAGITTARIUS & CAPRICORN	Jara	13 December - 28 December
CAPRICORN	Eoh	28 December - 13 January
CAPRICORN & AQUARIUS	Peorth	13 January - 28 January
AQUARIUS	Elhaz	28 January - 13 February
AQUARIUS & PISCES	Sigel	13 February - 27 February
PISCES	Tyr	27 February - 14 March
PISCES & ARIES	Beorc	14 March - 30 March

RUNE MESSAGES FOR THE ZODIAC ~ BY YOUR BIRTHDATE

ARIES ✶ *30 March - 14 April* ♈

RUNE NAME ✶ EOW, EHWAZ ~ Norse ~ EOH ~ A Horse

SPECIAL CRYSTAL ~ Iceland Spar
SPECIAL TREE ~ Oak / Ash

Positive Meanings ✶ Momentum, Cooperation, Teamwork, Trust, Horse, Stallion, Partnership, Progress, Transportation, New Home, New Goals, Steady Progress, Change for the Better

Magical Powers ✶ To call forth Divine aid in times of trouble, to facilitate change, to assist with astral travel, to travel safely, to bring good luck

BASIC DIVINATORY MEANING ✶ Progress / Horse. This rune concerns travel and transport, and also carries the energy for putting across ideas effectively to others. It implies the trust that a horse and rider share, and therefore has links with trustworthy partnership activities of all kinds. The energy of the horse is powerful and primal. It allows you to see the world from a higher perspective, helping you to avoid obstacles and to make swift progress along your path. The horse was regarded as a sacred animal throughout the old world and is recorded in many myths and legends as a loyal and faithful ally. The horse is also associated with fire, the element of free expression and our ever-unfolding destiny. The energy of the horse can help to clear stagnation and remove blocks, both external and internal. This makes it a valuable ally and partner to accompany you on the spiritual path. Ehwas helps one to make progress on the adventurous path of one's destiny.

MESSAGE FOR ARIES ✶ You have the support to be able to make swift progress along your path, but this is dependent upon you being as loyal and supportive to those around you as they are to you. The horse is a proud animal, but it does not let its pride get in the way of its purpose. In the same way, you too should be proud of your achievements and successes while remaining inwardly and outwardly humble to ensure your travels will be swift and sure.

✶ ✶ ✶

ARIES & TAURUS ✶ *14 April - 29 April* ♈ ♉

RUNE NAME ✶ MAN, MANNAZ ~ Norse ~ MADR ~ Man or Humankind

SPECIAL CRYSTAL ~ Garnet
SPECIAL TREE ~ Holly

Positive Meanings ✭ Man, and his connection to the Divine, Humanity, the Self, the World, Forethought, Expect Help, Lover, Husband, New Career Opportunities, Favours from the Gods

Magical Powers ✭ To attract goodwill, to gain assistance from others, to increase memory and mental powers, to know oneself

BASIC DIVINATORY MEANING ✭ Destiny / A Human / The Self. This rune represents a male figure, an authority figure or a professional man. If you need the help of a professional or an expert, this rune will bring the right person along. Destiny is all about choice. Every human being has a destiny and it is in every human being's capacity to fulfill that destiny. You can choose to take responsibility for your life, to be a spiritual being and to fulfill your rightful purpose, or you can choose to drift along by default, copping with whatever life throws at you. The path of destiny is not an easy path, for it holds many lessons and challenges along the way, but it is a path of fulfillment, richness, and growth. The other paths may appear easier, but they are filled with dissatisfaction. The Man rune also symbolises oaths and agreements.

MESSAGE FOR ARIES & TAURUS ✭ Your destiny awaits you, so claim it. For you to be a spiritual being, your body, mind, soul, and spiritual systems must be balanced. Embrace everything - the good and the bad - with total humbleness and acceptance, secure in the knowledge that everything that happens to you is there to teach you. By learning each lesson as it presents itself, you will go onwards and upwards to unimaginable heights.

✭ ✭ ✭

TAURUS ✭ *29 April - 14 May*

RUNE NAME ✭ LAGU, LAGUZ ~ Norse ~ LOGR ~ Lake or Water

SPECIAL CRYSTAL ~ Pearl
SPECIAL TREE ~ Willow

Positive Meanings ✭ Water, Womb of the Great Mother, Flow, Lake, Mysteries, Organic Growth, Psychic Matters, the Source, the Underworld, Renewal, Success in Travel, Life Energies, Movement Below Surface, Manifestation from Other Planes

Magical Powers ✭ To increase feminine life-force, to manifest intuition and psychic power, to increase magnetism

BASIC DIVINATORY MEANING ✶ Attunement to Creation / Water, Sea. This feminine rune is connected to the Moon Goddesses. It is particularly associated with women's health, fertility and childbirth. Water is the primal power that provides, nurtures and sustains all life. It aids change and helps you if you are going into unknown territory or are about to do something that is new or daunting. Water flows where it will, drawn back and forth by the power of the Moon. All fluids on the earth are governed in just the same way by the Moon. This includes the sea, the liquids that pervade all of nature, and the fluids within you. To be in harmony with the creative flow of water, you need to attune yourself to the seasons, to the natural ebbs, flows and cycles, and the Moon. Living in harmony with nature in this way, gives you a fresh perspective and opens up many possibilities to acquire new and greater knowledge and to transform it into wisdom. The Moon is exalted in the sign of Taurus, making its influence even more potent to the sign of the Bull.

MESSAGE FOR TAURUS ✶ It is only by attunement and connection to nature's creations and cycles, that your life will truly flow as it is meant to. The sea is ever fluid and moving, and is a powerful symbol of harmony and rhythm, so it should be a part of your life. But also stay open to and embrace change, for it is the only constant in life.

✶ ✶ ✶

TAURUS & GEMINI ✶ *14 May - 29 May*

RUNE NAME ✶ ING, INGWAZ ~ Norse ~ INGUZ ~ The Danes, the God Ing

SPECIAL CRYSTAL ~ Amber
SPECIAL TREE ~ Apple

Positive Meanings ✶ Peace, Harmony, Tribe, Fertility God, Hero God, Male Fertility and Drive, Growth, Inner Wisdom

Magical Powers ✶ To fascinate and influence others, to 'fix' the outcome, to gain influential position, to project sensual energy

BASIC DIVINATORY MEANING ✶ The Fire Within / The Fertility God, Ing. This rune has substantial associations with breeding, keeping, and maintaining cattle, which makes it, along with the first rune, Feoh, of particular interest to farmers and other agricultural workers. It also brings fertility, production, material results, harvest opportunities, and fruition to other fields as well. It is a feminine rune that can be used for sexual matters, female issues and children. Ing symbolises the spark of creation, the power to give life and to make the land fertile. As the

Divine spark, it represents the fire within everyone that drives them forwards and keeps them striving towards ever-higher spiritual fulfillment; and it is the potent force that propels you to keep going when things get tough. This inner fire can life dormant for many years, but when it is fuelled by the breath of recognition, it cannot be extinguished. This rune can be used for help with the completion of projects or dealing with something on a long-term basis, as well as for problem-solving. Ing teaches that you cannot change the past, and that the present moment is the only real place where you can truly exert any influence. In this way, Ing helps you to release the past, and keep your eyes on your dreams, while simultaneously living in the here and now.

MESSAGE FOR TAURUS & GEMINI ✯ You are on a specially carved spiritual path and although you may feel isolated at times, you can be safe in the knowledge that within you burns the fire of inspiration which propels you ever onwards and upwards. Feed the fire by always striving to learn more, never indulging in illusion or complacency. Never bog yourself down with too many questions; answers and solutions will come to you naturally if you allow them to. Live each day as it comes, with the wise knowledge that the past is just a memory, the future just a dream and the here and now is your one precious, graspable gift.

GEMINI ✯ *29 May - 14 June* ♊

RUNE NAME ✯ ETHEL, ODILA, OTHEL, OTHALA ~ Norse ~ ODAL ~ Possession

SPECIAL CRYSTAL ~ Ruby
SPECIAL TREE ~ Hawthorn

Positive Meanings ✯ Family, Ancestral Property, Home, Spiritual Heritage, Inheritance, Fundamental Values, Tangible Possessions, Spiritual Help, Group Order and Prosperity

Magical Powers ✯ To call on ancestral powers and spirits, to charm a female, to develop latent strengths and talents, to guard the family fortune, to protect the health of the elderly, to gain wealth and prosperity

BASIC DIVINATORY MEANING ✯ Focus / Freedom / Inheritance / Inherited Land / Possession ~ Othel means a possession. This rune concerns benefit through property, gifts, help from older relatives, legacies, heirlooms, and objects that have been left to you, as well as documents, wills, and legal and financial matters. It also denotes family lore and inherited talents. The Othel rune has an image of an enclosure of land or of a magical circle and is the rune into which energies can be concentrated and focused. Although Othel means 'a possession', it is in the sense of holding and enjoying rather than owning. After all, we own nothing; all things are merely loaned to us, including our bodies. For the power of Othel to be fully experienced, you need to be able to firmly focus but relax at the same time. Concentrate your mental energies upon a thought, then wait patiently for other energies to be attracted to it. Never try to force things, but always keep in mind where you want to go. The energy of this thought will direct and guide you in the right direction. Above and beyond all, never lose sight of your dream.

MESSAGE FOR GEMINI ✶ This is a time to re-focus. Fix your deepest desire firmly in your mind, trusting that your thoughts will attract the energies that you need to make your dream a tangible reality. Concentration and focus are needed if you are to receive and read all the signs that are appearing before you. Allow whatever must happen to proceed unhindered and do not try to force issues. Your dream is like a butterfly sitting in the palm of your hand - if you try to possess it, grasp at it or keep hold of it, you risk losing it.

✯ ✯ ✯

GEMINI & CANCER ✶ *14 June - 29 June*

RUNE NAME ✶ DAGAZ ~ Norse ~ DAEG ~ Day, The Light

SPECIAL CRYSTAL ~ Diamond
SPECIAL TREE ~ Spruce

Positive Meanings ✶ Transformation, Day or Dawn, Change, Growth, New Beginnings, Clarity, Breakthrough, Awakening, Release

Magical Powers ✶ To receive inspiration, to advance, to bring luck, to start over

BASIC DIVINATORY MEANING ✶ Day (Light). Daeg is the rune of midday and of midsummer. It represents the positive energy of light at its most powerful and potent and is therefore a rune of great protection when painted over doorways or window shutters. Daeg is positivity at its strongest, signifying success, progress, growth, clarity of vision and protection against harmful influences. It allows you to see the positive within every negative. Daeg also helps you remember that everything is given to you. If you do not use these given gifts with love and sincerity, they will be taken from you. You own nothing; everything is lent to you by the Higher Powers, so always use your gifts with respect, discernment, and wisdom. This rune is associated with success in studies and examination, as well as changes for the better and success generally.

MESSAGE FOR GEMINI & CANCER ✯ The power of the light shines upon the path ahead of you, guiding you clearly and lovingly. As long as you remain true to this path, only good fortune can come your way. You need have no fear, for you are well protected by the power of the light. The illumination it provides will give you clear vision so that you may see and avoid negative energies before they enter your life. The only warning this rune has for you is be wary of being blinded - although it is not the light that will blind you, it is your ego. The ego, if not mastered, will allow your success to blind you, so always remain humble, graceful and grateful for all the good things that come to you.

✯ ✯ ✯

CANCER ✯ *29 June - 14 July* ♋

RUNE NAME ✯ FEOH, FEHU ~ Norse ~ FE ~ Cattle

SPECIAL CRYSTAL ~Moss Agate
SPECIAL TREE ~ Elder

Positive Meanings ✯ Cattle, Wealth, Fulfillment, Nourishment, Possessions, Success, Good Health, Income, Luck, Property

Magical Powers ✯ Primal energy - to progress, to increase, to attract, to protect, to send, to strengthen

BASIC DIVINATORY MEANING ✯ Spiritual Richness / Wealth / Cattle. To the Nordic people, cattle were a sign of status and wealth. Like all animals, cattle were sacred, but they were also feasted upon at times of celebration, showing that wealth could and should be used for the benefit of all. Cattle represented prosperity and abundance in these ancient times, as they still do in many cultures throughout the world today. Feoh represents your position, funds, wealth, career and status, as well as emotional security, sustenance, and fulfillment of all kinds. This rune rules pregnancy, fertility and growth, and you can also use this rune to enhance your reputation. Just as cattle were shared in feasts and harvests, Feoh speaks of a spiritual richness to that is to be used for the benefit of all. It is a rune of unselfish abundance. Let your richness shine forth to lighten your path and the paths of others. The well of spiritual abundance never runs dry; however, you should not waste it on those who will take unfair advantage of it; discernment is important.

MESSAGE FOR CANCER ✯ While physical wealth is transient, spiritual wealth is permanent. The wisdom that you learn and integrate into your life can never be taken away from you, no matter how many times you share that wisdom with others. Everyone has spiritual gifts, and if you are unaware of your gifts it does not mean that you have none; on the contrary, it means that you have not yet uncovered or tapped into them. Each person has many gifts; once they are recognised they can be used to endless advantage.

✶ ✶ ✶

CANCER & LEO ✶ *14 July - 29 July* ♋ ♌

RUNE NAME ✶ URUZ ~ Norse ~ UR ~ Wild Ox or Aurochs, Strength

SPECIAL CRYSTAL ~ Garnet
SPECIAL TREE ~ Birch

Positive Meanings ✶ Strength, Wild Ox, Aurochs, Adulthood, Masculine Potency, Action, Courage, Energy, Freedom, Good Fortune, Health, Potential, Desire, Change, Potency

Magical Powers ✶ Manifestation - to start, to heal, to change

BASIC DIVINATORY MEANING ✶ Auroch / Strength. Aurochs were wild oxen and a powerful totemic animal of the Nordic tradition symbolising strength. Strength can be greatly misunderstood in today's cultures, with many people equating it with inflexibility, bullish behaviour, and dominance. Some also confuse pride with strength, whereas pride is actually a weakness borne out of an ego that has been allowed to run rampant. The Ur rune is for physical strength, masculinity, the active principle, and the physical and material planes. It offers opportunities for you to better yourself, and possibly also a financial improvement, but always with the expenditure of energy, effort, spiritual force or strength. It also promotes the acquiring and use of physical skill, or the training of such in others.

MESSAGE FOR CANCER & LEO ✶ You have the strength within you to fulfill all your dreams, but with that strength comes a deep responsibility. Strength is not a power with which to exert control over others, but a power to stop others exerting control over you. Use your strength to keep you focused on your path, to stop yourself being overpowered or off-balanced by others. There are always some people who are negative, and strength comes from not letting those people upset you; this is a special skill that comes from mastering the ego. True strength only comes once the ego is mastered, and to find your true strength, you must first face your shortcomings. Once you recognises where your weaknesses lie, you can then turn them into positive traits. This process can be daunting and confronting for many people and there are those who, out of deep-rooted fears, try to hide their weaknesses rather than face up to them. Have the courage to face and remedy your darker aspects and you will gain mastery over your ego.

✶ ✶ ✶

LEO ✶ *29 July - 13 August* ♌

RUNE NAME ✶ THORN, THURISAZ ~ Norse ~ THURS ~ Thorn

SPECIAL CRYSTAL ~ Sapphire
SPECIAL TREE ~ Thorn / Oak

Positive Meanings ✶ Thorn, Thor's Hammer, Giant, Non-action, Directed Force, Reactive Force, Masculine Sexuality, Catharsis, Good News, Happiness, Comfort, Inner Strength, Great Care in Decisions

Magical Powers ✶ Applied Power - to begin, to attract, to push, to defend

BASIC DIVINATORY MEANING ✶ Spiritual Authority. This rune is sacred to Thor, the Nordic Thunder god, and brings protection in all its forms, even spiritual and psychic protection. It can be used to give you the strength to stand up for and assert yourself when necessary. Don't use this rune if you want anything to happen swiftly, as it is better attuned to things that take their time and course in the Divine natural order. The shamans and magicians of northern Europe have long associated thorn trees with spiritual authority. Thorn trees are symbolic of protection and their wood was often used to make talismans to ward off harmful or negative influences. Blackthorn was particularly favoured as the material for making powerful staffs and wands. The blackthorn has a sister tree, the hawthorn, which, while being a similarly powerful protective tree, also has soothing and balancing feminine energies. The protection that comes from the thorn tree is the protection of spiritual authority and gives you the power to stand up for your truths and convictions, and to claim your true Path.

MESSAGE FOR LEO ✶ You have the power within you to face anything that might cross your path. Fear nothing, for you have the authority to claim your true destiny. Allow no one to deter you from your search for the truth. Hold tight and true to your birthright, be an enlightened spiritual being, and always remember to keep your feet firmly on the ground. Living from your authentic core brings personal power and it is up to you to use that power in an unselfish, humble and loving way, for power can corrupt if you do not have a true and honest heart. You should never need to tell others of your authority; knowing that you have it is always enough. To utilise the power of the Thorn rune fully, you must first master your ego. Spiritual authority, like strength, is a power that is designed to help you keep on your Path and not a force to exert over others for selfish ends.

LEO & VIRGO ✴ *13 August - 29 August* ♌ ♍

RUNE NAME ✴ OS, ANSUZ, ANSUR ~ Norse ~ ASS ~ A God

SPECIAL CRYSTAL ~ Emerald
SPECIAL TREE ~ Ash

Positive Meanings ✴ Odin, Sovereign Ancestor God, Messenger, Communication, Information, Incantation, Healing, Harmony, Blessings, Insight, Inspiration, New Life-Changing Goals, True Vision, Words of Power, Revealing Message

Magical Powers ✴ Communication - to convince, to know, to achieve, to increase

BASIC DIVINATORY MEANING ✴ A Message / A Mouth. In the Nordic tradition, the mouth is an overt symbol of communication. Messages come in many forms and communication problems arise from often an inability to decipher these messages correctly. A word can have completely different meanings and associations to different people. The same word can create very dramatically diverse pictures in the mind of each person, depending on the mind perceiving it. This rune is sacred to Odin, the chief god of magic, and represents authority, elders, superiors, our ancestors, parents, and all that can be inherited from them. Odin is also the god of storms, so protection from this powerful force of nature, is possible with this rune. This rune also brings spiritual progress and guidance from the Divine. It is especially useful for conjuring up sensitivity and inspiration and for anything that requires communication in all its forms.

MESSAGE FOR LEO & VIRGO ✴ The answers to your questions are already here: you have just not heard them yet. Look for the signs and confirmations which are everywhere and in everything around you. Check that you are not ignoring any messages because you do not like their contents. Trust that everything that comes to you comes to teach and guide you, and that by acknowledging the truth you will grow in knowledge and wisdom.

✴ ✴ ✴

VIRGO ✴ *29 August - 13 September* ♍

RUNE NAME ✴ RAD, RAIDHO ~ Norse ~ REID ~ The Wheel of Life, A Wheel, Chariot or the Act of Riding

SPECIAL CRYSTAL ~ Chrysoprase
SPECIAL TREE ~ Oak
Positive Meanings ✴ Getting to the Truth, Law, Travel, Wagon, Transportation, Journey, Relocation, Seeing Past Illusions, Journey of Life, the Path to Power

Magical Powers ✯ To bless, to travel safely, to obtain justice, to seek

BASIC DIVINATORY MEANING ✯ This rune represents journeys, movement and transport, as well as learning and imagination, change, movement in your affairs or the ability to control matters more successfully.

MESSAGE FOR VIRGO ✯ Recognise that everything comes in cycles and that by following these cycles, you will be able to progress quickly and efficiently. Align yourself to the seasons by honouring the turning of the year's wheel. Everything in life is cyclical. All things have a beginning, a middle and an end. All journeys and lessons of the heart and spirit have beginnings, middles and ends, too. Once you recognise this fact, you can 'go with the flow', and let things unfold rather than always resisting. Embrace hard times in the certainty that the more difficult things are now, the more beautiful they may be in the future in contrast. Indeed, everything has its opposite, and challenges bring both equal and opposite rewards. Life is a journey along which we encounter challenges that open the way for new opportunities to learn lessons. When times are difficult, be assured that they will not go on forever. Once you have learnt the lessons that the hard times are trying to teach you, you will no longer need to suffer them. Remember with humble grace that every situation has a potential lesson, and the faster you learn from them, the swifter you will progress and ascend. Embrace everything with pleasure and wisdom, in the knowledge that there are lessons encased within all your experiences, both good and bad.

VIRGO & LIBRA ✯ *13 September - 28 September* ♍ ♎

RUNE NAME ✯ KEN, KENAZ ~ Norse ~ KAUNAZ ~ A Bonfire, A Pitchbrand Torch

SPECIAL CRYSTAL ~ Bloodstone
SPECIAL TREE ~ Pine

Positive Meanings ✯ Beacon, Enlightenment, Controlled Energy, Boil, Hearth, Forge, Pyre, Sore, Swelling, Creativity, Inspiration, New Insights, New Strength & Energy, Revelation, Transformation

Magical Powers ✯ To banish, to restore self-confidence, to strengthen willpower

BASIC DIVINATORY MEANING ✯ Enlightenment / A Torch. This rune brings warmth and light, mental illumination and creativity, success, status and good health all round, and luck in celebrations and also in love, especially for females. Illumination allows one to see in the dark. Enlightenment is a spiritual illumination; it is arriving at a new understanding, like opening your eyes for the first time or turning on a light after a period of darkness. You are not seeing anything new - it has always been there - you are just seeing it for the first time. Enlightenment is a beginning, not an end, and this new understanding needs to be utilised and tempered with wisdom and discernment before its truth, power and worth can be fully known. With knowledge comes responsibility, because greater knowledge leads to greater personal power. It is vital that you use your knowledge and power only for what is good, just, truthful and right.

MESSAGE FOR VIRGO & LIBRA ✭ New insights abound; you are coming into a new understanding of life and its meanings and spirit. But you must not be complacent about it; you must use this new understanding, or it will be worthless to you. It is vital that you always look for ways in which you can use your insights for the good of yourself and others. Enlightenment is not the end of your journey. Rather, it is the starting point of an adventure of learning that, if followed with a true heart, will show you great wisdom and understanding.

✭ ✭ ✭

LIBRA ✭ *28 September - 13 October* ♎

RUNE NAME ✭ GEBO, GEOFU ~ Norse ~ GYFU ~ A Gift, Giving

SPECIAL CRYSTAL ~ Opal
SPECIAL TREE ~ Ash / Elm

Positive Meanings ✭ Gift, Love, Exchange of Powers Between Gods & Humans, Blessing, Hospitality, Generosity, Partnership, Weddings, Legacies, Promotion, Windfall

Magical Powers ✭ To create harmony in partnerships, to integrate the energies of two people, to remove a curse

BASIC DIVINATORY MEANING ✭ A Spiritual Gift. This rune could bring a gift, an offer, or an opportunity, and it can allow you the wondrous gift of knowing how to make the most of your talents. Because there is a strong element of give and take inherent in the Geofu rune, it brings happiness and success in all kinds of partnerships, as it teaches that to receive a gift, you must also be a giver. Likewise, if you give, you must be willing to receive. This cycle of giving and receiving must never be broken, for those who take without giving on a physical or emotional level break the links, create blockages, and ultimately lose their own spiritual gifts. To be truly balanced you must be able to receive a gift with total humility, knowing that if you abuse something given to you, you will lose it. Compassion is a to give a gift of love and understanding, while encouragement is to give the gift of empowerment.

Each person has many things to give; once your gifts are recognised, they can be passed on to others.

MESSAGE FOR LIBRA ✶ When a gift arrives in your experience, this presents you with a choice. You can either accept it or reject it. If you choose to accept it, you must be prepared to give back some form of energy in return. Everything has its price, but with spiritual gifts the cost is always worth it in the end. It is up to you to find the balance between giving and receiving and to learn the lesson of responsible giving. It is important to discern when to give, how to give it, and to whom to give. Obviously, it is not appropriate to give to everyone indiscriminately for there are those who do not wish to receive, so giving to them is a waste of your energy and corrupts your own spirit and the Laws of Nature.

✭ ✭ ✭

LIBRA & SCORPIO ✶ *13 October - 28 October* ♎ ♏

RUNE NAME ✶ WUNJO ~ Norse ~ WYN ~ Joy

SPECIAL CRYSTAL ~ Diamond
SPECIAL TREE ~ Ash

Positive Meanings ✶ Bliss, Delight, Joy, Gateway, Glory, Mystery, Hope, Pasture, Reward, Pleasure, Comfort, Happiness, Success, recognition of Worth

Magical Powers ✶ To bring happiness, fulfillment & spiritual transformation, to gain favour with others, to summon fellowship

BASIC DIVINATORY MEANING ✶ Balance and Happiness. True happiness only comes to those who are balanced and integrated. Happiness comes from seeking and finding the truth, then integrating it into every aspect of your life. It is found within and is not dependent on any other person or external circumstance. To have happiness, you must be at peace with yourself and with your place in life. This requires you to think and act in a balanced manner. If you seek balance and harmony within, you will attract peace, prosperity and happiness into your experience. This rune is associated with a mixed bag of ideas, including joy and bliss on an emotional level, as well as journeys over water, visitors from overseas, artistic and spiritual awakenings, gain, luck and success due to inspiration or creativity. Curiously, sometimes this rune brings a fair-haired man, and sometimes it means that a wish will be granted.

MESSAGE FOR LIBRA & SCORPIO ✶ Happiness is yours if you are willing to work for it. You must strive for inner integration, balance and harmony in your life. Always be looking for solutions rather than dwelling upon challenges. For happiness to last, it needs to be founded upon truth, integrity, authenticity, and honesty. If you hide from the truth, it will be most certain that you shall never experience true happiness. Seek only what is true and right, and good fortune must follow.

✯   ✯   ✯

SCORPIO ✯ *28 October - 13 November* ♏

RUNE NAME ✯ HAGAL, HAGALAZ ~ Norse ~ HAGALL ~ Hail

SPECIAL CRYSTAL ~ Onyx
SPECIAL TREE ~ Ash / Yew

Positive Meanings ✯ Ice, Hail, Snow, Natural Forces, Disruption, Bringing Opposites into Harmony

Magical Powers ✯ To attract positive influence, to gain mystical knowledge, to bring luck, edge and experience

BASIC DIVINATORY MEANING ✯ A Challenge. This rune signifies an unexpected bolt from the blue and can be good for those who need their lives shaken up a little.

MESSAGE FOR SCORPIO ✯ Challenges are occurring in your life, however these are not to be feared, but to be embraced. A symbolic hailstorm may seem daunting, but if you catch a hailstone you will realise that it is only water and nothing to be feared. And so it is with difficulties. Develop a steely resolve, fire up your determination, and face the obstacles and challenges head-on in the assurance that they are merely stepping stones to the realisation of your dream. Every adversity comes to teach you something. Remember, the greater the challenge, potentially the more wisdom you can acquire once you have overcome the blocks in your path. Because challenges occur to teach you, you should never shy away from them, for when you fix your mind a vision of how you would like your future to be, you send energy in the form of thought waves out into the Universe. These vibrations then magnetise to you all the things that need to be in place before that desire can become reality. You cannot know all the lessons at all times, but if you stay fixed on your dream, be assured that you will be attracting all the lessons you need to ensure it comes true. When you encounter difficulties, they are not signs to abandon your dream, they are simply stepping stones to the bigger Plan the Universe is responding to on your behalf. Challenges provide opportunities to learn and embrace the lessons that you will need when your deepest wish becomes a reality. Confront the challenges head-on - and once you have overcome them, you will be stronger and wiser, and will have cleared a Path directly to your dream.

✯   ✯   ✯

SCORPIO & SAGITTARIUS ★ *13 November - 28 November* ♏ ♐

RUNE NAME ★ NYD, NIED ~ Norse ~ NAUTHIZ ~ Need

SPECIAL CRYSTAL ~ Lapis Lazuli
SPECIAL TREE ~ Beech

Positive Meanings ★ Need, Necessity, Caution, Desire, Constraint, Survival, New Strength, Self-Reliance

Magical Powers ★ To achieve long-term goals, to attract a lover, to overcome stress, to develop spiritual power

BASIC DIVINATORY MEANING ★ Need. This rune brings whatever is necessary for survival or self-preservation. If you are short of the basic necessities or in need of employment, this rune's message is a good omen for you. In essence, it advises that you are getting exactly what you need at this moment to allow you to make the best progress on your spiritual path. Everything is in its proper place, how it is meant to be. It may appear to be the very opposite of what you are wanting, but this state is not permanent - just as nothing ever is - it is merely a series of lessons that must be embraced so that you can make the transition from perceived lack to abundance. You need to have total acceptance of what has occurred in the past, to keep your mind fixed on where you want to be, while trusting that everything in the current moment is supposed to be there and important lessons are to be drawn from it. Find your power in the now. After all, the past is just a memory, the future is just a dream, and the present is the only place over which you can have influence.

MESSAGE FOR SCORPIO & SAGITTARIUS ★ What we want and what we need in our lives are often two completely different things. If you want to be strong, you will need to examine your shortcomings closely. This creates a paradox. You hold an ideal, a vision of being strong, and yet all you can see are your weaknesses. It is only when you realise that the weaknesses need to be confronted and transformed into strengths, that you will begin to understand the difference between your wants and your needs. To achieve your wishes, you often need to experience the very opposite of them, just as to be strong you must first encounter weakness. To find your Path, you must first lose your way; to be beautiful within, you must first face up to and deal with your inner shadow self. Your weaker, darker side isn't always pretty, but it is a powerful, wonderful teacher.

✯   ✯   ✯

SAGITTARIUS ✷ *28 November - 13 December* ♐

RUNE NAME ✷ ISA ~ Norse ~ IS ~ Ice, Standstill

SPECIAL CRYSTAL ~ Cat's Eye
SPECIAL TREE ~ Alder

Positive Meanings ✷ Standstill, Contraction, Lack of Emotion, Psychological Blocks, Reinforcement, Patience, Careful Speech

Magical Powers ✷ To develop concentration and will, to halt unwanted forces, to make a situation 'static'

BASIC DIVINATORY MEANING ✷ Ice. This rune indicates that something is frozen or is about to freeze, including one's finances. It can teach you that you might need some patience to ride a wave of temporary discontent, or perhaps to preserve the status quo. Ice can serve as an impenetrable barrier, and the only thing you can do is to wait for the thaw. Nonetheless, winter is not a time for idleness; there is much that can be done in preparation for the thaw. Although nothing appears to be moving, everything must be in place and ready if you are to take full advantage of the impending melting of the ice. Winter is also a time of reflection and contemplation, a time to review the past, to assimilate all the lessons that the past has taught, and a time to look to the future and reaffirm your dreams. Recognise that the current moment you are experiencing is just another phase of your ever-unfolding path of learning; and when this phase is over, a new one will surely begin. Therefore, use this time to rest a while; for you will need to focus all your energies upon what is to come.

MESSAGE FOR SAGITTARIUS ✷ Things appear to be at a standstill and this is not a time to force any movement. Patience and wisdom are certainly called for: patience because you will have to wait until things change externally before you can proceed; and wisdom because you need to decide how best to use this waiting time. Now is not the time for abandoning your dreams; on the contrary, this is an opportunity for you to re-ingrain and reaffirm them. It is an opportue time for contemplation and preparation, not for sadness or regrets. Be assured that things will change as surely as winter transforms into spring and then into summer. The ice will slowly but surely melt away.

SAGITTARIUS & CAPRICORN ★ *13 December - 28 December* ♐ ♑

RUNE NAME ★ GER, YER, JERA, JARA ~ Norse ~ AR ~ Cycle or Harvest

SPECIAL CRYSTAL ~ Carnelian
SPECIAL TREE ~ Oak

Positive Meanings ★ Spear, Cycles, Good Year, Good Season or Harvest, Earned Success, Peace, Progress, Prosperity, Time to Reap Rewards

Magical Powers ★ To bring success in gardening and farming, to gain returns on good investments and hard work, to assist in legal matters

BASIC DIVINATORY MEANING ★ Harvest. This rune tells of a time of reaping rewards from the seeds sown in the past. It is a good rune to work with if you want to end a cycle and clean the slate, as it helps with such things as being able to clear debts or to get rid of outworn baggage, as well as being associated with rewards for past work. It also indicates a time of plenty and abundance, a period of joy and celebration. But it is also a time of great work with no room for complacency. After all, it is wise to acknowledge that the harvest does not last forever. The winter of further hard lessons lies ahead, and you would do well to make sure that you have stored enough knowledge and wisdom to face the next challenges this will present. This is simply another turning point in your life, not your goal. There are greater harvests for you to experience in the future, but before any harvest there has to be preparation of the land, sowing of the seed, tending of the seedlings, and of course support of the forming and growing fruits of your labour.

MESSAGE FOR SAGITTARIUS & CAPRICORN ★ Harvest is traditionally the time of the hardest work. The results of your labour must be collected and stored if they are not to spoil. It is a time of fore-planning, of preparation. Everything must be in its place before the first cold snaps of winter come. If the winter is to be survived, it is imperative that as much of the fruits of your past labour as possible are stored. Nothing must be overlooked, and everything must be done correctly. If your fruits are not stored in the correct way, they will ruin long before the winter is over. This is certainly not a time to be resting on your laurels, but rather a time of gentle, steady work. The harvest feasting takes place only after the harvest is finished, not before. You are at the end of a cycle but remember that endings only lead to new beginnings.

CAPRICORN ✶ *28 December - 13 January* ♑

RUNE NAME ✶ EOH, EEWAZ ~ Norse ~ EIHWAZ ~ Yew Tree or Yew Bow

SPECIAL CRYSTAL ~ Topaz
SPECIAL TREE ~ Yew

Positive Meanings ✶ Enlightenment, End of a Relationship or Matter, Change, Reliability, Trust, Strength

Magical Powers ✶ To banish, to protect, to remove obstacles, to communicate between levels of reality

BASIC DIVINATORY MEANING ✶ Transformation / Yew Tree. The yew tree has a long association with immortality and the cycle of death and rebirth. As a yew tree grows, its central trunk becomes soft and starts to decay. While this occurs, a new sapling begins to grow within the tree. When the tree matures, the same process continues until the tree is made up of many trees growing from the centre outwards. This amazing regeneration is what enables a yew tree to grow to an immense size and age. The yew tree is said to have known many lives and so can help you if you wish to remember past lives. Because of its longevity, the yew is also regarded as a keeper of ancient wisdom. The first idea with this rune, is based on the symbolism of the pliable yew wood, so you can use this rune when you need to adopt a more flexible approach to life, to become more adaptable or to turn an inconvenient situation into an advantageous one. The second is a wish for long, healthy life.

MESSAGE FOR CAPRICORN ✶ This is a time of transformation, a time of releasing the old and embracing the new. It is a time of metaphorical death, the dying of the past, and yet it is also a time of new beginnings, fresh life, and new hopes and dreams. The only constant is change, and if you want to make swift and efficient progress on your Path, you need to learn to embrace change instead of resisting it. To resist change is to cause oneself suffering, to risk stagnation, to risk becoming stuck at the point of spiritual death instead of walking forwards towards the new dawn that is awaiting you. Do not be afraid; change can be daunting, but if you remain true to yourself and keep to your true Path, you will soon find yourself basking under a Sun of new enlightenments.

CAPRICORN & AQUARIUS ✶ *13 January - 28 January* ♑ ♒

RUNE NAME ✶ PEORTH, PERTHRO ~ Norse ~ PERTHO ~ The Secret Rune, Dice Cup

SPECIAL CRYSTAL ~ Aquamarine
SPECIAL TREE ~ Beech

Positive Meanings ✶ Mystery, Evolutionary Force, Dice Cup, Chance, Science, Technology, Feminine Mysteries, Fate, Occult, Sexuality, Whisper, Initiation, Knowledge of Future, Nice Surprise, Unexpected Gain

Magical Powers ✶ To gain inner guidance, to protect against dark forces, to find lost things

BASIC DIVINATORY MEANING ✶ Choice / A Dice Cup. This rune is for those who seek knowledge or education or who want to increase or improve their psychic powers. It also indicates a lucky break! The dice cup is the receptacle from which dice are thrown; it is the source of chance, luck, and fate. A die which is not thrown is just a lump of wood or plastic with dots on it. It is only when the dice are thrown that they have significance, because the manner and position of their falling is in the hands of fate. People think of fate as an inevitable tide, but this is not so. Fate merely presents you with choices: there is the choice of whether or not to throw the dice, for example, and also whether to heed what the dice tell you.

MESSAGE FOR CAPRICORN & AQUARIUS ✶ Life is full of choices, but many people choose to let the hand of fate and chance guide them instead of taking charge of their destiny and claiming it in spite of what fate may bring. Peorth tells you that you always have a choice in anything. No one and nothing can upset you, you can only choose to be upset. No one can exert power over you, but you choose to allow them to. So claim your power of choice! Do not allow others to compromise your truth and do not let others prevent you from doing what you need to do in your heart. The only danger here is to not make a choice, to leave things to chance and fate, as that Path can only serve to disempower you.

✶ ✶ ✶

AQUARIUS ✶ *28 January - 13 February* ♒

RUNE NAME ✶ EOLHS, ELHAZ ALGIZ ~ Norse ~ YR ~ Protection, Elk

SPECIAL CRYSTAL ~ Amethyst
SPECIAL TREE ~ Yew

Positive Meanings ✶ Elk, Protection, Opportunity, Defense, Refuge, Yew Bow, Stone Axe, Channelled Energies, Removal of Blockages

Magical Powers ✶ To communicate with other worlds, to protect, to defend, to strengthen the life force, to promote luck

BASIC DIVINATORY MEANING ✶ An Elk / Protection. This rune brings artistry, creativity, poetry, literacy and success in crafts and hobbies. It may also mean joining a club or group that has a special language or meaning. It can even protect or defend against danger. To the Nordic people, the elk was a powerful totemic animal with very strong protective energies. The wearing of this rune is said to guard the wearer against all manner of attacks and adversities, both physical and psychic. The Elhaz rune is said to represent the elk when the animal is viewed face on. The antlers of the elk were thought of as psychic receivers which could pick up on the subtle vibrations of all living things around it. The protective energies of the elk come not only from its ability to sense danger, but also its speed and the skill with which it flees dangerous situations swiftly and efficiently. Therefore, the Elhaz rune can be used as a powerful ally to help you find a safe passage through difficult or challenging times.

MESSAGE FOR AQUARIUS ✶ Be assured that although your path ahead is fraught with dangers, you need have no fear for you have the power of protection within your very core. You will be safe as long as you do not act recklessly or take unnecessary chances for the sake of it. Risky ventures can be undertaken with favourable results but bear in mind that all things must be built on firm foundations. Do not become complacent and be ever-alert to malignant forces.

✯ ✯ ✯

AQUARIUS & PISCES ✶ *13 February - 27 February*

RUNE NAME ✶ SYGEL, SOWILO, SIGEL ~ Norse ~ SUNNA ~ The Sun

SPECIAL CRYSTAL ~ Ruby
SPECIAL TREE ~ Juniper

Positive Meanings ✶ The Sun, Sun-Wheel, Life-Energy, Revelation, Wholeness, Contact with the Higher Self, Advancement, Power for Change, Change of Residence, Time of Renewal, Turnaround, Victory

Magical Powers ✶ To increase good health, vitality and sexual magnetism, to strengthen psychic powers

BASIC DIVINATORY MEANING ✶ The Sun / Good Fortune. To the Nordic people, the Sun was considered the great life force, the giver and sustainer of life, for without its rays there would be no food, no sustenance, and certainly no life. The Sun is associated with all that is good, light, joyful, just and pure. The light of the Sun banishes darkness and rejuvenates the spirit. It is also the 'destroyer of ice', as one Icelandic runic poem describes it, and is therefore a powerful rune to counteract the negative aspects of the Is rune (which means a standstill and 'ice'). Hitler stole this rune from the Nazi SS because he knew it as a symbol of success. You can use it to bring optimism, vitality, success and victory in any undertakings or endeavour. It also augurs well for fame and the recognition of talent. Sigel is also a rune of truth; the power of light illuminates the darkness of deception and illusion, offering clarity of thought and vision. It will highlight not only deception in others, but also the ways you delude yourself. It will shine a light upon the Path of all who hold it.

MESSAGE FOR AQUARIUS & PISCES ✶ You have the power to bring your desires to fruition. Good fortune awaits you and there is a positive feel to everything you touch and are moved by. This is not a time to rest and relax, however, rather it is an ideal time to look within at the darker aspects of your nature so that they may be brought to light and dealt with. The power of the Sun will enable you to face those shadowy parts of your being fearlessly and finally to gain power over them. This is a good time to seek solutions to problems, as solutions are all within your reach.

PISCES ✶ *27 February - 14 March* ♓

RUNE NAME ✶ TIR, TIWAZ ~ Norse ~ TYR ~ The God of War, Justice, Initiation

SPECIAL CRYSTAL ~ Coral
SPECIAL TREE ~ Oak

Positive Meanings ✶ Warrior, Sovereign Order, the Sky God, Analysis, Authority, Rationality, Honour, Justice, Law, Order, Victory, Success, Wisdom, Finding True Strength

Magical Powers ✶ To achieve victory over adversity, to bind an oath, to fight, to defend against known enemies, to create ardent love

BASIC DIVINATORY MEANING ✶ Tyr, the Warrior God). The path of the warrior presents challenges and initiations. The warrior must learn many skills including patience, keenness of sense, speed and agility. He must be of a pure, vital and strong heart, with a firm belief in the sacredness of that which he protects. As a companion, one could not wish for a better ally, for the warrior has a natural instinct to protect, thrive and survive. He is always resourceful and focuses on solutions rather than problems. The wise warrior knows that mistakes are not failures, but rather lessons to be learned if one is honest and humble enough to seek and obtain the wisdom inherent in every adversity. The person who makes no mistakes in their life becomes an old fool.

MESSAGE FOR PISCES ✶ This rune symbolises new challenges and initiations into new understandings. It indicates a need for fearlessness, for your victory is already assured if your heart and spirit remain true and aligned with your highest purpose. This is a time to make use of all the skills and wisdom that you have learnt so far. Protect your faith and mind your beliefs, as they may be challenged, but the truth will always triumph in the end. The Tyr rune also represents justice, the ability to stand up for oneself and even to go into battle when necessary. It can be used to bring a love affair into being, but beware, as this may be of the passionate, tumultuous kind that may bring heightened energy into your experience.

✯ ✯ ✯

PISCES & ARIES ✶ *14 March - 30 March*

RUNE NAME ✶ BEORC, BERKANA, BERKANO ~ Norse ~ BJARKAN ~ Birch Tree

SPECIAL CRYSTAL ~ Moonstone
SPECIAL TREE ~ Birch

Positive Meanings ✶ Growth, Fertility, Spring, Rebirth, Personal Growth, Creativity, Desire, Marriage, New Beginnings

Magical Powers ✶ To conceal and protect, to heal, to nurture, to love

BASIC DIVINATORY MEANING ✶ New Beginnings / A Birch Tree. The birch tree is a pioneer tree. When forest or scrubland is destroyed by fire, the birch is one of the first trees to regenerate and re-colonise the land. Therefore, it is symbolic of birth and new beginnings, like the mythical phoenix rising from the ashes. The birch tree has long been associated with purification in magic. The birch broom was used to sweep negativity from an area, while the punishment of 'birching' was said to banish evil from criminals. The old pagan ritual of beating the bounds to mark land boundaries and to cleanse negativity from the soil also utilised birch wood. This ancient practice is still performed in remote regions of Scandinavia and the British Isles. As a symbol of the birch tree, the Beorc rune signifies a fresh start, new beginnings, expansion, awakening, fertility and overall growth. Beorc is a great rune for joy in the family, as well as weddings and other celebrations that mark new starts and horizons.

MESSAGE FOR PISCES & ARIES ✶ This is an exciting time of new beginnings and fresh adventures, a time of great energy and activity, a time to sow the seeds of the things you wish to grow. But remember that the harvest is still a long way off; do not expect to see immediate rewards for your efforts, as new ideas need nurturing, tending to, expressing and feeding before they will bear fruit. This is a time to make sure that the past is truly left in its place. If you have learned all the lessons that the past has had to teach, you need never revisit it. It can be left behind, and you can venture forth with boldness and fresh eyes to embrace new pastures. This is also a good time to think about undertaking a spiritual spring-cleaning of your mind, body, spirit and physical spaces, to effectively clear away the old to make way for the new.

Crystal Messages

ABOUT CRYSTALS

Beautiful and strong is the material of stones, but more beautiful and much more powerful is the mystery that emanates from them.

Li Po, Chinese Poet & Alchemist, 8th Century A.D.

Around six thousand years ago, in ancient Mesopotamia, the Sumerians started studying precious stones and minerals, as well as the stars, with a view of improving their lives in many ways by probing the secrets and mysteries of the Universe. Their esoteric interests and knowledge were such that they began to grasp the general connections between the Earth and the heavens, or the Solar system as they knew it, and the functions of stones and minerals as a link between the two. Their method of making these connections was by colour (for example the Sun was allocated all yellow stones), as well as many other spiritual links been the microcosm (humans and all other life on planet Earth) and the macrocosm (the Universe).

Each crystal and mineral of the Earth embodies different qualities, patterns or potential expressions of the Divine language, the silent whispers of the Universe. If we can accept the fact that the human body is a sophisticated, multi-faceted antenna system comprised of a crystalline matrix that is constantly transmitting and receiving all manner of energies, it could then be assumed that energy and body workers who use quartz, shells and stones, which are also crystalline materials, have the power to promote resonant interactions with the liquid 'crystal' structures found in human tissues. It could even be said that we are all made of essentially the same substances and structures, and that crystals and gemstones vibrate at varying energetic levels which can connect with our own in order to 'buzz' and dance together to make a harmonious Uni-verse both within and without.

All crystals work through vibrational balancing and by channelling energy. The magic of crystals is in their colour, which is determined by the rate at which their atoms vibrate; these vibrations can be matched to the energy given by your own body's aura. And just as light can be focused and refracted through gemstones, so too can all kinds of psychic energy, from healing energies to Divine communications.

Gemstones can help us attune to higher vibrations and bring them into our own experience and being. This theory of crystal resonance suggests that the characteristic energy patterns emanated by any stone can be transferred into the 'liquid crystal medium' of our bodies through resonance. Our bodies, being composed of these tuneable liquids, can mimic and mirror any consistent vibrational pattern with which we come into contact; we can therefore resonate with the healthful qualities of various crystals and minerals.

Crystals and precious stones have been valued throughout world cultures over many centuries for their healing virtues and capacities to imbue courage, strength, invulnerability, clairvoyance, love and numerous other qualities. Wearing gemstones is one of the simplest and most effective self-healing practices you can undertake and wearing or carrying those stones whose vibrations correspond with the qualities you wish to embody brings their energetic currents into engagement with your body.

Although it is untrue that the only stones you can usefully wear are the ones astrologically matched with your Sun sign or ruling planet, those which align with your Sun sign or ruling planet are your most fortuitous and therefore strongest 'attractors' and 'amplifiers'.

Nobody is under the rule of one planet or zodiac sign alone. We are all in essence a complex mixture of every planet, many elements, all the signs, and varying aspects, depending on their positions, placements and prominence in our birth chart. Everything that goes on in the skies above us affects what is going on here on Earth, and also *within* us.

Working mindfully with your star sign's special crystal is one way you can increase the flow of power and magic into your life ~ and ultimately, connect you with the Divine.

ZODIAC CRYSTALS

Here is a list of the birthstones for each zodiac sign, which have been passed on throughout the ages and have endured because their individual essence vibrates in harmony with that particular sign. Out of this list, I have chosen one as your Divine crystal (see following for this specially selected gemstone and its message for you), but of course you may choose any to work with from the list. As with everything else in the Divine realms, whatever resonates the most with you is likely to have the greatest effect on you.

♈ ARIES ✶ Bloodstone, Carnelian, Diamond, Aquamarine, Aventurine, Hematite, Lapis Lazuli, Malachite, Obsidian

♉ TAURUS ✶ Rose Quartz, Diamond, Sapphire, Emerald, Jade, Selenite, Carnelian

♊ GEMINI ✶ Citrine, Tiger's Eye, Agate, Alexandrite, Aquamarine, Jade

♋ CANCER ✶ Emerald, Chrysoprase, Moonstone, Pearl, Ruby, Aventurine, Carnelian

♌ LEO ✶ Clear Quartz, Onyx, Citrine, Ruby, Peridot, Carnelian, Jasper, White Onyx

♍ VIRGO ✶ Carnelian, Sapphire, Peridot, Sardonyx, Agate

♎ LIBRA ✶ Peridot, Jacinth, Tourmaline, Opal, Sapphire, Aventurine, Chrysoprase, Citrine, Jade, Moonstone, Rose Quartz

♏ SCORPIO ✶ Aquamarine, Topaz, Malachite, Peridot, Labradorite, Moonstone, Turquoise

♐ SAGITTARIUS ✶ Topaz, Zircon, Turquoise, Amethyst, Azurite, Labradorite, Obsidian, Smoky Quartz

♑ CAPRICORN ✶ Ruby, Garnet, Turquoise, Smoky Quartz, Fluorite, Amethyst, Tiger's Eye

♒ AQUARIUS ✶ Garnet, Turquoise, Aquamarine, Amethyst, Azurite, Hematite, Lapis Lazuli

♓ PISCES ✶ Amethyst, Bloodstone, Turquoise, Aquamarine, Blue Lace Agate, Chrysoprase, Fluorite

Additionally, there are certain gemstones which are deemed 'mystical' for each sign. They are:

MYSTICAL BIRTHSTONES OF THE ZODIAC

Aries ✶ Jade
Taurus ✶ Opal
Gemini ✶ Sapphire
Cancer ✶ Moonstone
Leo ✶ Ruby
Virgo ✶ Diamond
Libra ✶ Agate
Scorpio ✶ Jasper
Sagittarius ✶ Pearl
Capricorn ✶ Onyx
Aquarius ✶ Emerald
Pisces ✶ Bloodstone

CRYSTAL MESSAGES FOR THE ZODIAC

ARIES

DIVINE CRYSTAL ✶ DIAMOND

Diamond is pure crystallised carbon and is known as the ruler of the mineral kingdom, due to its hardwearing qualities, hardness and sheer brilliance. Diamond is the purest and hardest substance in nature. The word 'diamond' has its origin in the Greek word 'adamas', which means unconquerable. Mined for over 4,000 years, ancient civilisations discovered that this amazing gem could cut any other stone. The diamond is known universally as a token of love; quite simply, it is the ultimate symbol of purity. Psychologically, this precious gem imparts a sense of fearlessness, fortitude and invincibility, for diamonds are unbreakable in every sense of the word. Diamond is also an amplifier of any energy with which it comes into contact, therefore should only be used for positive magic, and is one of the few stones that never needs recharging or cleansing; in fact, it increases the energy of whatever it comes into contact with and is very effective when used with other crystals for healing as it enhances and draws out their power. Like the clear quartz, it is a master healer which accelerates the spiritual development of its wearer. As an amplifier of energy, the merciless light of diamond will highlight anything that is negative and requires transformation. Diamond has been a symbol for wealth for thousands of years and is one of the stones of manifestation, with the ability to attract abundance; the larger the diamond, the more abundance will be drawn to the requester. Indeed, clear crystals such as diamond will interact with your energy field by raising your vibration through clearing away any cloudiness or blockages within your subtle bodies. With it may be worn a bloodstone, another Arian gemstone, when the beneficent influence of the diamond will be greatly increased. A highly creative stone, stimulating imagination and inventiveness, and aiding spiritual evolution, it seems it was made for the pioneering, strong-as-steel, dynamic Arian nature.

DIAMOND'S DIVINE MESSAGE FOR ARIES ✶ "Aries, I am the King of the Crystal Kingdom, and your ultimate power stone. I am a luminously brilliant gem, and through my renowned purity and durability, I offer incomparable proof of total perfection expressed in a single element. My pure radiant white light can help to bring your life into a cohesive whole, the first step in using your power to optimum effect. I help to clear emotional and mental pain, alleviate fear, and bring about the new beginnings you desire. I also provide a link between your intellect and your higher mind, aiding clarity and overall enlightenment. On a spiritual level, I allow your soul's light to shine outwards, as I purify your aura of anything shrouding your inner light. I remind you of your soul's aspirations; I activate the Crown chakra, linking it to the 'Divine Light'. Like you, Aries, I am unconquerable, radiant, defeated by none. I am, hands down, the greatest."

TAURUS

DIVINE CRYSTAL ✶ EMERALD

Emerald is a vivid grass-green precious stone belonging to the beryl family, whose name is derived from the Greek *beryllos*, meaning a green stone. Emerald is mainly blue-green in colour but can also be green-yellow and even yellow. Virtues ascribed to this beautiful stone of Venus and Taurus, are those of hope, purity, prosperity, love, dreams, kindness, healing, fertility, and eternal youth; the ancients believed that it would bestow immortality and good fortune upon those who wore it. Emeralds were a prime source of wealth in Ancient Greece and Egypt, and this legacy endures today. With its dazzling green brilliance, emerald has long been prized for its magical properties and as such has a long history of myth and folklore. Most important of all was emerald's reputation as a link with the Divine forces. It is said to enhance psychic abilities and clairvoyance. The ancients believed that the Greek god Hermes inscribed the laws of 'magic' upon an emerald tablet, and indeed, emeralds were dedicated to Mercury, the winged messenger, by early astrologers. Connected with the Heart chakra, emerald opens and activates this vital organ to heal all problems associated with the heart, whether they be physical or emotional. It is known as 'the stone of successful love' with which unconditional love can be pledged to a partner. By promoting harmony and wholeness to every aspect of one's life, emerald dispels negativity and draws beauty, wisdom and healing to it. Emerald ensures emotional, physical and mental equilibrium and imparts strength of character to overcome setbacks and misfortunes. As a stone of regeneration and recovery, it can inspire a deep inner knowing, broaden vision, and enhance one's wisdom and integrity. It encourages us to follow the laws of nature and, by imbuing us with a sense of beauty and openness, enhances our ability to appreciate the wonders of life.

EMERALD'S DIVINE MESSAGE FOR TAURUS ✴ "Taurus, as the ultimate love and heart stone, I encourage you to stay open to love and to follow your heart in all that you undertake. Taurus, often fixated upon the material realm, sometimes needs reminding that the spiritual bank balance is the most important figure in life. As an ancient stone of wealth, I am believed to attract good fortune to you. But I also encourage gratitude, helping you to recognise abundance in all forms rather than just monetary. Life-affirming and inspirational, I am a brilliant stone of beauty, instilling a sense of growth and energy, which provides you with an overall uplifting and healing tonic for the mind, body and spirit."

✴ ✴ ✴

GEMINI

DIVINE CRYSTAL ✴ CITRINE

Citrine is known in crystal healing circles as the success, prosperity, abundance and happiness stone, and is an attractive, bright, golden-yellow gem that takes its name from the old French word 'citron', meaning 'lemon' or 'yellow'. The golden-yellow colour of citrine quartz is formed when high temperatures are applied to amethyst or smoky quartz. Natural citrine is said to contain solidified sunlight and never to absorb negativity, so never needs cleansing. Citrine carries the power of the Sun and has a particular affinity with the Solar Plexus chakra. Its beneficial energies also work well with the Sacral and Heart chakras. This is a willpower stone, being so Solar in energy, and is particularly helpful for helping to release old patterns of behaviours or thoughts that stand in the way of our achieving greatness. Being so highly Solar in nature, citrine energises every level of life, promotes clarity and puts us in touch with celestial Fire and the powers of our brightest luminary and the core essence of our self - the Sun; in this way, it can help to raise self-esteem and self-confidence. Because it is a stone of positivity, it dispels destructive tendencies, improves motivation, encourages self-expression, activates individuality, and is excellent for dissolving blockages to creativity. Further, it is useful for overcoming depression, fears and phobias, and promotes the inner calm that enables wisdom to emerge. Citrine awakens the higher mind, stimulates inspiration and frees the mind of limitations, helping to turn ideas into reality. It amplifies and regenerates energy and being the product of heat-treated amethyst or smoky quartz, it carries the forces of transmutation and inner alchemy. Its bright yellow colour is literally like a sunbeam shining into your life, helping you to gain insight or confidence when you need to manifest change. This stone helps you look forward optimistically to the future instead of hanging onto the past; it also promotes exploration and enjoyment of new experiences. It is an aura protector and has the ability to cleanse the chakras, especially the Solar Plexus and Sacral chakras. But it also activates the Crown chakra, opens the intuition and balances the subtle bodies, aligning them with the physical. Citrine is one of the stones of abundance. This dynamic stone teaches how to attract, manifest and keep wealth, prosperity and success.

CITRINE'S DIVINE MESSAGE FOR GEMINI ✶ "Gemini, I am the ultimate joy and abundance stone, thus providing a supremely uplifting tonic for your spirit. I am associated with good fortune, luck, manifestation, personal power, and overall energy. I am an exceedingly beneficial stone, a powerful cleanser and regenerator for your restless spirit. Warming, energising and highly creative, I help you to develop your psychic abilities, especially if you have problems trusting and acting on your instincts. Hold a piece of citrine in your hand when you are undertaking any psychic work, such as mediumship or scrying, and it will enhance your inspiration and reasoning capacities. I have the power to impart joy to all who behold me, and overall, I will promote joy in your life. I am a happy, generous stone that encourages wonder, enthusiasm and delight, filling any dark areas with cheer and light. My sunny nature means that I can enliven you and connect you strongly with the light of your inner being."

CANCER

DIVINE CRYSTAL ✶ MOONSTONE

An opalescent form of feldspar, resembling in its colour the pale lustrous gleam of moonlight, moonstone is traditionally regarded as a stone of the Goddess and is sacred to all things Lunar and celestial. Moonstone is a translucent, milky stone which occurs in yellow, peach, grey, blue and colourless. The beautiful sheen of this stone seems to wax and wane like its namesake and the crystal has featured in much Lunar folklore, being considered a sacred link to the Moon in many cultures. Moonstone improves emotional intelligence and provides deep healing within this realm and is believed to have the power to endow love, wealth and wisdom. Possessing a gentle nature which promotes kindness and peace, it is calming, balancing, soothing, healing, protective and uplifting, particularly to Cancerians whose birth stone this is. It helps to identify emotional patterns that are stored in the subconscious mind and can act as a guardian. Moonstone makes conscious the unconscious and promotes and enhances empathy, lucidity, clairvoyance, receptivity, serendipity and synchronicity - however, regarding these last two, care needs to be taken that it does not induce illusions in response to wishful thinking. It is helpful in times of shock, possessing a calm, flowing peace that helps restore emotional balance in everyday experiences too. Moonstone is the traditional birthstone of June and resonates most strongly with the sign of Cancer.

MOONSTONE'S DIVINE MESSAGE FOR CANCER ★ "Cancer, I open your mind to hoping and wishing, inspiration and impulse, magic and enchantment. I am believed to absorb the rays of the Moon, and with them some of the mystical attributes of that heavenly body. My potency is said to increase as the Moon waxes (or goes from New to Full) and lessens when that orb declines. I am a symbol of hope and a stone of new beginnings, and like the Moon, I am reflective and remind you that, as the Moon waxes and wanes, so too is everything a part of an ever-rotating cycle of Divine change. My most powerful effect is that of calming the emotions, and I am useful in honing your intuitive and psychic abilities. I am also a stone of wishes and for working towards goal manifestation, as I grant you intuitive recognition and flashes of insight, allowing you to absorb what is most needed from the Universe."

★ ★ ★

LEO

DIVINE CRYSTAL ★ RUBY

Ruby derives its name from the Latin *rubens* or *rubeus*, meaning 'red'. A variety of the mineral corundum, it has a hardness of 9. Because it symbolised happiness and brightness and was believed to be the most beautiful of gems, it came to be associated with the sign of Leo. This association was also made because of its power in bringing success, wealth and joy, and because its symbolic virtues included courage, nobility, spirit and loyalty. Ruby has long been regarded as a symbol of love, beauty, passion, success, strength, protection and power. It aids in strengthening and refining the natural abilities you were born with. A powerful energiser for the Base chakra, ruby signifies and arouses lust, and governs the sexual and reproductive organs. It can be used to release any energy blockages deep within the self, and to activate, vitalise, intensify and increase desire. It utilises infrared, the slowest vibration of the colour spectrum, giving a new boost to processes that have been sluggish or stagnant. Ruby is one of the stones of abundance and aids in retaining wealth and a healthy, driven passion. Ruby brings up anger or negative energy, transmutes them, and removes anything unfavourable from your path. Promoting lively leadership and confidence, ruby brings about a positive and courageous state of mind. Essentially, ruby is a dynamic stone which charges up passion, banishes sadness, warns of danger or imminent misfortune (by darkening in colour), attracts sexual activity, fires up enthusiasm, and helps one overcome exhaustion, apathy and lethargy by imparting potency and vigour. It can stop outside forces from draining your energy. Ruby renews one's passion for life, truth, courage, wisdom and perseverance, emitting an abundance of cheerfulness.

RUBY'S DIVINE MESSAGE FOR LEO ★ "Leo, I am your ultimate life force power stone. The ancients considered me to be the stone of the Sun, representing the life force, fire, and the Divine spark that resides in us all. The gem of northern summer, I burn with a captivating fire. Imparting vigour to your journey, I energise and balance your spirit. I encourage the setting of realistic goals, improve motivation, and stimulate your passion for living. I help to the Heart chakra and enliven this centre, encouraging you to 'follow your bliss'. I am a stone of immense power and vitality, and I can be worn to activate your pure life force energy. My essence is a great ally when you wish to work profound magic in your life."

✯ ✯ ✯

VIRGO

DIVINE CRYSTAL ✯ SAPPHIRE

The hardest crystal after diamond, sapphire has long held a reputation for its amazing spiritual as well as physical properties. A variety of the mineral corundum, sapphire is a symbol of ultimate truth and imminent justice. Sapphire is found in a variety of colours, including blue, yellow, white, black, purple and green - but the blue variety is probably the best known. Its name is derived from the Sanskrit word *Sani*, which means Saturn. Sapphire has always been associated with love, fidelity, joy, prosperity, the heavens and the angels. It was believed to encourage altruism and generosity, to stimulate the imagination and curiosity, and had the reputation of winning those who wore it numerous friendships. Especially prized by the ancient Greeks and appearing throughout their mythology, those who wished to put a question to the famous Delphic Oracle had to wear a sapphire. There are many legends surrounding this luminous blue stone: The Ten Commandments were said to be written on tablets of sapphire, and King Solomon was believed to have used one to commune with God. An old Persian myth tells that the Earth sat on a giant sapphire which gave the sky its brilliant blue colour. In Buddhism, sapphire is known as the 'stone of the stones' because of its connection with the qualities of devotion, happiness, spiritual enlightenment, and tranquillity. Due to its highly soothing and balancing effect, sapphire is beneficial for treating nervous conditions such as panic attacks, anxiety and stress. Sapphires (especially star sapphires *) are good stones to work with to improve your psychic faculties or astral travel, stimulating the Third Eye chakra to enhance psychic experiences. Use it to connect to your spirit guides and teachers and for interdimensional communication, as it connects mind, body and spirit.

SAPPHIRE'S DIVINE MESSAGE FOR VIRGO ✯ "Virgo, I am known as the wisdom stone, and labelled the 'Gem of the Heavens'. I am believed to bestow you with strengthened vision, including prophetic visions of the future. I am the ultimate symbol of truth and constancy, and effective at opening and activating your Crown Chakra, which is why I am an excellent tonic for improving mental focus and clarity. I have a calming and balancing effect on emotions. When used open up the Crown and Third Eye chakras, I allow you access to the angelic realms. Some sapphires are believed to be record-keepers and may aid you to access the knowledge of ancient civilisations and the Akashic Records, when dreaming, 'journeying' or meditating. Overall, I will encourage you to reach for the stars, speak your truth, and stay on your rightful spiritual path."

★ ★ ★

LIBRA

DIVINE CRYSTAL ★ JADE

Green jade is a calming, loving stone, connected with the Heart chakra and dreams. The most sought-after colouring is an intense apple green, an eye-catching, extremely rare and highly attractive gem also known as Imperial Jade. Jade brings peace through serenity and cleanses the energy centres. Green jade strengthens the Heart chakra and can be used to harmonise dysfunctional relationships. It calms the nervous system and channels passion in constructive ways. It increases love and nurturing and symbolises harmony, purity, protection, good luck and friendship. It is a serenity stone and is excellent for healing conditions associated with stress and feelings of overwhelming obligation. A wonderful ally in healing others, jade is a good stone for those who are beginner healers or who wish to give their healing skills an added boost. Jade has a long history of being used to attract wealth and prosperity due to its associations with royalty. Chinese business people have extensively used jade to attract new business and promote worthy causes and ventures. Placing a piece of jade in your work space is beloved to attract wealth and enhance calm and harmony in the work environment. Used with other stones or on its own, it is traditionally believed to generate abundance and attract good fortune in all areas of life. Jade is also a useful 'dream' stone; placed under your pillow, it encourages insightful dreams and will help you to not only remember your dreams, but also to interpret them. In addition, as a stone of wisdom, it assists us to reach decisions about meaningful things. Jade has the wonderful attribute of dispelling all negativity and indeed has been considered a sacred stone by various cultures for many centuries. The Chinese call jadeite 'Yu Shih' meaning Yu stone, believing it to contain all five cardinal virtues needed for a happy existence: modesty, courage, charity, justice and wisdom. Maori greenstone jade is a master healer and powerful manifestor.

JADE'S DIVINE MESSAGE FOR LIBRA ★ "Libra, I am your ultimate harmony, healing, and good fortune stone. The ancients considered me a sacred stone and I was traditionally worn as a stone of luck. On a spiritual level I have a deep affinity with the Heart chakra and I work with you to harmonise relationships, bring out compassion, and establish strong bonds with others. I bring composure when I am worn, carried or used, and instill in you wisdom, tranquillity, serenity, and stability of the temperament. Spiritually, jade encourages you to become who you really are. Awakening hidden knowledge within you, I assist you to recognise yourself as a spiritual being on a human journey. A profoundly sacred stone, I encourage you to recognise that you have access to much wider powers and dimensions than can be physically perceived, and I therefore motivate you to become all that you can be. I can also assist your understanding of any blocks which may be hindering the manifestation or progress of your goals and help you to open your heart to receive."

✫ ✫ ✫

SCORPIO

DIVINE CRYSTAL ✫ MALACHITE

Malachite is a striking, rich-green layered opaque stone of intense energy. Its dramatic patterns echo its versatile and vast healing qualities. It is so named because its layers resemble the soft green of the marshmallow plant, derived from the Greek word for the plant's colouring - *malache*. Malachite is a copper-rich crystal which can be used diagnostically to get to the heart of a problem. It is a stone of balance that soothes, but also strengthens, the nervous system. A resolute stone that draws insights out from deep within the subconscious mind and facilitates the regeneration of the self, with dedicated use, this intense stone can balance and bring harmony to the body and psyche. Malachite is an exceptionally evolving * stone that is perfect for all self-transformational explorations, and the more you work with it, the more expansive its influence becomes. It also has a detoxifying effect, cleansing the body of both physical and emotional impurities. Assisting in the release of outworn or restrictive patterns of thought or behaviour, it is both physically and psychologically vitalising. It also facilitates release and letting go, enabling you to move forward. Used in combination with other similarly acting crystals, malachite can heal grief, ease heartache, draw out toxic emotions, break unwanted ties, root out psychosomatic causes of bodily dis-ease, and teach you how to take responsibility for your thoughts, actions and feelings. Malachite is known as the 'sleep stone' because it has the effect of inducing drowsiness if gazed at for long enough. Indeed, it can ease insomnia, improve quality of sleep and dreaming, and offer protection from nightmares. Malachite is used for its protective properties as well. It absorbs pollutants and negative energies, picking them up from the atmosphere, the physical body and the aura. It guards against radiation of all kinds and soaks up plutonium pollution. It also clears electromagnetic pollution and heals Earth energies. Malachite can be used for scrying - journeying through its convoluted patterns can stimulate pictures and assist in receiving insights or messages from the future. Essentially, it is a true empowerment crystal, which helps you reclaim your power by bringing to the surface any hidden issues, toxic thoughts or repressed feelings that are holding you back. If this stone had an expression, it would be, "I Am." It will help those who are brave enough to work with it, to step into your true power. As a stone of transformation and change, life is lived more intensely and adventurously under the influence of this vivid gem. It will enhance spiritual rebirth and growth, and when placed on the Solar Plexus it will facilitate deep emotional healing, allowing one's deepest self to shift in a new, positive direction. This profound crystal will surprise you with its merciless spotlight on what has held you back for so long - and will further astound with the depth of transmutation that you can achieve with it.

* It is believed by some people that malachite is still evolving and will be one of the most important healing stones in years to come.

MALACHITE'S DIVINE MESSAGE FOR SCORPIO ✫ "Scorpio, I am the ultimate transformation and power stone, and as these are two vitally important components of your spirit, working with me will help you to access these higher states of being. I illuminate the darker corners of your mind, and in doing so I demand that you examine the deep-rooted causes of any physical or mental issues. I am connected with the Solar Plexus, Throat and Heart chakras, and although powerful and probing, I instill courage and determination, dissolve your fears and anxieties, and help you break free from limitations. I am also a stone of alignment so am an excellent aid in self-exploration journeys. Working with me ultimately helps you confront whatever it is that is blocking your spiritual unfolding and wellbeing. I am regarded as "the mirror of the soul" and so some crystal experts may advise against wearing malachite as it may prove too intense and confronting for some - but never for Scorpio, the very embodiment of deep change and sweeping transformation."

SAGITTARIUS

DIVINE CRYSTAL ✫ TOPAZ

A traditional stone of protection, topaz has long been believed to protect its wearer from harm. Usually orange-yellow or yellow-green in colour, topaz can also be found in blue, green, red, pink, yellow or colourless. It is believed that topaz originates from and bears the name of an island in the Red Sea off the coast of Egypt, which, according to legend, was plunged into thick fog day and night and solely inhabited by snakes. This island, known today as the Isle of St John, was infested with these snakes who were the guardians of the topaz. According to the legend, the flashes of these stones sparkling in the night gave a supernatural glow to the foggy island, and this famous luminosity which defied the dark forces of the night made the topaz gem a symbol of honesty, faith, purity, loyalty, and righteousness. In ancient times amulets were made from topaz to protect the bearer from evil spirits or accidents, and it was believed that it changed colour to warn the bearer of imminent danger. The ancients also believed in its ability to arouse passions and intense feelings, to inspire enthusiasm and commitment, to regenerate the body, and to uncover acts of treachery and deceit, hence its connection and resonance with the zodiac sign of Scorpio also. African tribal people use it in their ceremonies to communicate with the spirit world and to attract and manifest both wealth and health. An empathetic stone that directs energy to where it is needed most, it soothes, heals, recharges, stimulates, re-motivates, and aligns the meridians of the body. As well as promoting forgiveness and truth, it helps shed light upon one's path, tap into inner resources, and highlight goals. Eliminating doubt and uncertainty, topaz also encourages a sense of trust in the Universe, that enables you to simple *be* rather than *do*. This is an envisioning stone and helps you see the core of any issue. It has the capacity to see both the bigger picture and the minute detail, and to recognise how they interrelate. With an affinity for the Sacral and Solar Plexus chakras, topaz encourages one to be benevolent in outlook and helps to promote a more selfless approach to life and be more considerate of the needs of others. Encouraging relaxation and serenity, it is good for restoring calm and helping the mind to unwind. A piece of topaz can also be worn or carried when it feels like one's willpower is wavering, in any situation. As it enhances creativity, understanding and self-expression, topaz defines the essence of a true magic-worker; one who is courageous, a visionary, and filled with hope, inspiration and purpose.

TOPAZ'S DIVINE MESSAGE FOR SAGITTARIUS ✶ "Sagittarius, I am your ultimate stone to use for attraction and desire-drawing purposes, magnetising people and situations on friendship, love and business levels, attracting all your desires to you as long as they are for the greater good. I also have the power to magnetise prosperity, honour, glory, and recognition of your worth. My vibrant energy brings abundance, generosity, joy, success and good fortune, and I am particularly supportive of your affirmations and manifestations. Excellent for cleansing the aura and for inducing relaxation, I act like a battery and recharge spiritually and psychically, strengthening your faith and optimism, and reminding you of your Divine origins. I will help you discover your own inner wisdom and riches as well, making you feel confident and philanthropic and compelled to spread the good fortune and sunshine all around. One of my more unusual characteristics is my apparent ability to put you in touch with life in other parts of the galaxy. Try me out, you might just launch yourself into greatness with one momentous, bounding leap."

CAPRICORN

DIVINE CRYSTAL ✷ GARNET

Garnet is regarded as a symbol of sincerity, good faith, loyalty, and honesty. It is a stone of vitality and dreams and increases the flow of the body's natural energy systems. It inspires service, cooperation, relaxation and 'going with the flow'. Garnet has an affinity for the Base and Sacral chakras, where it breaks down blockages and stimulates our untapped creative energy. It will also revitalise and balance energy in these chakras, bringing serenity or passion according to the need. Sometimes known as 'carbuncles' (when they are cut *en cabachon*, that is flat at the bottom or with a convex rounded top instead of facets), garnets occur in many different shades, the most well-known being deep red. Garnet also keeps us grounded, making us feel safe and secure. It assists in boosting confidence, imparting courage, building strength of character, and enabling us to find our inner fortitude and resources. Garnet helps to dissolve unhelpful behavioural patterns and past hurts to allow you to become more self-empowered and move on. Further, if you are feeling impotent or stuck in plans that have not yet manifested, this stone assists in moving out of the stagnancy and into potent action. It is also useful in easing situations in which you feel trapped and there seems no way out, or where life has become chaotic or broken, offering hope in apparently hopeless circumstances. It can help with any sexual difficulties, both mentally and physically, and is a stone of love and commitment which brings warmth, devotion, constancy, faithfulness, understanding, sincerity, trust and honesty to a relationship. Innovative garnet encourages you to be more creative and stimulates the right brain, creating 'light-bulb' flashes of inspiration and thought. It is an energising and regenerative stone, especially for the two lowest bodily chakras, although it also works effectively on the Heart chakra. It can activate other crystals, amplifying their effect.

GARNET'S DIVINE MESSAGE FOR CAPRICORN ✷ "Capricorn, I am your ultimate strengthening and fortifying stone, helping you to overcome obstacles and dissolve discordant feelings. Relating to the mysteries of sex and regeneration, I am a stimulant and effective connector to your deepest memories. I am a useful stone to work with during life's challenges, where courage or fortitude may be called for. During such times of change or upheaval, I can provide you with a sense of grounding, calm and balance. I can also help lift melancholy and will help you tap into your inner resources and full potentials by releasing your fears. I am a powerful attractor of abundance and prosperity, and am an overall tonic for your mind, body and spirit, purifying, supporting, and strengthening you on all levels."

✶ ✶ ✶

AQUARIUS

DIVINE CRYSTAL ✭ TURQUOISE

A very ancient and powerful stone found mainly in Persia, where it is found in veins in rock, turquoise symbolises prosperity, strength, wisdom, justice, fairness, nobility and friendship. Magical attributes of this brilliant blue or green-blue stone are protection from the evil eye and dark forces and attracting good fortune. It is also known as the 'horseman's stone' due to the belief that it protected riders from falls. This also explains its connection to the zodiac sign Sagittarius (the centaur). Turquoise is a purification stone, dispelling negative energy and clearing electromagnetic 'smog', providing protection against pollutants and toxins within the environment. Empathetic and balancing, turquoise balances and aligns all the chakras with the subtle bodies. It was revered by the ancient Egyptians, and favoured by the Native Americans as a travelling stone and to connect with the sky spirit Father Sky, to ask him to bring rain to increase crop yields and thereby increase prosperity. Indeed, without possession of a turquoise, no medicine man could command the honour, respect and veneration his position demanded; nor would the spear or arrow of the hunter fly true to its target. As a protective amulet, it is believed to fade or change colour to warn of infidelity, danger or illness. Turquoise instils inner calm while remaining alert, assists in creative problem-solving, and aids creative expression. Psychologically, turquoise is a strengthening stone and dissolves unhelpful attitudes, mood swings and self-sabotage. It even has the power to prevent panic attacks and aids recovery after a nervous breakdown. Turquoise soothes the emotions and clears the way to enable you to go with the flow, to express and accept who you really are and to find your perfect life path with courage, conviction and fortitude. It encourages self-compassion and shields your aura from the negative influences or emotions of others, helping you to recognise any 'dramas' you may be caught up in that are blocking your progress or true individuality.

TURQUOISE'S DIVINE MESSAGE FOR AQUARIUS ✭ "Aquarius, I am your ultimate stone of friendship and good fortune. Also known as the Stone of Venus, my great quality lies in my ability to draw to myself any situation of conflict, my inner light acting as a barrier between you and any negative thought patterns or harmful situations. For this reason, the ancients termed me The Celestial Stone. I am a Divine symbol of generosity, sincerity, and affection and I am believed to preserve friendships and make friends of enemies. I am a most efficient healer, providing physical and spiritual solace and wellbeing. Placed on your Third Eye, I can enhance spiritual attunement, communication with the higher realms, and promote your intuition and meditative experiences. Used on the Throat chakra, I help to release and dissolve old beliefs, fears, karma, and inhibitions, allowing your soul to express itself freely once more."

PISCES

DIVINE CRYSTAL ✫ AMETHYST

Amethyst is the stone of spiritual power and psychic energy. It has a high ethereal vibration and is an extremely powerful yet tranquil stone. Amethyst is the birthstone for the month of February, and its name is derived from the Greek word *amethystos*, literally meaning "not intoxicated." Purple has long been considered a royal colour, so it is not surprising that amethyst has been so much in demand throughout history. Amethysts are featured in the English Crown Jewels and were also a favourite of Ancient Egyptian royalty. Leonardo da Vinci wrote that amethyst could dissipate evil thoughts and quicken the emotional intelligence. This charming stone awakens and activates our higher awareness and psychic abilities. Amethyst has strong cleansing and healing powers, and its serenity assists with enhancing meditation and the reaching of higher states of consciousness. Connected with the Crown and Third Eye chakras, amethyst offers protection, wisdom, focus, power, access to Divine understanding, ethereal awareness, and increases psychic abilities, healing, and inner peace. Its best-known use is for heightening and enhancing one's spiritual connections and insights; it can even open doors to other dimensions, planes and realities. The radiation of violet light issuing from amethyst has been placed on record as providing a calming influence upon the nerves, making it balancing and comforting to the wearer.

AMETHYST'S DIVINE MESSAGE FOR PISCES ✫ "Pisces, I am your ultimate healing power stone, comforting and supporting you in times of distress or challenge. As a serene and calm gem, I can act as a compassionate anchor for you, to ensure that you are emanating your energy from a place of peace, tranquillity, and understanding. Encouraging selflessness, intuition, spiritual wisdom, and Divine visualisation, I can transmute Earthly energies to the higher vibrations of the etheric realms. Wear or work with me to elevate you to higher places and to help open up your Third Eye energy system so that it may connect you with the Ascended Realms of Spirit. I am the supreme psychic battery, helping you to align yourself with your highest self, your deepest intuition, and that magical place where your wishes reside. After all, your dreams are waiting for you to join them up there … isn't it time you joined them?"

Numeric Messages

ABOUT NUMBERS & NUMEROLOGY

Everything that exists has a vibration. The vibration of sound, music, colour, matter, even our words, thoughts, and names show form. All vibration is measurable. To measure we need numbers. Numbers are the basis of all. Numbers are the key to all mysteries.

Shirley Blackwell Lawrence

Behind the wall, the gods play; they play with numbers, of which the Universe is made up.

Lilla Bek & Robert Holden

Numerology is essentially the metaphysical * 'science' of numbers. It is a system of divination based upon the concept that the Universe is constructed in a mathematical pattern and that all things may be expressed in numbers that correspond triple to vibrations. The use of numbers in magic is its cornerstone of power.

The contemplatives and thinkers of ancient times were the first to develop a science of numbers for the world of physical phenomena and material form. It became known as *the first science* and the *Mother of All Sciences*. The sciences of astronomy, economics, travel, trade, architecture, physics, chemistry, geometry, alchemy - indeed, every other science - owe their support and foundations to the science of numbers. The great minds of ancient times were equally interested in the seeking of an inner, philosophical and poetic meaning of numbers, and so this philosophical branch became referred to as numerology. The philosophers and contemplatives of ancient cultures and civilisations, such as the Babylonian, Phoenician, Hebrew, Greek, Celtic, Egyptian, Tibetan, and Mayan, each evolved a system of numbers to describe and explain what they regarded as 'the heartbeats of

Nature'. The great thinkers of ancient times believed that *the deeper you look into a number, the more you can see of the whole world.*

The ancient Greek philosopher and mathematician Pythagoras, born around 590 BC and named after Pythasis, the Oracle of Delphi at the time, became known to his disciples as the 'divine one'. Pythagoras flourished c. 530 BC, as he embarked on a 30-year spiritual quest studying with important religious and esoteric teachers and healers to find the mystery of 'The Hidden Light' and came to see mankind as living in three worlds: the natural, the human and the divine. It was he who coined the word 'Philosopher', meaning lover of wisdom. He settled in southern Italy where he founded the first university in history. It was here that he taught his students the hidden wonders of the divine essence of the cosmos, the science of number vibrations, the musical harmonies of the heavenly spheres, the theory of magnitude in relation to planets and the Earth (known as astronomy), sacred geometry, and what he is remembered for today - mathematics. He asserted that all things can be expressed in numerical terms, because they are ultimately reducible to numbers. Pythagoras stated that, "Numbers are the first things of all of Nature" and followed the theory that "Nothing can exist without numbers." He believed that all-natural phenomena could be reduced to terms of geometry and arithmetic. He founded his university/school of philosophy based on this doctrine, and numerology has long been regarded as a branch of his assertions. Many believe that numbers have an arcane, mystical relationship with words, and with inanimate and animate objects; the interpretations that arose from these relationships date back to a time when the dawning intelligence of primitive man first visualised the meaning of number and associated it with spiritual significance. Numerology is the science of the exploration of this relationship in order to discover hidden meanings, forecast the future or interpret the character of a person. In its more modern form, a series of figures which correspond to an individual's name and date of birth are calculated, and practitioners believe one's prospects, fortune and character can be deciphered from the results.

Each primary number is ascribed certain characteristics and values and a male or female aspect. Odd numbers are masculine, strong and creative, while even numbers are feminine and either weak, or nurturing and stable. In the Greek mysteries, the number 888 represented the 'Higher Mind', and in some systems the number 666 represented the 'Mortal Mind' (in others it is called the 'Number of the Beast').

So, what is numerology and how does one use it? Everything in the Universe has a vibrational frequency, an energy, a force, all vibrating at various rates, and we as humans are no exception, the difference between one person and another is their rate of vibration. This force or energy is constantly in motion and changing, and we can even 'tune into' and feel our vibrations if we are still for long enough.

Along with letters, sounds, colours, crystals, and many other things, it is believed that numbers also have vibrations, and when we are able to familiarise ourselves with our own numerical frequencies, we can use this familiarity to add power and magic to our lives. The numbers of our birth date and the letters of our names have a vibrational frequency, and herein lies the key to understanding our self and our journey through life. Numerology refers to the knowledge contained within the numbers of our birth date and our name. This inherent power contains the secrets of our own personal magic that can assist us and light the way through life.

* Metaphysics is the study of those sciences that extend beyond the physical or tangible

'THE MUSIC OF THE SPHERES'

Numbers are indestructible, they are the key to the eternal plan.

Hettie Templeton

Among the most resonant ideas bequeathed to the world by Pythagoras of Samos was his conception of the Music of the Spheres, the celestial refrain that the great mathematician imagined was made by the movement of the stars and planetary bodies as they whirled along their courses. He famously came to this theory while listening to the sounds of hammers banging on anvils in a smithy's forge, noticing that a heavy hammer produced a frequency twice as long as half its weight, an octave lower. It was then seen that the musical scale worked in accordance with mathematical principles. Music and the cosmos, reasoned Pythagoras, were organised on the same harmonious, mathematical, numerological basis.

The Music of the Spheres became part of the hermetic conception of the world, reiterated by such great minds as Plato and Ptolemy, and illustrated by the English alchemist Robert Fludd. Two thousand years after Pythagoras, Johannes Kepler showed that the theory was also a physical 'reality' - that the planets did indeed move according to the same mathematical template that operated in music. Kepler's measurements showed that the ratio between Jupiter's maximum and Mars's minimum speed corresponds to a minor third; that between Earth and Venus to a minor sixth. Even modern astronomy accedes that the correspondence between musical ratios and planetary velocities is correct and accurate, or in the words of Fred Hoyle, 'frighteningly good'.

The concept of the Music of the Spheres carries an important corollary: that if humanity were to create music in tune with the celestial laws of harmony, the perfection of heaven can be replicated on Earth in the time-honoured principle of 'As Above, So Below'. The Pythagoreans were consequently interested in the healing, balancing and civilising power of music, which, as Shakespeare so eloquently observed, can 'soothe the savage beast'.

OTHER IMPORTANT NUMBERS FOR YOUR LIFE'S JOURNEY

Through the study of numbers, we embark upon the study of ourselves. Numbers are like cosmic clues. They shed conscious light upon our unconscious darkness. Through the study of numbers, we realise something of our unlimited potential. The energies which amalgamated to create and to manifest Suns, Galaxies, and Universes are the very same energies which have amalgamated to create and to manifest ourselves. Through numbers we discover our place in a world of all possibilities.

Lilla Bek & Robert Holden

As I am primarily focusing on *Divine Zodiac Messages*, delving into the meanings behind all the other personal numbers that influence your character is beyond the scope of this book. However, I will briefly outline how to calculate each one and what it can tell you about yourself so that yuou may explore each further through other sources, to decipher its special messages should you wish to.

1	2	3	4	5	6	7	8	9
A	B	C	D	E	F	G	H	I
J	K	L	M	N	O	P	Q	R
S	T	U	V	W	X	Y	Z	

YOUR OVERALL NUMEROLOGY NUMBER ~ Your numerology number is determined by adding up all the numbers in your birth date until they reach a two digit figure. The two resulting numbers are then added together again to form a single digit, which is your personal numerology number. Each primary number or birth number from 1 to 9 has a specific meaning and is governed by a planetary force. The principle of numerology reduces all numbers down to the following: 1 to 9, 10, 11, 13 and 22. The last four numbers only apply to people specially concerned with the occult and spiritualism - and can be studied at greater length through other sources if so desired - and can in any case be reduced further to a single digit if preferred. Your birth number contains a unique power, and therein lie your strengths, shortcomings and opportunities.

PERSONALITY NUMBER ~ This is calculated from the day of the month that your birthday falls on. Your Personality Number will never change. You carry it with you through life. This number is an expression of your outward personality, the way you meet the world and the impression you make. Although it goes deep, permeating through all your experience and all you do, it is also on the surface. It makes a statement about you.

LIFE PATH NUMBER ~ Totalling all the digits in your birth date (your overall numerology number) ~ Your Life Path Number is also something unchangeable. It relates to the path you are on, your tasks and self-development. In many ways it is linked to spirit.

SOUL NUMBER ~ Add the value of the vowels in your name, for these are the out-breath of your essence ~ Your Soul Number tells of your instincts and feelings and may also be about the groups you connect with on a culture and intuitive level. This number may not be so conscious at first, and people who get to know you may gradually become aware of this deeper self and its values. Your soul number tells you about your yearnings and dreams, even your purpose in living.

DESTINY NUMBER ~ Translate each of the letters in your full name (as it appears on your birth certificate) into numbers. This number relates to family heritage, to the expectations that are placed upon you, and the ones you have for yourself. It reflects the path you are on in life in a subtler way and is less about what you create and more about what you learn. You may change your name through choice or marriage, and this will have an effect on your destiny, which will overlay the original number, and may become more important. However, the original destiny number stays with you.

HERE-&-NOW NUMBER ~ Comes from your first name, nickname and/or the name you are generally known by.

Your first name carries the vibrational key that unlocks your soul's Akashic records, or your Book of Life. In fact, it's hand-selected by Heaven prior to your incarnation so that it best suits your life's purpose. You or the angels whispered your intended name to your parents before your birth. If they were listening, they gave it to you. If they called you something different … you can always change it to something that feels more suitable. Each person's first name has a specific and unique vibration.

Doreen Virtue

The Power of Name ~ Naming a force, creature, person, or thing has several connotations. In cultures where names are chosen carefully for their magical or auspicious meanings, to know a person's true name means to know the life path and the soul attributes of that person.

Clarissa Pinkola Estes

The Here-and-Now Number holds a very important vibration because you may hear it many times a day. This number is very powerful and very obvious, but not so deep. It reveals the way you are seen on an immediate level and also the image you wish to project. It is like a strong wave passing through the surface of your life, but it may leave the depths undisturbed and unexplored. This number is changeable and if you want to shift your vibration or numerology profile, you could start with a new nickname in a new group and see what happens.

☆ ☆ ☆

NUMERIC MESSAGES FOR THE ZODIAC

ARIES ~ MESSAGES FROM MARS'S NUMBER ~ 9

★ NINE ★

(The number 9) is the number of man due to the nine months of embryonic development. The key words connected with 9 are ocean and horizon, since the ancients believed them to be infinite. Ennead (9) is an infinite number, since it is followed by nothing other than the infinite number 10 ... Enead is the sphere of the air.

Martin Ivanov

At the current level of development, we live in a third dimension where the number 9 dominates above everything.

Linda Goodman

This is the hermit of the Tarot; the number which refers to initiates and to prophets. The prophets are solitaries, for it is their fate that none should ever hear them. They see differently from others; they forefeel misfortunes.

The Key of the Mysteries, **Eliphas Levi, Rider & Company**

NINE'S MESSAGE & MEANING FOR ARIES ★ "The number 9 relates to the symbolism of the triple power of 3. In China it is highly auspicious because it is the number of the celestial spheres. Among the Aztecs, a 9-storey temple echoed the 9 heavens or stages through which the soul must pass. In the Native American Earth Count, 9 signifies the Moon, change and movement. Ruled by Mars, 9 is a multiple of the lucky 3, so 9 is also a lucky number. The number 9 is usually regarded as second in significance only to number 3 among the odd numbers, primarily because it is the product of 3 by 3. It is sometimes considered the ultimate number, with special and even sacred significance. The Nonagon, the number 9, or the Ennead was known to many ancient cultures as Perfection and Concord, and as being unbounded. Magicians of former times would draw a magic circle - 9 feet in diameter, in which to practice their magic. It is the number of the Universe and of vision, representing spiritual ideals, philosophy and perfection. Nine is the number of completion, bringing together all the creative forces to reach a conclusion. It is almost the most indestructible of the odd numbers in the sense that all its multiples reduce to nine if we add together the digits of which they are composed. Consequently, it is considered the number of ultimate achievement and without interruption, and along with the number 8, as the symbol of eternal life. Cats are thought to have nine lives and are often connected to witchcraft and other magical doctrines. Number 9 is a tolerant, impractical and sympathetic vibration. The power and potential of the number 9 is linked to the powers of Law, balance and completion. Nine, being the number of vision, compassion, imagination, intuition and holistic perception, liberates the inner artist in you. It also stirs your natural, innate healing potential and your deepest psychic self. You hear the music of the spheres and the cries of all others in the world. You are often delighted with the sheer wonder of life, with all its colour and scope, and its opportunities for great happiness. You may be drawn to the peace of ashrams, monasteries or churches, because they answer a deep need in you. You are aware of the Higher Powers, and even if you have no specific religious beliefs, you are aware of the spiritual dimension. Culture and the arts are very important to you, and music can transport you into another world. You have a secret yearning to be an exceptional artist and, if more mundane numbers such as Four or Eight are strong in your make-up, you may feel that your genuine creativity is stifled. You need to value anything creative that you produce as unique and carrying the Divine spark, and you should never compare yourself to the great masters or you may become lost in profound despair. Your spiritual source constantly beckons you and you search ceaselessly for flashes of Divine light that can carry you towards it. I can provide that guidance for you. Through my vibration, you are fortunate enough to be blessed with natural gifts and should do all in your power to put these to the best purpose for benefiting both yourself and the world at large. At its best, number 9 will influence the highest qualities of courage, humanity, service and brotherhood. Number 9 people should try to carry out their plans on a Tuesday, the day governed by their planet, Mars."

MAGICAL & ALCHEMICAL MESSAGE ★ "Nine is a significant and magical number. It equals three times three, and in mythology, we often find an original trio who have expanded to nine. Each point of the triangle can generate another triangle. In this sense, nine has an essentially expansive, lively form of energy, that can include detail and diversity expanded from the basic three. It is a neutral, balanced potential that feeds Universal truth, cosmic law & pure perception. Nine is a symbol for the Higher Self, the Divine Spark, the *I am* & the perfected part of us. Dignity, honour, conduct, service, leadership & the 'watching mechanism' are all inspired by number nine. Representations of nine usually combine the three triangles in some way. It represents completion - life flows in cycles of 9 - 9 years, 9 months, 9 days - and throughout life our major changes tend to happen with our personal 9 year. Numbers 1 to 9 are the basic vibrations and represent our 9 basic experiences of life. These experiences relate to our inner world and also to our outer world, and with a deeper understanding of the correlations between our experiences and the identifying numbers 1 to 9, we have an excellent reference for all aspects of our self and our journey through life. In sacred geometry the power of nine is linked to the power of three triangles, which is a common symbol for perfection and completion. Ancient alchemical lore states that to travel around the triangle twice you become wisdom - the completion of this law states that to travel around the triangle thrice you become Law. With the advent of nine, the full course for the journey of involution and evolution has now been set."

★ ★ ★

TAURUS ~ MESSAGES FROM VENUS'S NUMBER ~ 6

★ SIX ★

The figure 6 is similar to the ancient form of the spiral, found on many prehistoric artefacts. This symbol means the passage into and out of manifestation ... six is concerned with the meaning of creation, wanting it to be a perfect expression of something absolute. The six-pointed star, the Star of Solomon, is a potent magical symbol composed of two interlocking triangles. The triangle that points downwards signifies the Great Feminine, while the triangle pointing upwards represents the Great Masculine - the interplay of spirit and matter. Together they are complete and symmetrical. Six is aware of the beauty that exists all around and seeks to extend it.

Theresa Morey

SIX'S MESSAGE & MEANING FOR TAURUS ★ "Ruled by Venus, the number 6 is a loving, stable and harmonious vibration. A perfect number because it is the sum of its factors (1, 2, 3), 6 is balanced, and is associated with family love, peace and domesticity. In the context of numerology, 6 is the number of harmony. Its power can be obtained by doubling the power of three. Therefore, powers of six and of three have certain similar inherent potentials that centre on and around knowledge, intellect and reason. In fact, it is one of the fundamental tenets of numerological lore that when a number is doubled to form a new number, that new number is a complete transformation of the old number, taking on twice as much power and drive. This makes the potential of six stand out not only for knowledge, intellect and reason, but also for the profound and special qualities of insight, wisdom and knowing. Six is indeed a symbol for a pure and profound potential. The Hexagon, the number 6 or the Hexad is represented geometrically as a 6-sided, balanced figure. It is also symbolised by two intersecting triangles known as the Seal of Solomon. Considered a sacred number to some religions who believe that the world was created in 6 days, as such the double triangle was and is frequently carved in stone or painted on windows in old monasteries and churches. In nature we find many examples of the hexagonal in the form of crystals, which are a complete and very comprehensive class in themselves. On the whole, the Hexas has always been considered one of the happiest numbers, since it represents perfect harmony and completion. As well, 6 has long been regarded as a particularly lucky number, with great balance. It possesses an extremely harmonious nature, associated with love, service and responsibility. Symbolised by the 6-pointed star, its colours are pale blues, turquoises, greens and indigo. It denotes equilibrium, and the six-pointed star is comprised of two triangles, one pointing upwards towards the 'spirit' or heavens, and the other pointing down towards the body or earth, symbolising balance between them. This association with balance is partly due to the qualities of a cube, a six-sided figure which shows great stability whichever way up it appears. The cube also displays an equal face in all four directions, plus a face pointing towards the heavens, the so-called fifth or esoteric dimension. Each side of the die is numbered, with six the highest and therefore the most fortuitous of the numbers. Opposite sides of the die often add up to 6 also. In Buddhism, there are several groupings of 6, including the 6 realms of existence. But 6 is associated with sin in the New Testament Book of Revelation: as 666, it becomes the number of the beast of the Apocalypse. Carrying the vibe of Venus, it is the number of family, comfort, graciousness and beauty but also represents duty and responsibility. Six is also the number of the voice, and therefore highly beneficial for anyone interested in a singing career. Number 6s are born to sing, so a musical path is well suited to these types. You resonate with others who are sympathetic and compassionate and sincere appreciation means a lot to you. Your luckiest day is Friday. Beauty and tranquility are as necessary to you as the air you breathe, and in fact without them you can become unwell. The Chinese say, 'Have nothing in your home that is neither useful nor beautiful.' You follow this as far as possible, being very aware of the aesthetic appeal of your surroundings."

MAGICAL & ALCHEMICAL MESSAGE ★ "Six is the principle of reconciliation. In alchemy, it represents the union of fire and water, brought into a harmonious relationship. Six is shown as a hexagon, or a six-pointed star made up of two interlaced triangles, which point above and below, symbolising unity between heaven and earth."

★ ★ ★

GEMINI ~ MESSAGES FROM MERUCRY'S NUMBER ~ 5

★ FIVE ★

Number five takes us beyond the material plane and into the realms of mind and spirit, into ideas, abstracts and mental constructs. In the Western esoteric traditions, five relates to the fifth element, which is ether. This is symbolised by the pentagram, or five-pointed star, which is a potent magical symbol.

Theresa Morey

FIVE'S MESSAGE & MEANING FOR GEMINI ★ "Ruled by Mercury, this is a changeable number by nature. The number 5, symbolised by the five-pointed star pentacle, is an intellectual vibration and is connected with freedom and movement, spirit, energy, travel, adventure and creativity. The Yogis of Tibet, the Indians of North America and the Taoists of China are just a few of the many varied cultures which have revered the number five as a power of Nature, seeing it as an expression of the vital, Universal life-force which sustains, pervades, connects and interweaves throughout everything that exists. The power of five was also regarded by these cultures as the 'gate of heaven' and as 'a doorway to the collective'. The Greeks considered the pentagram as a sacred symbol of light, health and vitality. But the number 5 also represents unpredictability and instability, owing to the unstable and unbalanced nature of this number. This fickleness and uncertainty is associated with the number 5, as it carries no constant vibration and may change or shift. In the context of numerology, 5 is the number at the centre of the soul plane and you are a 'soul' child. Bright, creative, happy, high-spirited, adventurous and not conscious of restrictions, you engage with life freely and trustingly. This is the number of the easily led mischief-maker, so make sure you choose your friends carefully, as you can get into all kinds of trouble quiet innocently. As a result of your not being aware of others' wrongdoings or the world's limitations, you can experience many hurts at a soul level and will need understanding, sympathy, love and support from loved ones. You have the potential to be wild and uncontrollable, again due to your impressionable and trusting nature. But you possess a great imagination and take a keen interest in everything you do. Given the opportunity and well-structured support, you can become a great student or worker. Five - the number of the physical senses - symbolises the planet Mercury, and people born under this number are mercurial in qualities and characteristics. It is a quixotic number of quicksilver temperament and ideas, and signifies communication, an artistic streak and extreme creativity. Carrying the Mercurial vibe, this is the number of adventure and communication which embodies the concept of 'variety is the spice of life'. People under its influence will likely have many irons burning on as many different fires as possible at the same time. It can also indicate travel and movement so is perfect for all those with wanderlust and who welcome the world and new experiences with open arms. Love of home is strong to you, but you often feel like running away; similarly, if freedom is denied to you on a long enough basis, you may become rundown with nervous problems. Time out for yourself, away from chaos and activity, is therefore vital if you are not to burn yourself out. You make friends easily with people born under any other number, but close friends will probably be fellow number 5s. Wednesday is the luckiest day for the quicksilver number 5."

MAGICAL & ALCHEMICAL MESSAGE ★ "Five stands for dynamic focus, a combination of two and three. It can be sparkling, sexual or charismatic, or on the other hand, a decisive act of destruction. It can also represent the quintessential element which is a distillation of all four basic elements. A five-pointed star, the pentagram (five points joined by one line) or a pentagon (a five-sided figure) are its main representations. Pentacle magic could work wonders for you. The quincunx, the number 5, or the Pentad, was regarded by the followers of Pythagoras, as well as other philosophers, as the symbol of health and prosperity, but on the whole, it seems universally to have symbolised marriage, fecundity and propagation, this belief probably having its origin in the idea of 5 being the union of 3 and 2, or a male and female number (in Ancient Rome, its significance was emphasised by the burning of 5 tapers during the marriage ceremony). A fifth element indeed exists, and was described by Plutarch in the 1st century AD, in these words: 'If we assume that the World in which we live is the only one there is ... then it is itself made up of, as it were, five worlds which make Harmony of it: one is the Earth, another

Water, the third Fire, the fourth Air, and the fifth Sky, with the last one being called Light by some and Ether by others and by yet others, Quintessence'. It could be said that 5 is the number of transformation, representing the combination of the four elements plus spirit (or ether). The magical symbol of the five-pointed star is an Egyptian hieroglyph for the womb, as well as one form of the ancient Seal of Solomon. Five is associated with magical gateways, and indicates that there may be challenges ahead, but these will help you develop your skills."

★ ★ ★

CANCER ~ MESSAGES FROM THE MOON'S NUMBER ~ 2

★ TWO ★

After the impetus of one comes the balance of two, representing the first stirrings of self-awareness. Two is about relationships (and as such) is the gateway to the emotions.

Theresa Morey

TWO'S MESSAGE & MEANING FOR CANCER ★ "Number 2 is ruled by the Moon, the luminary which fosters harmony by favouring love, union, cooperation, compromise, passivity, diplomacy, tact, negotiation, settlements, and all mutually beneficial ventures. In the context of numerology, 2 is a soul vibration, making those under its influence sensitive to everything around them. As two is linked to the instinctive, unconscious and creative, an innate urge to dance, write, sing, compose, draw, act and create are marked characteristics. The number 2 is a feminine energy which is sensitively tuned to emotion, empathy, instinct, caring and intuition. You will seek out quiet, peaceful environments if you can and throughout life you are unlikely to be involved in any serious or willful trouble. A gentle, considerate and sensitive vibration, number 2 is the mediator and peace-maker. The number 2 represents the first divergence from the unity represented by the number 1. As such, it signifies the first opportunity for diversity and conflict. On the other hand, it represents the first flowering of the creative principle, and is a symbol of fertility, for male and female, positive and negative, spirit and matter, and also for that part of ourselves that enables us to turn and look at ourselves, allowing for self-reflection and therefore, greater conscious awareness of self. Duality, the number 2, or the Duad as it was called by Pythaogreans, represents both diversity and equality or justice. This idea of diversity originates from the idea of two opposites, such as good and evil, night and day, joy and pain, love and hate, riches and poverty. Yet, at the same time, both sides of a question must be always heard, so the number 2 also stands for concord, harmony, response, balance and sympathy. Arguably one of the most beautiful symbols representing the perfect unity formed by the number 2, is that of yin and yang, as depicted in the Tao in China. Indeed, Chinese numerology is based on the number 2, as in Taoist belief the Universe is made up of polarity, which is expressed in various complementary forces. Many cultures regard sets of two, such as twins, as especially lucky. In the Native American Earth Count, 2 represents Grandmother Earth, the body, death and introspection. When early humankind became aware of the binary rhythms upon which the great symphony of nature is based, and which is at the heart of nature itself, it became aware of everything which is double: sky and Earth, male and female, hot and cold, day and night, high and low, life and death, Sun and Moon, inside and outside, pure and impure, good and evil. The cross symbol is sometimes described as a map of the world: the centrepoint is the power of one, the Monad, or Divine Spark, from which all things originate; the arms of the cross represent the power of two (vertical, masculine; horizontal, feminine) upon which all the multifarious forms of life are propagated and supported. Carrying the vibes of the Moon, it stands for social enjoyment, cooperation and companionship. Since it soothes an aggressive spirit, it is suited to those who like a gentle, congenial way of life, those who wish for nurturing, intimate partnerships, and who love to pass their time daydreaming. Monday is your special day."

MAGICAL & ALCHEMICAL MESSAGE ★ "Two represents two forces opposing *or* complementing one another. It often stands for male and female, positive and negative, light and dark, and heaven and Earth. In spiritual teaching, it can be used to represent the division between God and man, sometimes known as the 'Lover and the Beloved'. In alchemy, a separation from one into two is essential to release the vital energy that a polarity generates. In magic, two carries a feminine, nurturing and unifying potential, promoting feelings, empathy, intuition, romance, soul healing, creativity, imagination and the free-flowing unconscious. Ultimately, the number two has the potential for both contrasts and union, its links with the Lunar Rays cannot be underestimated, especially for the sign of Cancer."

★ ★ ★

LEO ~ MESSAGES FROM THE SUN'S NUMBER ~ 1

★ ONE ★

Good luck lies in odd numbers ... They say there is divinity in odd numbers, either in nativity, chance or death.

William Shakespeare

(Monad) is so called since it always remains in one and the same condition, i.e., separated from the multitude. It is also referred to as the birth mind, since it is the beginning of all thoughts in the Universe. Monad is the father.

Martin Ivanov

One relates to beginnings, potentials and initiative. It brings with it courage, energy and positivity, but it is not so much about concrete achievement as the creation of opportunity.

> One is the flash of inspiration, the pure urge to action ...Without the impetus of one nothing can ever come into being.

Theresa Morey

> The Tao is the origin of the One,
> The One created the two,
> The two formed the three.
> From the three came forth all life.

Tao Te Ching, Chapter 42

ONE'S MESSAGE & MEANING FOR LEO ★ "Ruled by the Sun, number 1, which is truly indivisible, signifies power, stoutness of heart, independence, action and responsibility. Number 1 represents beginning and the primal cause. A symbol of creation and the human species, it is depicted in the standing stone, the upright staff and the erect phallus. In the Native American Earth Count, 1 represents Grandfather Sun and fire, the spark of life. We use the expression 'number one' to refer to our own importance as an individual. A very powerful number, it represents unity and wholeness. In Pythagorean theory 1 represents the masculine principle and is the first masculine number and the number of beginnings and is therefore considered to be the number of the Universe and the highest order. Symbolising the Sun and Leo, its colours are yellow, red, orange and gold. The power and potential of this number is linked traditionally to the vibrations of the colour red. It is associated with the physical body, and is a number which represents manifestation, and, in particular, the impregnation of spirit into matter. The numerological history of Creation states that the first objective of God, the Creator, was to make the world appear, and that to do this God had to invoke the power and potential of the number one. In sacred geometry, one is linked to the Greek primordial Monad., which, when interpreted, means 'Divine Fire', 'Divine Spark' or 'Logos of Life'. In essence, one represents the first dawn, the beginning of life for all Galaxies, all the worlds and all life (if indeed there *is* a beginning). In astrology one is linked with the Sun and Mars, and to the signs Aries ('I Am') and Taurus ('I Have'). In sacred anatomy the number one has a precise relationship with all the centres of sacred energy, called the chakras, in the body. In particular it is connected with the red base chakra, often described as the *chakra of physical life* and of *survival and reproduction* and procreation; it is also connected with the yellow Solar Plexus chakra, described as the *chakra of the Sun* and as the *Great Energy Battery Chakra*. It is also linked with the mystical power of *kundalini* (life force) and to climax, birth and re-birth. The number 1 stands for all that is strong, individual, original, protective and creative. This is a powerful number and it augurs success; woe betide anyone who dares to threaten those ruled by this mighty number! One is a strong vibration and indicates the ability to stand alone. As it is governed by the life-force of the Sun, it stands for independence, the development of ideas and the courage to follow them through. It also represents the ego and selfishness so lessons concerning those issues will probably arise, for the betterment of the person. It is a perfect number for those who want to run their own show in some way, and for those who wish to get ahead. The number of innovators and winners, but also tyrants, number 1 people are born leaders, ambitious and active, and well as often dominant and aggressive. Those who come under the influence of the Monad (Unity, as expressed by the figure 1) will show great tenacity and singleness of purpose. This indicates self-reliance, an unswerving desire for action, resolve, ingenuity, concentration, great achievement and possibly even genius. You can be implicitly relied upon, as you seem to take pleasure in the assumption of great responsibilities. Sunday is your special day."

MAGICAL & ALCHEMICAL MESSAGE ★ "Oneness preserves the integrity of creation and cannot be divided without losing its integrity. In the beginning, there was one: the absolute, the all in one, the one in all. This one is the 'I' of the Universe, represented by a rod or, in alchemy, a serpent. It is the absolute symbol of masculinity, the active, engendering principle. But how can there be masculinity when there is, as yet, no femininity? What came first, the chicken or the egg? Alchemy answers this perplexing riddle with another: the figure of the ouroboros, the serpent with its tail in its mouth. This symbol is potentially both male and female, both I and O. It is the beginning and the end of the Great Work in alchemy. It is all or nothing. It is male and female, but also neither. Alchemists talk about one truth, one matter, one process: 'One is the All, and by it the All, and in it the All, and if it does not contain the All it is nothing.' It is usually represented as a point or circle. Finally, there is the monad, considered by the Renaissance alchemists, philosophers and esoteric practitioners to be the great, unifying principle and soul of the world."

☆ ☆ ☆

VIRGO ~ MESSAGES FROM MERCURY'S NUMBER ~ 5

★ FIVE ★

The pentacle, all five-lobed leaves, and five-petaled flowers are sacred to the Goddess as pentad. The apple is especially her emblem, because, when it is sliced crosswise, the embedded seeds form a pentacle.

Starhawk

FIVE'S MESSAGE & MEANING FOR VIRGO ★ "Ruled by Mercury, this is a changeable number by nature. The number 5, symbolised by the five-pointed star pentacle, is an intellectual vibration and is connected with freedom and movement, spirit, energy, travel, adventure and creativity. The Yogis of Tibet, the Indians of North America and the Taoists of China are just a few of the many varied cultures which have revered the number five as a power of Nature, seeing it as an expression of the vital, Universal life-force which sustains, pervades, connects and interweaves throughout everything that exists. The power of five was also regarded by these cultures as the 'gate of heaven' and as 'a doorway to the collective'. The Greeks considered the pentagram as a sacred symbol of light, health and vitality. But the number 5 also represents unpredictability and instability, owing to the unstable and unbalanced nature of this number. This fickleness and uncertainty is associated with the number 5, as it carries no constant vibration and may change or shift. In the context of numerology, 5 is the number at the centre of the soul plane and you are a 'soul' child. Bright, creative, happy, high-spirited, adventurous and not conscious of restrictions, you engage with life freely and trustingly. This is the number of the easily led mischief-maker, so make sure you choose your friends carefully, as you can get into all kinds of trouble quiet innocently. As a result of your not being aware of others' wrongdoings or the world's limitations, you can experience many hurts at a soul level and will need understanding, sympathy, love and support from loved ones. You have the potential to be wild and uncontrollable, again due to your impressionable and trusting nature. But you possess a great imagination and take a keen interest in everything you do. Given the opportunity and well-structured support, you can become a great student or worker. Five - the number of the physical senses - symbolises the planet Mercury, and people born under this number are mercurial in qualities and characteristics. It is a quixotic number of quicksilver temperament and ideas, and signifies communication, an artistic streak and extreme creativity. Carrying the Mercurial vibe, this is the number of adventure and communication which embodies the concept of "variety is the spice of life." People under its influence will likely have many irons burning on as many different fires as possible at the same time. It can also indicate travel and movement so is perfect for all those with wanderlust and who welcome the world and new experiences with open arms. Love of home is strong to you, but you often feel like running away; similarly, if freedom is denied to you on a long enough basis, you may become rundown with nervous problems. Time out for yourself, away from chaos and activity, is therefore vital if you are not to burn yourself out. You make friends easily with people born under any other number, but close friends will probably be fellow number 5s. Wednesday is the luckiest day for the quicksilver number 5."

MAGICAL & ALCHEMICAL MESSAGE ★ "Five stands for dynamic focus, a combination of two and three. It can be sparkling, sexual or charismatic, or on the other hand, a decisive act of destruction. It can also represent the quintessential element which is a distillation of all four basic elements. A five-pointed star, the pentagram (five points joined by one line) or a pentagon (a five-sided figure) are its main representations. Pentacle magic could work wonders for you. The quincunx, the number 5, or the Pentad, was regarded by the followers of Pythagoras, as well as other philosophers, as the symbol of health and prosperity, but on the whole, it seems universally to have symbolised marriage, fecundity and propagation, this belief probably having its origin in the idea of 5 being the union of 3 and 2, or a male and female number (in Ancient Rome, its significance was emphasised by the burning of 5 tapers during the marriage ceremony). A fifth element indeed exists, and was described by Plutarch in the 1st century AD, in these words: 'If we assume that the World in which we live is the only one there is ... then it is itself made up of, as it were, five worlds which make Harmony of it: one is the Earth, another Water, the third Fire, the fourth Air, and the fifth Sky, with the last one being called Light by some and Ether by others and by yet others, Quintessence'. It could be said that 5 is the number of transformation, representing the combination of the four elements plus spirit (or ether). The magical symbol of the five-pointed star is an Egyptian hieroglyph for the womb, as well as one form of the ancient Seal of Solomon. Five is associated with magical gateways, and indicates that there may be challenges ahead, but these will help you develop your skills."

★ ★ ★

LIBRA ~ MESSAGES FROM VENUS'S NUMBER ~ 6

★ SIX ★

(The number 6) is a symbol of the creation of the world, as described by the prophets and ancient Mysteries.

Martin Ivanov

SIX'S MESSAGE & MEANING FOR LIBRA ★ "Ruled by Venus, the number 6 is a loving, stable and harmonious vibration. A perfect number because it is the sum of its factors (1, 2, 3), 6 is balanced, and is associated with family love, peace and domesticity. In the context of numerology, 6 is the number of harmony. Its power can be obtained by doubling the power of three. Therefore, powers of six and of three have certain similar inherent potentials that centre on and around knowledge, intellect and reason. In fact, it is one of the fundamental tenets of numerological lore that when a number is doubled to form a new number, that new number is a complete transformation of the old number, taking on twice as much power and drive. This makes the potential of six stand out not only for knowledge, intellect and reason, but also for the profound and special qualities of insight, wisdom and knowing. Six is indeed a symbol for a pure and profound potential. The Hexagon, the number 6 or the Hexad is represented geometrically as a 6-sided, balanced figure. It is also symbolised by two intersecting triangles known as the Seal of Solomon. Considered a sacred number to some religions who believe that the world was created in 6 days, as such the double triangle was and is frequently carved in stone or painted on windows in old monasteries and churches. In nature we find many examples of the hexagonal in the form of crystals, which are a complete and very comprehensive class in themselves. On the whole, the Hexas has always been considered one of the happiest numbers, since it represents perfect harmony and completion. As well, 6 has long been regarded as a particularly lucky number, with great balance. It possesses an extremely harmonious nature, associated with love, service and responsibility. Symbolised by the 6-pointed star, its colours are pale blues, turquoises, greens and indigo. It denotes equilibrium, and the six-pointed star is comprised of two triangles, one pointing upwards towards the 'spirit' or heavens, and the other pointing down towards the body or earth, symbolising balance between them. This association with balance is partly due to the qualities of a cube, a six-sided figure which shows great stability whichever way up it appears. The cube also displays an equal face in all four directions, plus a face pointing towards the heavens, the so-called fifth or esoteric dimension. Each side of the die is numbered, with six the highest and therefore the most fortuitous of the numbers. Opposite sides of the die often add up to 6 also. In Buddhism, there are several groupings of 6, including the 6 realms of existence. But 6 is associated with sin in the New Testament Book of Revelation: as 666, it becomes the number of the beast of the Apocalypse. Carrying the vibe of Venus, it is the number of family, comfort, graciousness and beauty but also represents duty and responsibility. Six is also the number of the voice, and therefore highly beneficial for anyone interested in a singing career. Number 6s are born to sing, so a musical path is well suited to these types. You resonate with others who are sympathetic and compassionate and sincere appreciation means a lot to you. Your luckiest day is Friday. Beauty and tranquility are as necessary to you as the air you breathe, and in fact without them you can become unwell. The Chinese say, 'Have nothing in your home that is neither useful nor beautiful.' You follow this as far as possible, being very aware of the aesthetic appeal of your surroundings."

MAGICAL & ALCHEMICAL MESSAGE ★ "Six is the principle of reconciliation. In alchemy, it represents the union of fire and water, brought into a harmonious relationship. Six is shown as a hexagon, or a six-pointed star made up of two interlaced triangles, which point above and below, symbolising unity between Heaven and Earth."

☆   ☆   ☆

SCORPIO ~ MESSAGES FROM MARS'S NUMBER ~ 9

★ NINE ★

With nine there is a sense of returning to source. Nine is a number of completion and transition. The first set of numbers has come to a culmination and there is both fulfilment and dissolution before re-remerging into a new cycle. Three, the number of generation, has now been repeated three times - creation is complete. If nine features in your personality, you will have an urge to move beyond ... Above all, you seek spiritual meaning.

Theresa Morey

Nine are the interlocked dimensions,
and Nine are the cycles of space.

Nine are the diffusions of consciousness,
and Nine are the worlds within worlds.
Aye, Nine are the Lords of the cycles
that come from above and below.
Space is filled with concealed ones,
for space is divided by time.
Seek ye the key to the time-space,
and ye shall unlock the gate.
Know ye that throughout the time-space,
consciousness surely exists.
Though from our knowledge it is hidden,
yet still forever exists.

Contained in *The Emerald Tablets*

At the current level of development, we live in a third dimension where the number 9 dominates above everything.

Linda Goodman

NINE'S MESSAGE & MEANING FOR SCORPIO ★ "The number 9 relates to the symbolism of the triple power of 3. In China it is highly auspicious because it is the number of the celestial spheres. Among the Aztecs, a 9-storey temple echoed the 9 heavens or stages through which the soul must pass. In the Native American Earth Count, 9 signifies the Moon, change and movement. Ruled by Mars, 9 is a multiple of the lucky 3, so 9 is also a lucky number. The number 9 is usually regarded as second in significance only to number 3 among the odd numbers, primarily because it is the product of 3 by 3. It is sometimes considered the ultimate number, with special and even sacred significance. The Nonagon, the number 9, or the Ennead was known to many ancient cultures as Perfection and Concord, and as being unbounded. Magicians of former times would draw a magic circle 9 feet in diameter, in which to practice their magic. It is the number of the Universe and of vision, representing spiritual ideals, philosophy and perfection. Nine is the number of completion, bringing together all the creative forces to reach a conclusion. It is almost the most indestructible of the odd numbers in the sense that all its multiples reduce to nine if we add together the digits of which they are composed. Consequently, it is considered the number of ultimate achievement and without interruption, and along with the number 8, as the symbol of eternal life. Cats are thought to have nine lives and are often connected to witchcraft and other magical doctrines. Number 9 is a tolerant, impractical and sympathetic vibration. The power and potential of the number 9 is linked to the powers of Law, balance and completion. Nine, being the number of vision, compassion, imagination, intuition and holistic perception, liberates the inner artist in you. It also stirs your natural, innate healing potential and your deepest psychic self. You hear the music of the spheres and the cries of all others in the world. You are often delighted with the sheer wonder of life, with all its colour and scope, and its opportunities for great happiness. You may be drawn to the peace of ashrams, monasteries or churches, because they answer a deep need in you. You are aware of the Higher Powers, and even if you have no specific religious beliefs, you are aware of the spiritual dimension. Culture and the arts are very important to you, and music can transport you into another world. You have a secret yearning to be an exceptional artist and, if more mundane numbers such as Four or Eight are strong in your make-up, you may feel that your genuine creativity is stifled. You need to value anything creative that you produce as unique and carrying the Divine spark, and you should never compare yourself to the great masters or you may become lost in profound despair. Your spiritual source constantly beckons you and you search ceaselessly for flashes of Divine light that can carry you towards it. I can provide that guidance for you. Through my vibration, you are fortunate enough to be blessed with natural gifts and should do all in your power to put these to the best purpose for benefiting both yourself and the world at large. At its best, number 9 will influence the highest qualities of courage, humanity, service and brotherhood. Number 9 people should try to carry out their plans on a Tuesday, the day governed by their planet, Mars."

MAGICAL & ALCHEMICAL MESSAGE ★ "Nine is a significant and magical number. It equals three times three, and in mythology, we often find an original trio who have expanded to nine. Each point of the triangle can generate another triangle. In this sense, nine has an essentially expansive, lively form of energy, that can include detail and diversity expanded from the basic three. It is a neutral, balanced potential that feeds Universal truth, cosmic law & pure perception. Nine is a symbol for the Higher Self, the Divine Spark, the *I am* & the perfected part of us. Dignity, honour, conduct, service, leadership & the 'watching mechanism' are all inspired by number nine. Representations of nine usually combine the three triangles in some way. It represents completion - life flows in cycles of 9 - 9 years, 9 months, 9 days - and throughout life our major changes tend to happen with our personal 9 year. Numbers 1 to 9 are the basic vibrations and represent our 9 basic experiences of life. These experiences relate to our inner world and also to our outer world, and with a deeper understanding of the correlations between our experiences and the identifying numbers 1 to 9, we have an excellent reference for all aspects of our self and our journey through life. In sacred geometry the power of nine is linked to the power of three triangles, which is a common symbol for perfection and completion. Ancient alchemical lore states that to travel around the triangle twice you become wisdom - the completion of this law states that to travel around the triangle thrice you become Law. With the advent of nine, the full course for the journey of involution and evolution has now been set."

✯ ✯ ✯

SAGITTARIUS ~ MESSAGES FROM JUPITER'S NUMBER ~ 3

★ THREE ★

Look at the triangle and your problem is two thirds solved. Everything in nature consists of three parts.

Pythagoras

One engenders two, two engenders three, while three engenders all things.

Lao Tzu

(Triad) is the first really odd number … the number of knowledge of music, geometry, astronomy and the science of heavenly and earthly bodies. … the cube of this number possesses the power of the Lunar cycle. The sacred role of the triad and its symbol - the triangle - originates from the fact that it consists of monad and duad. Monad is the symbol of the Holy Father, and the duad the Great Mother. (The) creative aspect is always symbolised by the triangle.

Martin Ivanov

With number three we take a creative step towards the generation of new form. Three creates abundance, laughter and confidence.

Theresa Morey

THREE'S MESSAGE & MEANING FOR SAGITTARIUS ★ "Ruled by Jupiter, 3 is a lucky number which enhances optimism, self-expression and sociability. Number 3 is a sociable, outgoing and friendly vibration. Associated with spring, and consequently beginnings, new ventures and fertile phases, 3 is the number of growth and expansion. Number 1 contains the idea, number 2 is the pair which comes together to carry it out, and number 3 bears the fruit. Three also signifies initial completion, the first stage being achieved. In numerology, odd numbers are viewed as stronger and more spiritual than even numbers, partly because, when divided by even numbers, they leave a remainder and are therefore indestructible. Three symbolises the creative process that begins after one becomes two and starts to culminate into 'ten thousand things' - the essence of creation. In most great spiritual traditions, 3 carries a special meaning. Symbolised by a triangle, it is linked to the symbols of the astrological elements and the colours mauve and amethyst. The number 3, or the Triad, was esteemed by many ancient philosophers as the perfect number. From an early age, the idea of 'three wishes' becomes a part of our mythology, it is a part of our collective lore that 'things happen in threes', and it is regarded as powerful and sacred as it represents the manifestation of life itself: number one is the potential seed; number 2 brings complementary opposites together (e.g. male and female); and number 3 completes a dynamic triangle, energy is created, and everything begins to expand. It represents the three common stages we all encounter: birth, life and death; and the vessels through which we experience these: body, soul and spirit, or body, mind and spirit. There are three primary colours - red, blue and yellow - from which all other colours originate. The Pythagoreans believed in three worlds - the Inferior, the Superior and the Supreme - while followers of Socrates and Plato acknowledged three great principles - Matter, Idea and God. There are three dimensions of space - height, length and breadth; three stages of time - past, present and future; three states of matter - solid, liquid and gaseous; and three kingdoms of nature - animal, vegetable and mineral. Three is a magical number associated with the triple Goddess who moves through the experiences of maiden, mother and crone, and is linked to the Waxing, Full and Waning phases of the Moon. The basic area of Pythagorean teaching is that everything in nature is divided into three parts and to be truly wise one has it imagine every problem in the nature of a triangular diagram. He divided the Universe into three parts, which consisted of the Supreme World, the Higher World and the Lower World. (The Pythagorean thinkers did not consider 1 and 2 as numbers, since they define the two spheres of the Lower World. Pythagorean numbers begin from 3, the triangle, and 4, the square. Added to each other, plus 1 and 2, they produce the number 10, the great number of all things, the archetype of the Universe). A superficial 'show' may hide considerable spirituality in those born under the influence of this number, since 3 is the number of the Trinity. Number 3 is considered a masculine number, and Thursday is your luckiest day."

MAGICAL & ALCHEMICAL MESSAGE ★ "According to many schools of thought, the number 3 reigns everywhere in the Universe. The 'Threefold Law' is deeply ingrained in the minds of philosophers, theosophists and creators of religious movements. Pythagoras established an understanding of the vital importance of the Threefold Law and he placed huge significance upon it, putting it in the heart of all sciences. Practically every religious or wisdom tradition has a trinity at its core. The three ingredients of alchemy are known as Salt, Mercury and Sulphur, or body, soul and spirit. With the operation of three forces, we have a living and dynamic situation. There are possibilities for change and growth. Two opposing forces can be reconciled by the third in a new and creative solution. Three encapsulates the essence and concept of a triangle."

★ ★ ★

CAPRICORN ~ MESSAGES FROM SATURN'S NUMBER ~ 8

★ EIGHT ★

EIGHT'S MESSAGE & MEANING FOR CAPRICORN ★ "Universally, 8 is the number of cosmic balance. Number 8 is a strong, successful and material vibration. The Octahedron, the number 8, or the Ogdoad was greatly esteemed in Ancient Egypt, where it was customary to have 8 people in each boat taking part in sacred processions on the River Nile. In Buddhism it relates to the dharmachakra, or 8-spoked wheel of life, and the 8 petals of the lotus, representing the 8 paths to spiritual perfection. Taoists revere the Eight Immortals and Eight Precious Things, and the Hindu god Vishnu has 8 arms which correspond to the 8 guardians of space. In African belief among the Dogon, there are 8 hero-creators and 8 primal ancestors. Eight is the most balanced of numbers - a fact that, whether by accident or design, is perfectly reflected in the symmetrical Arabic symbol or numeral '8' that we use to represent it. Eight is the number of material success, prosperity and abundance. Financial troubles are said to ease by moving to a dwelling with a number that adds up to eight. Similarly, the number 8 can be used in all money magic. Eight remains a whole number when divided by one half and one quarter and is therefore the most indestructible of the even numbers. It is twice 4, and so incorporates the rebellious contradictions of that number. The symbol '8' also demonstrates indestructibility in that no matter at which point we start to draw it, we always end up where we started. Like the zero symbol or the circle, it has no end and no beginning, and therefore stands as a symbol of eternity; in fact, when placed on its side, the figure '8' is a symbol for everlasting life. In the Major Arcana of the Tarot, the eighth card 'Justice' shows a woman sitting on a throne which resembles the capital letter H - Heith in Hebrew stands for H, the eighth letter of the Hebrew alphabet. In China, the lotus flower with eight petals symbolises the eight paths to follow in order to find the way of the Buddha. The potential eight is linked to profound feminine intuition and insight. Number eight people often have an instinctive feel for what they do and are often described by others as 'naturals'. Success would appear to come easily and effortlessly to number eights, for it is a number with many golden and gifted qualities. Number 7 is the number of self-mastery, importance, success and abundance. It's a very powerful number for business and commerce, and is also the number of Divine law, so some sort of karmic situation may manifest which will teach those under its influence an important lesson or lessons. Overall, number 8 governs the material world and is ruled by the planet which aligns with this realm: Saturn. Its special day is Saturday. The number 8 promotes prosperity and encourages us to understand the exchange of energy and to concentrate on what we give and, perhaps more importantly, how we receive."

MAGICAL & ALCHEMICAL MESSAGE ★ "Eight stands for the octave. It is also the number of architecture and structure, where two sets of four can be combined elegantly together. The steps of the octave, which we associate mostly with notes in music and also possessing a vibrationally-connected connotation, are said to represent a cosmic order, in which you find a similar note at the top to that at the bottom, but at a different pitch or level. The octave is generally seen as a 'vertical' structure. Eight can be found in the octagon, or can be seen as two interlaced squares, or an eight-fold star. Ancient numerologists sometimes interpreted the potential of eight as an Energy which networks, connects, circuits and organises the Worlds. It represents the point at which the infinite and finite merge, where the spiritual materialises and matter spiritualises, where the unconscious becomes conscious and conscious becomes unconscious, and also where life follows death and death follows life. It is through the power of eight that

Spirit dissolves into matter and matter can be transmuted into Spirit. In sacred geometry the number eight is drawn up and down the staff of the caduceus symbol (two snakes entwined around a rod). This symbol is thought to symbolise the circuits and cycles that support and perpetuate life; it is the spiral, the stairway and the spiritual DNA that leads from Heaven to Earth and back again, because eight and its two eternal circles, never really begin and never end."

★ ★ ★

AQUARIUS ~ MESSAGES FROM URANUS'S NUMBER ~ 4

★ FOUR ★

(The number 4) is considered by the Pythagoreans as the beginning which precedes every number, the root of all things, the source of nature and the most perfect of all numbers.

Martin Ivanov

FOUR'S MESSAGE & MEANING FOR AQUARIUS ★ "Ruled by Uranus, the number 4 which brings efficiency, industriousness and practicality to those born under its influence. Four is the number of stability, providing physical structure, balance and integrity. The Quaternary, the number 4, or the Tetrad, was regarded by many ancients as symbolic of truth, while the Greeks considered it to be the root of all things. Traditionally the number of the Earth - there are four seasons and four primal elements (Fire, Earth, Air, Water) - four can be said to represent many other things also: the four liberal sciences were considered to be astronomy, geometry, music and arithmetic, four accepted states of death, judgement, heaven and hell, four compass point directions, four winds, four Archangels guarding the Earth (Uriel, Michael, Raphael and Gabriel) and four humours (phlegmatic, melancholic, choleric and sanguine), four limbs of the human body, Four Noble Truths (in Buddhism), the perfect number according to Pythagoras, being the source of ten (1 + 2 + 3 + 4 = 10), and significantly, the four suits of the Minor Arcana (Wands, Swords, Pentacles, Cups) - the number four brings structure and order, which is demonstrated perfectly in the square, an equal-sided, balanced, stable and dependable shape. It is the number of reality, logic and reason. Four is an unlikely number for Uranus, for this is the number of will, purpose, construction and discipline - and does not like the boat being rocked, unlike Uranus itself. Number 4 - the number of the seasons, the elements, the points of the compass - is oriented to the Earth, and its subjects are usually steady and practical, with great endurance. Yet number 4 - the square - contains its own opposite, and number 4 people often see everything from the *opposite* point of view, making them seem rebellious and unconventional. But in the end, if you haven't already, you will realise that what does endure is love, and each moment, if properly lived, is a kind of eternity. Sunday is your special day."

MAGICAL & ALCHEMICAL MESSAGE ★ "Four stands for the four elements of Earth, Water, Fire and Air, the 'building blocks' of creation and All That Is. The essence of man's threefold nature - mind, body and spirit - is brought to the material plane, to form a square, symbolising reality and solidity. Four also signifies two sets of polarities, but although this creates tension, this tension can be used to create a house, for example, or to lay out an arena for action. It can also create an enclosed area such as a philosophical rose garden. There are always battles where four is involved, but there is also potential for constructive work. The usual representation of four is the cross or the square. Four is associated with the four arms of the cross, a very common Earth symbol in ancient cultures and civilisations. Both the square and the cross have also been revered as power symbols which impart strength, will and inspiration."

★ ★ ★

PISCES ~ MESSAGES FROM NEPTUNE'S NUMBER ~ 7

★ SEVEN ★

(The number 7) is the sum of the number 3 (spirit, body, soul) and 4 (world) or the mystical nature of man, which consists of the triple spiritual body and four elements in material form.

Martin Ivanov

Seven planets light the heavens.
Seven metals rule the stars.
Seven angels stir the magick.
Seven spirits bring the charge.
Seven chakras, seven days.
Seven pillars, seven rays.
Blend together into one.
As I will it shall be done.

Silver RavenWolf

Seven is a magical number, relating to changes we may make in the world around us through the powers of our will and imagination. Seven looks beyond this world.

Theresa Morey

All human actions have one or more of these seven causes: chance, nature, compulsion, habit, reason, passion, and desire.

Aristotle

SEVEN'S MESSAGE & MEANING FOR PISCES ★ "Ruled by Neptune, 7 is a considered a very lucky number. A mystical number which is associated with philosophy, spiritual insights and inner contemplation, it is linked with the dreamy planet Neptune and its colours are sea greens and aquamarines. Seven is the number of mysticism and illusion, meditation and contemplation, profundity and depth, vision and perception. The Septenary or the Heptad as it is sometimes known, is the most interesting and mysterious of the primary numbers. To the Greeks and Romans, it was the symbol of good fortune, being connected with periodical changes of the Moon; and the seven notes in music gave rise to the philosophy of the 'harmony of the spheres' and the depiction of the Universe as one vast musical scale. Often linked to the world of dreams, 7 governs the imagination and the study of magic. Number 7 is a deep-thinking, spiritual vibration; symbolically it is the number for perfection. It signifies fine powers of sympathy, intuition and insight, and has long been regarded as symbolising spirituality, mystery, magic and the occult. Seven is the number of wisdom and relates to the completion of cycles. There are seven personal planets in astrology, seven days of the week, seven pillars of wisdom, seven chakras, seven wonders of the world, seven musical notes, seven Gothic gods, seven earths and seven hells and seven heavens in Islamic tradition, seven worlds believed in by the Chaldeans, seven degrees of initiation in various eastern orders, seven colours in a rainbow, seven crystalline systems, seven seas, seven continents, seven virtues, seven vices and seven deadly sins. Seven is a sacred number to the Native American Cherokee nation; it represents seven directions: north, south, east, west, above, below, centre. There are also seven sacred ceremonies in Native American tradition, and they have seven clans, each with interesting names: Blue Holly, Long Hair, Deer, Paint, Wolf, Bird, and Wild Potato. There are seven components of the personality - instinct, emotion, intelligence, intuition, reason, will and awareness - and in Buddhist thought humans are made up of seven primordial principles. On the seventh day, according to the Bible, God rested. Number 7 is thought to have occult significance, and people born under its influence often have a strongly spiritual or philosophical outlook - they are usually not so interested in material things. Carrying the Neptune vibe, it is the number for spiritual purpose, contemplation and evolution, therefore is the most appropriate for those wishing for peace, quiet and periods of solitude. It also attracts learning and education associated with personal development of some sort and is very nurturing for those who enjoy or prefer their own company, are self-motivated and have their spiritual growth and way of life as a focus, but not so compatible with those who do not like to be or live alone. Number sevens may be highly intuitive, even psychic, and need to take time and space to consider the effects of love, life and the Universe as a whole. Liking to delve into all things mystical, they would make great occultists, witches, wizards, magicians, musicians and artists. Number 7 people often exert a mysterious influence over others but may also have a tendency to become too introverted. Moodiness, depression, social awkwardness, aloofness, leaving too much to chance, cowardice and duality, may be negative associations. Number sevens are also unusual, psychic, wise, reserved, knowledgeable, serious, intelligent, analytical, contemplative, persevering, focused, studious, introspective, gracious, refined, and possess great inner wisdom. They are original thinkers and regularly experience the inherent luck associated with their number. However, they do need substantial amounts of understanding, because they often find it extremely difficult to understand themselves. Seven's planet is Neptune, which is associated with the Water element, and number 7 people often have a deep love of travel and the ocean. Monday is your special day."

MAGICAL & ALCHEMICAL MESSAGE ★ "Seven signifies a full range of differences. It contains diversity within a recognisable order, like the spectrum of colours in the rainbow. The seven days of the week are a familiar version of this, each day with its own character and magical correspondences. Something that has seven components in it has an identity of its own, above and beyond the individual ingredients. For this reason, a group is said to function effectively only when it has seven members or more. The warring fours and harmonious threes, their sum equalling seven, find their first conjunction here. In some schools of alchemy, the power of seven has been described as the *Power of Fusion*. The power of seven is connected with oneness, community and Cosmic consciousness, and describes a poetic, mystic ability to tune in and to be at one with all life and All That Is."

✭   ✭   ✭

Chakra Messages

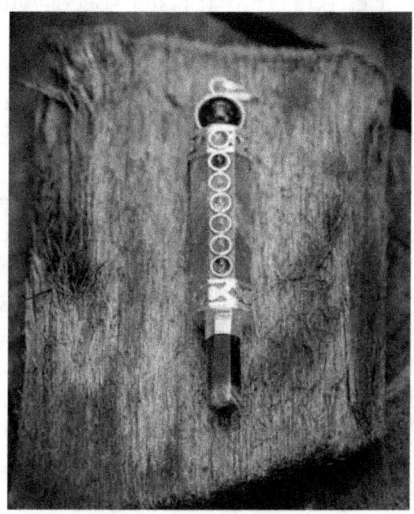

ABOUT CHAKRAS

Kundalini, the *Serpent Fire*, is generally imaged as a serpent coiled at the base of the spine until it is 'awakened'. Then the serpent becomes erect, like a cobra ready to attack, and moves up the spine to the Crown chakra, energising each chakra as it proceeds. Ultimately, kundalini is a transforming force. We are born with this force coiled at its 'home base'. Doesn't that say that *we are born to be transformed?*

Unknown

The word 'chakra' comes from the Sanskrit and means 'wheel', disc' or 'circle'. Chakras are vitally important to your physical health, emotional wellbeing and spiritual growth, and are regarded as a complete integrated system that works holistically. Chakras have no physical reality but are rather vortexes of consciousness forming a kind of 'management system' that transforms energies to meet the needs of the evolving body-mind-spirit complex operating as a human entity. They are actually located on the *surface* of the etheric double.

The chakras are funnel-shaped spinning energy vortexes of multicoloured light. These swirling vortexes of energy absorb and distribute life-force, the subtle energy known as *prana*. The seven master chakras - Root (Base), Sacral, Solar Plexus, Heart, Throat, Third Eye (Brow), and Crown - lie in the centre line of the body, with the first five embedded within the spinal column. Each chakra vibrates at a different vibrational frequency and on a different note and responds to specific life issues or 'thought forms'.

The lower body chakras deal with physical issues. As we move up the body, the chakras correspond to increasingly spiritual concerns. As a consequence, each chakra's energy vibrates at a different rate, depending on whether they govern earthbound or ethereal issues. The lower chakras have slower and denser vibrations, while the higher chakras spin at faster speeds with higher vibrations.

Because the chakras have no physical manifestation and cannot be located using any scientific instrument, they have tended to be viewed with scepticism by many Western medical professionals, a distinction they share with energy points in acupuncture and the notion of meridians. Instead, they are believed to have been sensed intuitively by many people over many centuries, and indeed people in yoga positions and in deep meditation have reported experiencing the sensation of a surge of energy rising from the base of the spine and emerging through the top of the head. Some people have even said they have seen points of blue light when their *kundalini* * energy has risen from the lowest chakra to the highest, as well as experiencing a profound sense of happiness and ecstasy.

In summary, the Universal Life Force enters the body through the Crown chakra at the top of the head. As it works its way through the body, it flows through the other centres. As it spreads to the Base chakra, it is said to arouse the kundalini energy, which yogis believe sleeps in a coiled serpentine form.

* *Kundalini* is a primary energy found at the base of our spine. It is said to symbolise and look like a coiled snake. In most of us, this serpent power is lying dormant, awaiting our spiritual actualisation and awakening. The Tantras, which are spiritual texts on some Hindu, Buddhist and Jain practices, teach that when we begin to work with our spiritual and soul energy system, this force will begin to uncoil and move up through our being, allowing for our primal and most sacred power to unfold, helping us to attain a deep state of enlightenment. This potential for transformation has been with us from the beginning as intrinsic to the Great Plan of personal growth and development, of *becoming more than you are*. *Kundalini shakti* is the transformative power or creative force inside you. It is your individual manifestation of the larger Shakti, which is the creative force of the Universe (counterpart to the cosmic consciousness identified with Shiva). On kundalini ★ "She is beautiful like a chain of lightning and fine like a lotus fibre, and shines in the minds of the sages. She is extremely subtle; the awakener of pure knowledge; the embodiment of all bliss, whose true nature is pure consciousness. Shining in her mouth is the *Brahmadvara*. This place ... is sprinkled by ambrosia." - **Sat Cakra Nirupana**

CHAKRA MESSAGES FOR THE ZODIAC

ARIES & LEO ★ SOLAR PLEXUS CHAKRA

The chakra associated with Aries and Leo is the third, or Solar Plexus chakra, which governs confidence, personal power and control.

SOLAR PLEXUS CHAKRA

Power & Confidence

Located in the region of the navel, this chakra is the focus of your Fire ... Mastery is the key word. This chakra supports clear thinking, strong vision, and assertive action. This is also the control centre for your physical vitality. The nerve centre that anatomists call the solar plexus is the largest mass of nervous tissue outside the skull and spinal canal – a sort of abdominal mini-brain.

Dr Rudolph Ballentine

Location ★ Behind the Navel
Colour ★ Yellow
Element ★ Fire
Planets ★ Mars, Sun
Zodiac Signs ★ Aries, Leo
Flower ★ 10-petalled Lotus
Energy State ★ Plasma
Mantra * ★ RAM
Concerned with ★ Personal Power, Confidence & Control
Gland ★ Adrenals
Body Function ★ Digestion
Tarot Card & Suit ★ The Tower, Wands
Psychic Powers ★ Empathy, psychic diagnoses
Alchemical Elements ★ Gold, Tin
Goddess-form Egyptian ★ Tefnut
God & Goddess forms Hindu ★ Braddha-Rudra, Lakini (Authority)
God-form Greek ★ Apollo, Athena
Animal ★ Ram
Shape ★ Downward Triangle
Crystals ★ Citrine, Amber, Ametrine, Yellow Jasper, Amblygonite, Golden Beryl, Sunstone, Yellow Sapphire, Tiger's Eye, Yellow Tourmaline

* Mantras are sounds or words that are repeated to aid concentration in meditation. These sacred syllables, when charged with the spiritual attention of an enlightened being, have the power to attract the attention to the point where it can contact the Light and Sound that pervade the Universe.

Positive Expression ★ Intelligent, optimistic, forgiving, thoughtful, perceptive
Negative Expression (Blockage) ★ Impractical, daydreaming, imbalance between the heart and head, lack of confidence, difficulty manifesting desires, low self esteem, misuse of power, over-reliance on will, dominance, shame

At the root of the navel is the shining lotus of ten petals, of the colour of heavily laden rain clouds. Meditate there on the region of Fire, triangular in form and shining like the rising Sun. Outside of it are three Svastika marks, and within, the seed-mantra Ram. By meditating in this manner upon the navel lotus the power to create and destroy the world is acquired.

Sat Cakra Nirupana

The Solar Plexus chakra is located at the diaphragm. Its Sanskrit name is *manipura*, and its symbol is a ten-petal yellow lotus flower whose centre contains a red downward-pointing triangle. This is the home of your inner power, a golden, bright sphere of light and pure being. You are able to access your force and strength through this centre. Balance in this chakra is expressed as self-confidence, a feeling of personal empowerment, logical thought processes and goal manifestation. It corresponds to the pancreas and the solar nerve plexus. If the Solar Plexus chakra is weak, wear yellow for power, confidence, and the ability to manifest your desires.

✴ MESSAGE FOR ARIES & LEO FROM YOUR SPECIAL ENERGY CENTRE ✴

"My subtle force is called *Tejas*, the prana of Fire, and I am concerned with your expansion, the energy of colour and form, the energy of sight, and your personal force and magnetism. I distubute my yellow rays to both the blood, and the brain and crown chakra. I give you the gift of awareness of the feelings of others and comprehension of astral vibrations. When combined with your willpower, which you can strengthen through balancing me, you can use this understanding and feeling to manifest your deepest desires. Because I am the centre from which you assert yourself in the world, I can increase your magnetic powers to draw towards you the things, people, circumstances and events you wish to experience in your life. To activate, open and energise me, try this exercise: Hold a piece of amber or topaz over your Solar Plexus (navel area). Take a deep breath, and as you exhale, imagine a beam of glowing white light moving from above your Crown chakra down to your Base chakra. Inhale again, and envision the white light rise to fill your Solar Plexus area and, as you gently hold your breath, see and feel that light morphing into a bright yellow blazing ball of warmth. While holding that vision and feeling, exhale and inhale again, holding your breath as you feel yourself becoming filled with the qualities of clarity, vitality, personal power, and the ability to assert your personal goals, values and needs. Finally, exhale and visualise the yellow ball of light and the qualities you summoned gradually dissolve into the ether around your auric body, and then take gentle flight into the wider Universe. Know that your message has been received by the Universe and is now in the process of Divine manifestation. Repeat as often as you like, until your dreams and desires materialise."

★ ★ ★

TAURUS & LIBRA ✯ HEART CHAKRA

The chakra associated with Taurus and Libra is the fourth, or Heart chakra, which governs all matters of the heart, namely love, openness, wellbeing and compassion.

HEART CHAKRA

Love & Compassion

Location ★ Heart Region
Colour ★ Green
Element ★ Air
Planet ★ Venus
Zodiac Signs ★ Libra, Taurus
Flower ★ 12-petalled Lotus
Energy State ★ Gas
Mantra * ★ YAM
Concerned with ★ Love & Compassion
Gland ★ Thymus
Body Function ★ Respiration
Tarot Card & Suit ★ The Wheel of Fortune, Swords
Psychic Powers ★ Hands-on Healing
Alchemical Elements ★ Copper, Gold
God-form Egyptian ★ Ma'at
God & Goddess forms Hindu ★ Ishana Rudra (Devotion), Kakani
Goddess-form Greek ★ Aphrodite
Animals ★ Antelope, Dove, Birds, Deer
Shape ★ Hexagram
Crystals ★ Rose Quartz, Jade, Green Aventurine, Rhodonite, Watermelon Tourmaline, Emerald

* Mantras are sounds or words that are repeated to aid concentration in meditation. These sacred syllables, when charged with the spiritual attention of an enlightened being, have the power to attract the attention to the point where it can contact the Light and Sound that pervade the Universe.

Positive Expression ★ Loving, accepts self and others, innate healer, generous, compassionate

Negative Expression (Blockage) ★ Selfish, envious, jealous, possessive, egotistical, melodramatic, loneliness, lack of emotional fulfillment, difficulty giving or receiving love, lack of compassion, unhealthy relationships, loving too much, unresolved sorrow

The Heart chakra is located in the region of the physical heart. Its Sanskrit name is *anahata*, and its symbol is a twelve-petal green/grey lotus flower whose centre contains a green circle and two intersecting triangles making up a six-pointed star representing balance (six is also the number of Venus, the planetary energy with which the Heart chakra is linked). This chakra blockage is especially significant because it is in the middle, uniting the upper and lower chakras. Among other things, a blockage can manifest as a lack of overall emotional fulfillment and difficulty receiving or being in a state of love. Balance in this chakra is expressed as unconditional love for ourselves and others, as well as openness to give, accept and receive compassion. This centre of the human body is the generator of all emotions: kindness, jealousy, empathy, hatred, anger, etc. It can be considered the most powerful of all the chakras because it has complete authority to create or destroy; as such, living from a place of pure heart energy may also be the most challenging to master. The spiritual lessons of this chakra are to learn compassion, practice forgiveness, and the meaning of conscious love, often referred to as 'unconditional love', which makes the heart a potential universal instrument of goodness. It corresponds to the thymus and the cardiac nerve plexus. If the Heart chakra is weak, wear light green or rose pink for love and emotional health.

✴ MESSAGE FOR TAURUS & LIBRA FROM YOUR SPECIAL ENERGY CENTRE ✴

"My subtle force is called *Vayu*, the prana of Air, and I am concerned with the healing of yourself and others, movement, the energy of touch and the gentle potency of emotional intimacy and affection. I distubute my rich forest-green rays through my twelve spokes. I give you the gift of love, compassion, authentic connection, and understanding. Because I am the centre from which you extend love outward, and through which you receive love, I can increase your magnetic powers to draw towards you the things, people, circumstances and events that will help enhance your experiences of loving, giving and receiving from the heart. Love from the Heart chakra is never needs-based and is therefore unconditional and egoless. Let yourself flow without restraint, seeing and feeling the beauty around you where before you saw limitations or even pain. With such unconditional love emanating from my centre, you will become an attractor for all of the love and abundance you can ever desire. To activate, open and energise me, try this exercise: Hold a piece of rose quartz over your Heart area. Take a deep breath, and as you exhale, imagine a beam of glowing white light moving from above your Crown chakra down to your Base chakra. Inhale again, and envision the white light rise to fill your Heart area and, as you gently hold your breath, see and feel that light morphing into a rich green ball of light. While holding that vision and feeling, exhale and inhale again, holding your breath as you feel yourself becoming filled with the qualities of acceptance, awareness, non-judgment, and self-worth. Finally, exhale and visualise the green ball of light and the qualities you summoned gradually dissolve into the ether around your auric body, and then take gentle flight into the wider Universe. Know that your message has been received by the Universe and is now in the process of Divine manifestation. Repeat as often as you like, until your heart's dreams and desires materialise."

★ ★ ★

GEMINI & VIRGO ★ THROAT CHAKRA

The chakra associated with Gemini and Virgo is the fifth, or Throat chakra, which governs self-expression, speech and communication, and corresponds to our beliefs, thoughts and actions involving communicating with others.

THROAT CHAKRA

Communication & Expression

Location ★ Throat Region
Colour ★ Blue
Element ★ Spirit/Ether
Planet ★ Mercury
Zodiac Signs ★ Gemini, Virgo
Flower ★ 16-petalled Lotus
Energy State ★ Vibration
Mantra * ★ HAM
Concerned with ★ Communication, Speech & Self-Expression
Gland ★ Thyroid
Body Function ★ Speech
Tarot Card & Suit ★ The Empress, Swords
Psychic Powers ★ Telepathy, Mediumship, Channelling, Clairaudience
Alchemical Element ★ Copper
God-form Egyptian ★ Seshat
God & Goddess forms Hindu ★ Pancha-Vaktra (5-faced Shiva), Shakini (Knowledge)
God-form Greek ★ Hermes
Animals ★ Bull, Elephant, Lion
Shape ★ Downward Triangle
Crystals ★ Amber, Blue Lace Agate, Amazonite, Blue Fluorite, Chrysocolla, Blue Chalcedony, Angelite, Aquamarine, Azeztulite, Azurite, Blue Calcite, Larimar, Lapiz Lazuli, Aqua Aura Quartz, Malachite, Blue Sapphire, Turquoise, Blue Tourmaline

* Mantras are sounds or words that are repeated to aid concentration in meditation. These sacred syllables, when charged with the spiritual attention of an enlightened being, have the power to attract the attention to the point where it can contact the Light and Sound that pervade the Universe.

> Positive Expression ★ Spiritual, self-expressive, willing to work with the Divine, articulate, cooperative, effective communication
> Negative Expression (Blockage) ★ Indecisive or willful, idealistic versus realistic, arrogant, deceptive to self or others, judgmental, problems with self-expression (expression of own truths), inability to communicate ideas or uncontrolled, low-value or inconsistent communication, problems with creativity, manipulative

The Throat chakra is located at the base of the throat. Its Sanskrit name is *vishuddha*, and its symbol is a sixteen-petal blue lotus flower whose centre contains a downward-pointing triangle within which is a circle representing the full Moon. The purpose of this chakra is to help you express energy by verbalising your emotions, desires and thoughts with clarity and integrity. It is possible to listen to and speak angelic wisdom through this centre, and this process is also referred to as channelling. Balance in this chakra is expressed as easy communication with ourselves and others on all levels. It corresponds to the thyroid and parathyroid glands and the pharyngeal nerve plexus. If the Throat chakra is weak, wear blue, aqua or turquoise for communication, expression and clarity.

★ MESSAGE FOR GEMINI & VIRGO FROM YOUR SPECIAL ENERGY CENTRE ★

"My subtle force is called *Akasha*, the prana of Ether, and I am concerned with your speech, particularly inspired speech, space, expression, the energy of hearing, and the action of the mouth. I am a silvery sky-blue and receive my primary force from the corresponding astral centre and the violet-blue ray from the sacral centre, which divides into a light blue ray to vivify the throat centre and the function of speech, then distributes the dark blue and violet ray to the upper part of the brain and the outer part of the Crown Chakra, bestowing the gifts of spiritual thoughts and emotions, and stimulating thought power. I give you the gift of inspired expression through speech, but because much of the time inspiration is linked to creativity, as such it may not always be from your own truth centre. Your task is to discover and express your true beliefs and understandings. I give you the message to not speak to hear your own voice; do not dominate conversations with your constant chatter. Simply uncover your profound inner truths and speak on their behalf. This requires silence, introspection, and stillness. When combined with your personal truth, which you can strengthen through balancing me, you can use this understanding to manifest your deepest desires by expressing them in the proper way so that they may be directed to the higher forces without blockages. Because I am the centre through which you communicate and express yourself in the world, I can increase your magnetic powers through the correct use of your words and thoughts. To activate, open and energise me, try this exercise: Hold a piece of turquoise over your Throat area. Take a deep breath, and as you exhale, imagine a beam of glowing white light moving from above your Crown chakra down to your Base chakra. Inhale again, and envision the white light rise to fill your throat area and, as you gently hold your breath, see and feel that light morphing into a bright sky-blue ball of light. While holding that vision and feeling, exhale and inhale again, holding your breath as you feel yourself becoming filled with the qualities of smooth expression, conviction, integrity, effective communication, inspiration, creativity, and the ability to express your personal truth. Finally, exhale and visualise the sky-blue ball of light and the qualities you summoned gradually dissolve into the ether around your auric body, and then take gentle flight into the wider Universe. Know that your message has been received by the Universe and is now in the process of Divine manifestation for your highest good. Repeat as often as you like, until the qualities you desire materialise."

✯ ✯ ✯

CANCER & SCORPIO ✯ SACRAL CHAKRA

The chakra associated with Cancer and Scorpio is the second, or Sacral chakra, which governs sexual, physical, material and creative desires and expressions.

SACRAL CHAKRA

Creativity & Sensual Pleasure

Location ★ Below the Navel
Colour ★ Orange
Element ★ Water
Planets ★ Moon, Pluto
Zodiac Signs ★ Cancer, Scorpio
Flower ★ Six-petalled Lotus
Energy State ★ Liquid
Mantra ^ ★ VAM
Concerned with ★ Physical, Sexual, Creative & Material Desires
Gland ★ Cells of Leydig *
Body Function ★ Sexuality, Pleasure
Tarot Card & Suit ★ The Sun, Cups
Psychic Powers ★ Empathy, psychic diagnosis
Alchemical Element ★ Iron
Goddess-form Egyptian ★ Tefnut
God & Goddess forms Hindu ★ Vishnu (Preserver), Rakini (Sexuality)
God & Goddess forms Greek ★ Pan, Diana

Animals ★ Sea Creatures, Crocodile
Shape ★ Light Blue Crescent
Crystals ★ Carnelian, Amber, Orange Calcite, Citrine, Golden Labradorite (Orange Sunstone), Topaz, Tangerine Quartz, Thulite, Coral

* The Sacral chakra regulates what are called the 'cells of Leydig', which are testicular or ovarian cells that produce and secrete testosterone.

^ Mantras are sounds or words that are repeated to aid concentration in meditation. These sacred syllables, when charged with the spiritual attention of an enlightened being, have the power to attract the attention to the point where it can contact the Light and Sound that pervade the Universe.

Positive Expression ★ Balanced, creative, personally vital
Negative Expression (Blockage) ★ Imbalanced, over- or undersexed, inflexible, emotionally cold, low energy, low libido, inhibiting, difficulty changing, difficulty experiencing joy, hyper-emotional, overly focused on physical pleasures

The Sacral chakra is located around the sexual organ region. Its Sanskrit name is *svadhisthana*, and its symbol is a six-petalled orange lotus flower containing a second lotus flower and an upward-pointing crescent Moon in a white circle. This is the home of your pleasure. The purpose of this chakra is to express your identity, personal power, personality and sexuality by using your creative drives. Balance in this chakra is expressed as originality, creative flow, and vitality. It corresponds to the reproductive sex glands and the sacral nerve plexus. If the Sacral chakra is weak, wear orange for creativity or procreation.

★ MESSAGE FOR CANCER & SCORPIO FROM YOUR SPECIAL ENERGY CENTRE ★

"My subtle force is called *Apas*, the prana of Water, and I am concerned with your self-preservation, pleasure-seeking, sex-drive, contraction, the energy of taste, and sexual attraction to others. I am orange-red in colour, radiant, and Sun-like. My primary function is to absorb vitality from the atmosphere and distribute the component atoms charged with specialised prana energy to the various parts of your body through my six spokes. I also receive a primary force from the corresponding astral centre, giving the astral body the power to travel consciously. When combined with your sexual power, which you can strengthen through balancing me, you can use this understanding and feeling to manifest your deepest desires. You will realise, when I am harmoniously balanced, that in the past your seeking pleasure can easily become obsessive and compulsive, in which case you need to slow down, and realise that pleasure is always available to you - you don't have to relentlessly pursue it. My magnetism will eventually bring it to you. To activate, open and energise me, try this exercise: Hold a piece of red coral over your Sacral area (the genitals). Take a deep breath, and as you exhale, imagine a beam of glowing white light moving from above your Crown chakra down to your Base chakra. Inhale again, and envision the white light rise to fill your Sacral area and, as you gently hold your breath, see and feel that light morphing into a deep orange ball of warmth. While holding that vision and feeling, exhale and inhale again, holding your breath as you feel yourself becoming filled with the qualities of magnetism, vigour, vitality, sensuality, and the ability to attract all that you need and desire. Finally, exhale and visualise the deep orange ball of light and the qualities you summoned gradually dissolve into the ether around your auric body, and then take gentle flight into the wider Universe. Know that your message has been received by the Universe and is now in the process of Divine manifestation. Repeat as often as you like, until your dreams and desires materialise."

★   ★   ★

SAGITTARIUS & PISCES ✶ THIRD EYE CHAKRA

This so-called Third Eye is the source of clairvoyance and clear-seeing. When this occurs, the vision beams out from the centre of the forehead. It does not stem from the physical eyes, but from this curious gland, which has the ability to 'see' past, present, or future conditions … If an individual is aware of its worth as an important part of the human body, it can be nursed into activity through meditation and ritual.

Patricia Crowther

For the medieval mystics, the 'eye of the heart' was a metaphor for intuition. In many traditions, the right eye represents the Sun's perception of the active and the future, the light of reason, whilst the left eye represents the Moon's perception of the passive and the past, or the sight which comes from emotion. But there is also a 'third eye', which symbolises the two and gives us wisdom. In Hinduism, this third eye sits in the middle of the god Shiva's forehead: 'This third eye corresponds to fire. It reduces everything to ashes'. In Buddhism, it is the All-seeing Eye of the Buddha which sits 'at the edge' between unity and multiplicity, between emptiness and non-emptiness.

Danah Zohar & Ian Marshall

The chakra associated with Sagittarius and Pisces is the sixth, or Third Eye chakra, which governs spiritual sight, Divine connections, intuition, psychic vision, wisdom and clairvoyance.

THIRD EYE CHAKRA

Intuition & Wisdom

Location ★ Between the Physical Eyes
Colours ★ Dark Blue/Indigo
Element ★ Light, Avyakta

Planets ★ Jupiter, Neptune
Zodiac Signs ★ Sagittarius, Pisces
Flower ★ Two-petalled Lotus
Energy State ★ Imagery
Mantra * ★ OM
Concerned with ★ Clairvoyance, Wisdom, Clear-seeing, Intuition & Vision
Gland ★ Pineal
Body Function ★ Sight, consciousness
Tarot Card & Suit ★ The High Priestess, Cups
Psychic Powers ★ Precognition, aura reading, clairvoyance, remote viewing
Alchemical Element ★ Silver
Goddess form Egyptian ★ Isis
God & Goddess forms Hindu ★ Shiva-Shakti (Male and female in union), Hakini (insight)
God-form Greek ★ Apollo
Animal ★ Owl
Shape ★ Downward Triangle
Crystals ★ Lapis Lazuli, Amethyst, Azurite, Charoite, Lepidolite, Sugilite, Azeztulite, Turquoise, Iolite, Larimar, Blue Calcite, Moldavite, Angelite, Phenacite, Tanzanite, Purple Fluorite

* Mantras are sounds or words that are repeated to aid concentration in meditation. These sacred syllables, when charged with the spiritual attention of an enlightened being, have the power to attract the attention to the point where it can contact the Light and Sound that pervade the Universe. According to many Eastern belief systems, in the beginning there was 'Om', the Universal sound of creation. It wasn't just a sound - it was a vibration moving through the whole Universe, the seed of the ultimate life-force.

Every high thought of beauty and love looks far ahead, as through a wizard's telescope, up to the sixth world, the realm of pure insight.

Robert Ellwood

Positive Expression ★ Spiritually wise, intuitive, personal awareness of the Divine
Negative Expression (Blockage) ★ Too self-sufficient, lack of imagination, vision or concentration, clouded intuition, inability to see the bigger picture, delusional, distorted imagination or intuition, over-reliance on logic and intellect

Ajna is like the Moon, beautifully white. It shines with the glory of meditation. Within this lotus dwells the subtle mind. When the yogi ... becomes dissolved in this place, which is the abode of uninterrupted bliss, he then sees sparks of fire distinctly shining.

Sat Cakra Nirupana

The Third Eye chakra is located between and just above the physical eyes. Its Sanskrit name is *ajna*, and its symbol is two large white lotus petals on each side of a white circle, within which is a downward-pointing triangle. This is the home of your intuition or sixth sense; your mind's eye. The purpose of this chakra is to help you to perceive unseen energies such as spirit guides and angels, using your innate clairvoyant, or psychic, skills. You are able to recognise and process spiritual information and wisdom through this centre, as it is connected to your conscious mind also. The seat of the soul is said to lie at this point, between and behind the two eyebrows, in a place known as the third or single eye. It is also referred to as the tenth door, *daswan dwar, tisra til*, and mount of transfiguration. By concentrating on this point, we can gain access to the soul, as this point is a doorway through which the soul can enter into the spiritual realms within. These are inner dimensions that exist concurrently with our physical Universe. Balance in this chakra is expressed as developed and sound senses of intuition, clairvoyance, clairaudience and clairsentience. It corresponds to the pituitary gland and the carotid nerve plexus.

✶ MESSAGE FOR SAGITTARIUS & PISCES FROM YOUR SPECIAL ENERGY CENTRE ✶

"My subtle force is called *Manas* connecting with mental energies, and I am also known as 'the Eye of Horus', 'The Horn of the Unicorn', and 'the Command Centre'. I am concerned with your intuition, Divine expansion, clairvoyance, and the imagination and its need to find the meaning in life. I am indigo-blue in colour and have ninety-six spokes, divided into two wing-like halves of forty-eight spokes each - one wing is purplish-blue, the other wing is rose and yellow. Because I am connected strongly with your purpose in life, you can meditate on me to uncover this and start living more authentically. I wish to tell you that seeing 'Divinity' in all things is not to do with religion, or even with belief in God (or Goddess), but rather it is seeing the creative force behind all manifestation everywhere, in all things, in all entities, in all energies, and in all beings. Even if outer manifestations appear 'bad' or 'disastrous', I assist you in believing that you can assert your own love, your own will, your own belief in goodness into reality, effecting transformation and needed change. To activate, open and energise me, try this exercise: Hold a piece of amethyst quartz over your Third Eye (brow area). Take a deep breath, and as you exhale, imagine a beam of glowing white light moving from above your Crown chakra down to your Base chakra. Inhale again, and envision the white light rise to fill your Third Eye area and, as you gently hold your breath, see and feel that light morphing into a bright indigo-blue ball of light. While holding that vision and feeling, exhale and inhale again, holding your breath as you feel yourself becoming filled with the qualities of clear-seeing, the awareness of both physical and etheric levels around you, and the ability to perceive from a higher spiritual perspective. Finally, exhale and visualise the indigo-blue ball of light and the qualities you summoned gradually dissolve into the ether around your auric body, and then take gentle flight into the wider Universe. Know that your message has been received by the Universe and is now in the process of Divine manifestation. Repeat as often as you like, until your dreams and desires for the discovery of the greater purpose of your life materialise."

★ ★ ★

CAPRICORN ★ BASE CHAKRA

The chakra associated with Capricorn is the first, the Root or Base chakra, which governs and regulates issues of security, survival and fulfilment of our physical needs for food and shelter.

BASE (ROOT) CHAKRA

Survival & Security

Location ★ Base of Spine
Colour ★ Red
Element ★ Earth
Planets ★ Saturn, Earth
Zodiac Sign ★ Capricorn
Flower ★ Four-petalled Lotus
Energy State ★ Solid
Mantra * ★ LAM
Concerned with ★ Security, Survival & Procreation
Gland ★ Gonads
Body Function ★ Elimination
Tarot Card & Suit ★ The World, Pentacles
Psychic Powers ★ Pain control, telekinesis, dowsing, psychometry
Alchemical Element ★ Lead
God-form Egyptian ★ Geb
God & Goddess forms Hindu ★ Bala Brahma (Child God), Dakini (Security)
God-form Greek ★ Gaia, Demeter
Animals ★ Bull, Elephant, Ox
Shape ★ Yellow Square
Crystals ★ Garnet, Fire Agate, Bloodstone, Boji Stone, Red Calcite, Carnelian, Cuprite, Hematite, Brecciated Jasper, Brown Jasper, Red Jasper, Obsidian, Smoky Quartz, Ruby, Black Sapphire, Zircon, Black Tourmaline, Lodestone

* Mantras are sounds or words that are repeated to aid concentration in meditation. These sacred syllables, when charged with the spiritual attention of an enlightened being, have the power to attract the attention to the point where it can contact the Light and Sound that pervade the Universe.

Positive Expression ★ Energetic, vital, affectionate, productive, grounded, stable, serves others, committed

Negative Expression (Blockage) ★ Angry, self-indulgent, aggressive, plodding, habitual, tied down, prone to anxiety, ungrounded, fearful about security and survival, flighty, difficulty letting go, lack of sense of belonging, weak constitution, overly practical, lacking dreams and imagination

The Base chakra, otherwise known as the Root chakra, is located at the base of the spine. Its Sanskrit name is *muladhara*, and its symbol is a four-petalled crimson lotus flower around a yellow square containing a downward-pointing white triangle. This is the home of your physical reality and is important for health and vitality. The purpose of this chakra is to ground your body and promote awareness of your life on Earth. With healing of and balance in this area, you will be able to heighten your consciousness and feel empowered to transform from merely having to survive to wanting to strive and achieve in greater things. Harmony in this chakra is expressed as groundedness, stability, ability to express and be aroused by physical affection, and reliability. When this chakra is balanced you are caring, focused, self-confident, secure, strong and happy, but out of balance it can make you sexually predatory or frigid, manipulative or guilt-ridden. It corresponds to the adrenal glands and the coccygeal nerve plexus.

★ MESSAGE FOR CAPRICORN FROM YOUR SPECIAL ENERGY CENTRE ★

"My subtle force is called *Prithivi*, the prana of Earth, and I am concerned with your survival, preservation, health, vitality, and procreation. I help keep you grounded, stable, and fixed to your true path once you have found it. To activate, open and energise me, try these two exercises: (1) Imagine your spine extending deep into the ground below you like a root, and imagine any excessive stress or blockages dissolving, then streaming down and dissipating into the Earth. Imagine you are drawing up healing energies from the ground, strengthening and vitalising your entire body, mind and spirit; (2) Hold a piece of ruby or garnet over your Base (area between the anus and genitals). Take a deep breath, and as you exhale, imagine a beam of glowing white light moving from above your Crown chakra down to your Base chakra. Inhale again, and envision the white light filling your Base area and, as you gently hold your breath, see and feel that light turning a deep red colour. While holding that vision and feeling, exhale and inhale again, holding your breath as you feel yourself becoming filled with the qualities of strength, energy, courage, and deep passion for life. Finally, exhale and visualise the deep red ball of light and the qualities you summoned gradually dissolve into the ether around your auric body, and then take gentle flight into the wider Universe. Know that your message has been received by the Universe and is now in the process of Divine manifestation. Repeat as often as you like, until your dreams and desires materialise."

★ ★ ★

AQUARIUS ★ CROWN CHAKRA

The chakra associated with Aquarius is the seventh, or Crown chakra, which governs spiritual wisdom, higher communication and enlightenment. This is the highest chakra of the seven master chakras and is a receptacle for guidance and understanding from higher 'planes', letting in Universal and Divine knowledge.

CROWN CHAKRA

Wisdom & Enlightenment

Location ★ Top of Head
Colours ★ Purple, Violet, White
Element ★ Consciousness/Knowing/Cosmic
Planet ★ Uranus
Zodiac Sign ★ Aquarius
Flower ★ 1,000-petalled Lotus (or 960 plus 12 at its centre)
Energy State ★ Information, Enlightenment
Concerned with ★ Spiritual Wisdom, Divine Connection & Enlightenment
Gland ★ Pituitary
Body Function ★ Superconsciousness
Tarot Card & Suit ★ The Magician, All
Psychic Powers ★ Astral projection, prophecy
Alchemical Element ★ Mercury
God-form Egyptian ★ Nut
God & Goddess forms Hindu ★ Brahma Vishnu (Inner teacher), Maha Shakti (Union)
God-form Greek ★ Zeus
Animals ★ No Animals
Shape ★ Upward Triangle
Crystals ★ Amethyst, Clear Quartz, Diamond, Angelite, Danburite, Ametrine, Charoite Azeztulite, Lepidolite, Phenacite, Selenite, Tanzanite, Sugilite

Positive Expression ★ Spiritual, At Oneness, Connectedness, Divine Love
Negative Expression (Blockage)★ Self-Righteous, spacey, ungrounded, impractical, alienated, indecisive, lack of common sense, difficulty with finishing things, depressed, confused, plagued by a sense of meaninglessness, delusional

The lotus of the thousand petals, lustrous and whiter than the full Moon, has its head turned downward. It charms. It sheds its rays in profusion and is moist and cool like nectar. The most excellent of men who has controlled his mind and known this place is never again born the Wandering, as there is nothing in the three worlds which binds him.

Sat Cakra Nirupana

The Crown chakra is located just above the crown of the head and does not, therefore have a 'physical' position. Its Sanskrit name is *sahasrara*, and its symbol is the thousand-petal white lotus flower. This is the level of super-consciousness or *samadhi*, a plane beyond time, space and consciousness. Balance in this chakra is expressed as cosmic connection and consciousness. The purpose of this chakra is to keep your soul connected to your angelic body and to All That You Are. You are able to access Divine, Angelic and Spiritual wisdom through this chakra, as it is connected to your higher, astral *, and subconscious mind. It corresponds to the pineal gland and the cerebral cortex nerve plexus.

* The astral body is the third body or level of consciousness, also called the desire or emotional body. The astral body is the Lower Self of emotion, imagination, memory, thinking, and will - all the mind functions in response to sensory perception. In the process of incarnation, the astral body is composed of the planetary bodies in their aspects to one another to form a matrix for the physical body. This matrix is, in a sense, the true horoscope guiding the structure of the body and defining karmic factors. It is the field of dreams and the subconscious mind and is the vehicle for most psychic activities. It is a doorway to the superconscious mind and the Collective Unconscious.

✵ MESSAGE FOR AQUARIUS FROM YOUR SPECIAL ENERGY CENTRE ✵

"My subtle force is called *Bindu*, and I am concerned with your superconsciousness, Higher Self, and the eternal continuity of both. I am perceived to have 960 spokes plus another twelve in my centre, which is gleaming white withhold at its core within the violet vortex. My function is to allow for the flow of consciousness, enabling you to leave your physical body and then return to it in full awareness. I reveal to you the true secret of 'Letting Go', not by surrender *of* self, but the merging of self *with* the Divine everywhere. It truly means *becoming more than you are* through becoming one with the All. By meditating upon me, you can do this anytime, anywhere. Be open to the experience that may take the form of experiencing Oneness with the flow of Universal energy. Or it may take the form of actual 'enlightenment', where you are filled with Light. When combined with Divine Love, which you can strengthen through balancing me, you can use this understanding and feeling to manifest your deepest desires. To activate, open and energise me, try this exercise: Place a piece of diamond a few inches above your Crown (top of head) whilst lying down. Take a deep breath, and as you exhale, imagine a beam of glowing white light moving from above your Crown chakra down to your Base chakra. Inhale again, and envision the white light rise to fill your Crown area again, and as you gently hold your breath, see and feel that light turning to a bright violet glowing light. While holding that vision and feeling, exhale and inhale again, holding your breath as you feel yourself becoming filled with the qualities of total awareness and oneness with all creation, the ability to sense and feel the Divine presence everywhere and in everything, and the deep knowing that you have a role to play in the Great Plan of continuing evolution. Finally, exhale and visualise the violet glowing light and the qualities you summoned gradually dissolve into the ether around your auric body, and then take gentle flight into the wider Universe. Know that your message has been received by the Universe and is now in the process of Divine manifestation. Repeat as often as you like, until your dreams and desires for ultimate connection and Unity with all materialise."

✫ ✫ ✫

Deva Messages

ABOUT DEVAS

Through magick we do conjure the Elements, evoking unto us the special properties of the Life-force for our learning and our coming-into-light. And yet are there secret paths of knowledge that have fallen from the minds of men ... For the way of Magick is a path to sacred knowledge, of reverence and humility - and the world is a wondrous place. Yet how many amongst us have fathomed these depths?

Nevill Drury

There are three groups of beings in the Universe: the nonhuman creatures, humans, and finally, the seemingly invisible and largely forgotten Divine helpers ... in Sanskrit they are called *Devas*, and they work on behalf of the Supreme Being in the ongoing maintenance of the Universe and as the manifestation of the Laws of Nature. Deva, which is the root of the English word *divine*, means 'playing in the light'.

Jeffrey Armstrong

Deva is a Sanskrit word that means 'shining one'. Devas are the life force within nature, and there are four devic realms - Fire, Earth, Air and Water - which contain ethereal elemental spirits or sprites. Elementals are the building blocks of nature, and close to being true energy and consciousness. The four elements correspond to four different states of matter: energy/transmutation (Fire), gas (Air), liquid (Water) and solid (Earth), which are linked to the four human states of consciousness: inspiration, thought, feeling and practicality. There are four spirits, or elementals, which reside in the devic realms, associated with each element.

People have been painting pictures, telling stories and writing about these devic realms for hundreds of years, albeit sometimes through disguised mediums such as fairytales or children's fantasy stories like Tolkien's *Lord of the Rings*. The power of the natural world is easily observed and since ancient times primal forces have been ascribed to various spirit beings. Indigenous cultures understood that Mother Nature did not do Her work alone but employed billions of Divine helpers to assist in the biosphere's ongoing unfoldment and renewal.

From the point of view of science, the devas remain unseen but are evident as the Laws of Nature. Belief in nature spirits is of such ancient origin and is Universal; cultures everywhere have names or words to describe them. In the sixteenth century, a famous Swiss physician, alchemist and mystic called Paracelsus * defined these beings as 'Elementals', classifying them according to the element of nature they inhabit. There are four main levels of elemental beings: Gnomes (Earth), Undines (Water), Sylphs (Air), and Salamanders (Fire). The gnomes are the 'knowing ones', from the Greek *gnoma*, meaning 'knowledge'. Undine is from the Latin *unda*, meaning 'wave'. Slyph is from the Greek *silphe*, meaning 'butterfly'. Finally, the salamander comes from the Greek word *salambe*, meaning 'fireplace'. The fifth element of Ether is the element from which came forth the other four, and Ether, or Spirit, has never been defined in any particular category, and encompasses the aspects and beings of all the other elements.

Elementals are usually benevolent guardian beings or spirits that look after nature's secrets and treasures in whatever part of the natural realm they occupy. They can only be seen or 'felt' by those possessing heightened psychic abilities, yet they can be summoned by those practising alchemy, spells and magic in order to harness the forces of nature for their own particular intentions. In our modern lives, it may seem as though this magic doesn't exist, but the truth is that most of us are simply less in touch with it than ever before. The consequence of this is that we are destroying vast areas of land, polluting waters, creating toxic landscapes, and disrespecting the laws of nature, which often whisper their messages softly. It is therefore important for us to look at the beauty that surrounds us with true appreciation and genuine regard, and to open ourselves up to the magic resides within it. The four devic realms can teach us much about nature; they act as custodians for the four elements and learning to work with them is a way of attuning to all the energies and beings of nature. Elementals are four-dimensional and have nothing to obstruct their movements. Therefore, they move as easily through matter as we do through air and space. They do require some contact with humans for their own evolution. Helping to direct them is an overseer, traditionally called the King of that element, and an archangel. Each of these elements is affiliated with one of the four directions and each elemental spirit embodies its own special energy. If you wish to re-connect and re-harmonise yourself by working with nature and its messages and lessons, you could begin by learning a little about your element's realm.

* Philippis Aureolus Paracelsus is considered the most original medical thinker of the sixteenth century. A Swiss chemist, physician, astrologer, botanist and philosopher who lived from 1493 - 1541, he is credited with the Doctrine of the Four Elements, from which early nineteenth-century occult practitioners drew the belief that an element (Fire, Earth, Air and Water) is not only physical, but also contains a spiritual essence. His belief in supernatural beings, intuition and the invisible causes of illness helped him discover

hydrogen and nitrogen. His hermetical views were that the health status of the body relied on harmony between the macrocosm (nature) and the microcosm (the individual). Paracelsus believed that "Elementals are unlike pure spirits for they are mortal, but they are not like man for they have no soul."

MAKING A WISH USING YOUR DEVA

All things within the cosmos are interrelated and it is only natural for kindred souls to come to the aid of their own kind, especially when threatened from alien or non-harmonious frequencies. The secret lies in being able to become one of that 'kind', whatever it may be, so that you attract its help in time of need.

Murry Hope

Deva: The Hindu word for god, especially a nature god. This term has been used to refer to entities of mental and/or astral matter who rule nature and guide natural evolution. They range from mighty beings enthroned over great mountains or seascapes to tiny elfin creatures who may be the spirit of a single flower. Some consider them as on a separate line of evolution from animals and humans.

Robert Ellwood

Magic is a journey of discovery for the brave and stable individual ... Discovery cosmic truths for oneself can open up a world of wonderment. The path of the magical initiation calls for the journeying of the spirit to be armed with the stability and practicality of the elements of Earth (gnomes); the loyalty, ardour and creativity of the elements of Fire (salamanders); the mental speed, communication and inventiveness of the elements of Air (sylphs), and the receptivity, understanding and adaptability of the Water elements (undines). In other words, man needs his fourfold nature fully verified and readily available.

Murry Hope

Wish magic is associated particularly with the Air elementals, as wishes made through them are carried away with the winds and released into the cosmos, though you can also burn wishes with candles or pass them through fire to activate the Fire spirits (and send your wish into the Universe in the form of smoke), 'plant' wishes in the ground or etch a symbol onto a stone to activate the Earth essences, or sprinkle blessed water over a wish or release flower petals as offerings into a fast-flowing stream to carry your desires far and wide using the Water elementals' powers.

When the four elementals are combined, they can magically create the fifth, powerful energy known as *Ether*, *Aether* or *Akasha*, in which the centre of the circle forms a swirling vortex, allowing desires, wishes, hopes and dreams to be transformed into material reality.

☆ ☆ ☆

DEVA MESSAGES FOR THE FIRE ELEMENT

★ DIVINE MESSAGE FROM THE SALAMANDERS FOR ARIES, LEO & SAGITTARIUS ★

"You, Aries, Leo and Sagittarius, light the Divine Fires of the Earth, bringing out the inner spark within all that exists. You spread your light, illumination and ideals wherever you go, leaving a trail of Divine sparks as you blaze your uniquely inspiring and uplifting trail wherever you go. Call upon me, the Salamander, to help you to use this Divine gift, using a red or orange candle, any kind of fire, and requesting my presence of the flames."

THE DEVIC REALMS & FIRE ★ SOUTH: REALM OF THE SALAMANDERS

The Fire element, comprising of the three zodiac signs Aries, Leo and Sagittarius, is connected with the South direction and the realm of the Salamanders.

★ SALAMANDERS ★

These are not to be confused with the reptile salamanders, although they have the same name. Fire spirits are described as thick, red and dry-skinned beings called salamanders, which look similar to the common scaleless lizard-like amphibians that share their name. Elemental salamanders are sometimes visible as small balls of fire and have also been seen in the shape of tongues of flame that can run over fields and peer into dwellings. No fire is lit without their help. In fact, the salamander comes from the Greek word *salambe*, meaning 'fireplace'. These spirits control all manner of flame, lightning, explosions, volcanoes and combustion. Mostly they are active underground and internally within the body and mind. Salamanders evoke powerful emotional currents in humans and stimulate fires of spiritual idealism and perception. Their energy is much like that of the Tarot Card, The Tower, assisting in the tearing down of the old and the building of the new - as fire can be both constructive and destructive in its creative expression.

The salamanders are the guardians of summer and Fire, and reside in the realm of passion, change, prophetic visions, personal power, inspiration and the inner child. They function in the physical body by aiding circulation and in maintaining proper body temperature and working with the body's metabolism for greater health.

Fire elementals work with humans via heat, fire and flame. This includes everything from the flame of a candle to the ethereal flames and daily light of the Sun. They can be powerfully effective in healing work, but must be used carefully for such applications, as their energies are dynamic and difficult to control. They are almost always present when there is any healing going to occur. Fire provides us with warmth, fuel and heating, and voraciously destroys the old so new life can spring forth out of the ashes - it is the essence from which the legendary phoenix arises. Fire also represents the inner child, that place of innocence from which we all stem. As it gives rise to sexual fervour it is also the root of our creative spirits. The fire elementals can indeed awaken in us higher spiritual visions and aspirations. They strengthen and stimulate the entire auric field to enable easier attunement to and recognition of Divine forces within our lives.

Despite their luminosity and warmth, Fire spirits are the most unpredictable and volatile of the elementals. They are elusive, fierce, and untameable, and because they are made of balls of energy or light, they tend to be far shorter-lived than other elemental nature forms. In fact, the smaller ones may even literally burn themselves out. They vary in size and intensity, from mighty dragons to tiny but potent fire fairies. They may also manifest as glow worms or fire flies, dancing over sacred sites or within caves.

The salamanders can be seen in the heart of fires, dancing like dragons in the flames, and this dragon symbology is used in many Eastern religions to pay homage to them. Salamanders love the Fire for it is nourished by it - yet it is so cold within itself that it cannot be harmed by the flames. Fire spirits are of immense magical value as light-bringers; they inspire us to reach up and out to fulfill our loftiest dreams and ambitions. They help blacksmiths in their task of forging mighty swords and armour, feeding strength into the flames to have it then yield into the blacksmith's purpose. And yet the salamander is a mighty and tenacious defender of Fire. Only the strongest powers can hold it at bay - it can then be a loyal ally and not an enemy to bar us on our quest. The King of Fire is Belenos or Djinn *, its archangel is Michael, its magickal tool is the wand (which calls down the spirits into form), and its sacred ceremonial stones are Yellow Topaz, Amber and Citrine.

* Djinn is a fiery elemental spirit who, being made of pure fire, is a glorious flamelike creature with flashing luminous ruby eyes. He is never still and lives in the mystical Emerald Mountains of Kaf, ruling over all other fire beings. Djinn is called the 'wish-granter' and is an efficient shape-shifter and magician who travels with the speed of light. Although his natural home is in the Emerald Mountains, he can appear almost anywhere, especially in bottles or lamps as a genie. As well as granting wishes, Djinn can endow the powers of creativity, inspiration, small miracles, travel, change, and courage.

INVOKING THE FIRE DEVAS

If you wish to increase your sexual prowess, inspiration, creativity or overall success, need some career or goal luck, are fearful of an imminent but necessary change or move, or you are in need of courage or energy to meet a challenge, ask the fire devas for their help. Suitable offerings you can use to attract their energy, are fires (obviously), candles, anything gold or glittery, certain crystals *, some essential oils ^, sparkling stones, fibre-optic lamps, mirrors, jack o' lanterns, sun catchers, clear crystal spheres, golden fruits, and golden flowers.

You can encounter salamanders most easily in a bonfire or open hearth. Some see them as sparks or flashes of colour. Dragon-like beings that live within flames, you can see them coiling within the swirling and lapping heat of the flames, and watch others dance and crackle in the sparks. They also reside in every beam of sunlight and flow of electricity. If you do not have access to a proper fire, a candle can serve the same purpose: call upon their help by meditating upon a lit candle. Lighting several at once, particularly in the colours of red, gold or orange, may heighten the power.

* Some crystals you can use to attract salamander activity and illumination in your experience, are hematite, obsidian, amber, ruby, bloodstone, carnelian, pyrite, lava, dragon's eggs, garnet, Boji stone, and topaz.

^ Some essential oils you can use to invoke the Fire elementals are basil, frankincense, chamomile, allspice, orange, clove, nutmeg, cinnamon, dragon's blood, cedar wood, angelica, rosemary, and tangerine.

★ ★ ★

DEVA MESSAGES FOR THE EARTH ELEMENT

✶ DIVINE MESSAGE FROM THE GNOMES FOR TAURUS, VIRGO & CAPRICORN ✶

"You, Taurus, Virgo and Capricorn, are the caretakers of the Earth, bringing out the inner Earth Mother within all that exists. You spread your love, nurturance and gentle ways wherever you go, leaving a trail of Divine abundance, treasures and material goodness, as you blaze your uniquely giving trail wherever you go. Call upon me, the Gnome, to help you to use these Divine gifts, using a brown or green candle, any kind of Earth mineral such as a crystal, rock salt or fertile soil, and requesting my presence to guide you."

THE DEVIC REALMS & EARTH ★ NORTH: REALM OF THE GNOMES

The Earth element, comprising of the three zodiac signs Taurus, Virgo and Capricorn, is connected with the North direction and the realm of Gnomes.

★ GNOMES ★

All things within the cosmos are interrelated and it is only natural for kindred souls to come to the aid of their own kind, especially when threatened from alien or non-harmonious frequencies. The secret lies in being able to become one of that 'kind', whatever it may be, so that you attract its help in time of need. It is said, for example, that he who relates to the gnome kingdoms never wants for a penny.

Murry Hope

Gnome: *noun* - A legendary dwarfish creature, supposed to guard the Earth's treasures; diminutive spirits or small fey 'humanoids' in Renaissance magic and alchemy, first introduced by Paracelsus in the 16th century, known for their eccentric sense of humour, inquisitiveness, and engineering prowess; are typically said to be small, humanoid creatures who live underground.

Gnomes are a race of small, misshapen, dwarf-like creatures that dwell in the Earth and often protect secret treasures in vast caverns. Their actions are reflected in the presence of mineral deposits and other kinds of geological formations. Gnomes are the beings of craftsmanship. They are needed to build the plants, flowers and trees. It is their task to tint them, to make crystals and gems and to maintain the Earth so that we have a place to grow and evolve. As guardians of the treasures of the Earth, they are attuned to helping humans find the treasures within the Earth or part of it; this can be hidden riches, the energy of crystals and stones, or the finding of gold within one's life. Ultimately, they work with humans through nature. They give each stone its own individuality and essence. Indeed, they do this with every aspect of nature, and thus we can learn from each one, for every tree, rock and flower has something it can teach us.

According to Paracelsus, gnomes cannot stand the light of the Sun, and even one ray would turn them to stone. If you wish to retrieve any treasures that are buried underground or associated with the Earth, you must first appease the gnomes, or they will cause you mischief.

The gnomes are the 'knowing ones', from the Greek *gnoma*, meaning 'wisdom and knowledge'. In fact, gnomes are extremely wise and knowledgeable about how all things of this Earth work. Another theory regarding their naming is that of Paracelsus, who was the first to use 'gnome' as a collective term for the spirits of the Earth. It is believed that he probably based this usage on the Greek term ge-nomos, meaning Earth-dweller. As knowing ones, the gnomes teach us respect and reverence for the collective wisdom and traditions of old age. They wish us to learn the knowledge garnered over many lifetimes of experiences, and the wisdom of our elders, our crones and sages. Gnomes stand for respect for old and advanced age, and they ensure that the two stages of life represented by the crone and the sage are upheld, respected, honoured and learned from.

The gnomes are the guardians of winter, the direction of the north, the physical world, and of fertility and abundance. The north is traditionally known as the gateway to inner wisdom. The Earth provides us with food and beauty in many forms. The gnomes are caretakers of everything that grows, from tiny flowers to towering trees. Their role is to protect the soil, mountains, trees, sacred sites, plants, minerals, and land. Their Goddess is Cerridwen, and the King of Earth is Cernunnos, Ghob or Geb *, its archangel Uriel, its magickal tool the pentacle or disc (which calls down the spirits into form), and its sacred ceremonial stone is the garnet in all its four colours. Perhaps Merlin sums up the gnome realm best: "From time to time, no doubt, these gnomes do make merry with the lives of humanfolk, having their ways in mischief and making jokes. And yet, for all their pranks and mischief, are these gnomes good and virtuous within their natures, and offer gifts of kindness when hard times come upon our lives."

* Geb was the Egyptian god of the Earth and a member of the Ennead of Heliopolis. An elemental fey king whose throne is covered in silver and gold crystals, Geb is the guardian of miners and others who work within the Earth. He can endow those who invoke him with the powers of prosperity, skill

in all practical crafts, moneymaking by steady means, success in property matters, older people, animals, and finding and restoring what is lost.

INVOKING THE EARTH DEVAS

Gnomes are said to be the easiest of the devas to sense since their energy is almost tangible. Earth spirits can be very helpful since they embody practicality and common sense, and have an innate knowledge base around money, the material, and how to grow things. They relate to food, nourishment, health, healing, tree magic, treasures, fertility, gardening, protection, wealth, all craft skills, and all Earth magic.

Although they can be connected with at all times, they are easier to contact at midnight and throughout winter. They tend to prefer to emerge after dark. Their colours are black, dark green, browns, and all hues of the Earth. They associate strongly with ancient trees, particularly the hawthorn, the oak, the Moreton Bay fig, and ancient eucalypt forests, in whose roots they dwell. Other places they live are anywhere close to the Earth, caves, gardens, mines, old stone and crop circles, near ley and psychic power lines, and in mounds or hillocks. Suitable offerings to attract the Earth guardians are: flowers, herbs, salt, corn and wheat, crystals ^, stones, coins, certain essential oils *, nuts, berries, sand, small wooden items, and petals.

As keepers of the precious things of the Earth, they are able to awaken us to our planet's treasures. Therefore, salt, crystals, quality soil, minerals, ores and all solid landforms come under their domain. Many of us who work in mining, or with gemstones and metals, are also working with the gnomes.

Gnomes can also assist with the security of your home and are excellent guardians, so it is no accident that many gardens around the world are filled with representations of these powerful beings, as they are said to protect the home they are attached to. Gnomes can also be called upon to bring financial stability to your household, attracting the funds needed to pay a bill or to meet an urgent expense.

If you have a laborious task ahead, have job or financial worries, need to ground your ideals, or are in need of developing a special hands-on skill, ask the earth devas for their help. The easiest way to contact them is to spend some time outdoors around the Earth element and natural features, particularly rocks and thick-trunked trees. It is best to invoke the gnomes using a wand made of crystal, linking to the Earth kingdom, or an athame, as things of the Earth such as steel and iron are also directly in tune with the gnomes. You may find it helpful to hold a crystal or stone of resonance when asking the Earth elementals for assistance.

^ Some crystals to attract the Earth spirits are most agates (especially moss and tree agate), boulder opal, malachite, emerald, red or gold tiger's eye, aventurine, jet, petrified or fossilised wood, smoky quartz, and all stones with holes in the centre.
* Some essential oils to attract the Earth spirits are geranium, tea tree, cypress, vervain, oakmoss, honeysuckle, vetiver, patchouli, and magnolia.

☆ ☆ ☆

DEVA MESSAGES FOR THE AIR ELEMENT

★ DIVINE MESSAGE FROM THE SLYPHS FOR GEMINI, LIBRA & AQUARIUS ★

"You, Gemini, Libra and Aquarius, provide the Divine Breath of Life to all who dwell upon the Earth, bringing out the inner spirit within all that exists. You spread your knowledge, ideals and wisdom wherever you go, leaving a trail of Divine breezes as you blaze your uniquely uplifting and life-sustaining trail wherever you go. Call upon me, the Sylph, to help you to use your Divine gifts, using a blue candle, some incense or a dream catcher, and acknowledging my presence in all the winds that blow."

THE DEVIC REALMS & AIR ★ EAST: REALM OF THE SYLPHS

The Air element, comprising of the three zodiac signs Gemini, Libra and Aquarius, is connected with the East direction and the realm of Sylphs.

★ SYLPHS ★

Sylph is from the Greek *silphe*, and the word means 'butterfly'; these spirits control all winds. Sylphs are fairy-like spirits that inhabit the air, winds and atmosphere as well as high mountain tops (not all sylphs are restricted to living in the air, however). They are probably more closely in line with our concept of fairies and angels than the other elemental beings; and indeed, they work alongside the angels. Always active and extremely quick of movement and sound, Air Elementals are also known to be highly intelligent as they can gather vast amounts of information in a short period of time. They are aloof and detached and usually very subtle in their persuasiveness. People with strong sylph influence or activity often find that sexuality is not high on their list of priorities and may not understand how it can be so with others. But the sylphs stimulate the expression of the creative sexual drive into other avenues of one's life, such as work or hobbies.

The sylphs are guardians of spring, the direction of the east and the wind. Therefore, they are chiefly concerned with communication, the mind, the intellect and the kingdom of the feathered and winged creatures. As the east is the doorway to new beginnings and the direction through which the sacred circle is always entered, air has a uniquely ethereal, otherworldly, wispy quality to it. It makes its presence felt through its four winds: the north brings cold and withering; the east brings new life and freshness; the south brings vitality and warmth; and the west brings fertility and gentle abundance. Air, and its various components, is our vital life force, enabling us to exist. It also supports that which flies - from birds to human-made technology. It allows fire to burn and for communication with others and with the ether to flow with ease and stimulates our intellect, so we can exercise good reason, judgment and rational thought to enhance our lives. Air makes its home in the heavens and yet it flows freely as a gift for all to share. It moves among us like an unseen visitor, giving us life and strength, and carrying our wishes into the breeze for them to return in the form of free-flowing bounty in our physical world. Air inhabits our hearts, bring joy and wisdom and knowing, and sylphs guard these mind treasures as they are pure spirits of truth and beauty whose ways are not sullied by Earthly restrictions. The King of Air is Lugh or Paralda *, its archangel is Raphael, its magickal tool is the athame (which calls down the spirits into form), and its sacred ceremonial stones are Lapis Lazuli, Sapphire, Blue Topaz and Azurite. Perhaps Merlin sums up the sylph realm best: "For these beings are like unto jewels of light, their wings glistening as crystal butterflies in the first Dawn. We may see them in a dance of light upon a leaf or petal, perchance amidst the forest dells or in the hidden glades where few have ventured."

* Paralda, King of the Air elementals, is a mysterious, misty being who lives on the highest mountain on Earth, who shimmers in the early morning sunlight and breaks through the mist in an occasional flash of radiance. He has appeared both as a quick and youthful being, and as a wise and elderly scholar.

INVOKING THE AIR DEVAS

Sylphs are best contacted in high, open spaces where the wind blows freely, such as hillsides, mountains, grasslands, meadows, and open planes. They can be found in wind, clouds, rain, storms, and snowflakes. They can travel in the form of butterflies, ribbons, birds, feathers, dream catchers, thistledown, or dandelion seeds. Air spirits are he fastest moving in nature and form, changeable in action and mood, and unpredictable. They are movers of energy, carrying seeds for new life, stripping dead leaves from trees, and assisting birds on their migratory paths. To attract sylph energies, use wind chimes, trailing scarves, fragrances, feathers, mobiles, mist, bubbles *, and bird-call music. Make a wish on each butterfly you see or blow dandelion seeds softly into the air while stating your desires out loud or in your mind. If you are in need of clearer thought and memory, greater freedom or better communication skills, ask the Air devas for their help. They can help guide you if you have an important exam or journey to undertake, if you have to give a speech, or if you are doing anything that requires clear, swift thought and self-expression. To make contact with a sylph, make or acquire a dream catcher. A Native American craft, usually hoop-shaped with dangling beads and feathers, these are designed to 'catch' bad dreams and protect you while you sleep. Dream catchers can be adapted to attract sylphs however, although they can never really be caught, since they embody the essence of liberty and unencumbered flight. Perhaps you could get a new dream catcher for this very purpose and imbue it with your positive intentions through a special affirmation. When you become aware of your sylph stirring your dream catcher, ask for the specific help you are requiring, thank the sylph for his or her help, then set them free back into their realm of flight and freedom, knowing that their help has been given and their work done. Sylphs also respond well to the burning of incense, conscious breathing, and music. Suitable offerings are the crystals amethyst, diamond, sapphire, blue lace agate, sodalite, citrine, lapis lazuli, clear quartz, and turquoise, and essential oils and fragrances of lemongrass, bergamot, lavender, fennel, dill, almond, peppermint, sage, anise, and lemon verbena.

* You can send your wishes into the Air in the form of bubbles. Bubbles rise high and can carry them to the Air spirits who can transform your dreams and desires into reality. Wednesday and Thursday are particularly good days for Air elemental wish magic. Dawn is a good time to undertake your wish, especially when the wind is blowing noticeably but gently enough to carry your desire into the unseen ether.

★ ★ ★

DEVA MESSAGES FOR THE WATER ELEMENT

★ DIVINE MESSAGE FROM THE UNDINES FOR CANCER, SCORPIO & PISCES ★

"You, Cancer, Scorpio and Pisces, provide the Divine Life-Giving Waters of Life to all who take in your elixir, bringing out the inner emotional worlds within all that exists. You spread your kindness, love and compassion wherever you go, leaving a trail of Divine mist as you blaze your uniquely inspiring and life-sustaining trail wherever you go. Call upon me, the Undine, to help you to use your Divine gifts, using a blue candle, a chalice containing some sacred water, and honouring my presence in all bodies and droplets of my liquid essence that you encounter."

THE DEVIC REALMS & WATER ★ WEST: REALM OF THE UNDINES

The Water element, comprising of the three zodiac signs Cancer, Scorpio and Pisces, is connected with the West direction and the realm of Undines.

★ UNDINES ★

Undine is from the Latin *unda*, meaning 'wave', and therefore these spirits are said to control the waters of the Earth. Undines are perhaps the best known of the four elementals as they appear frequently in stories and legends. Usually female nymph-like beings, they are beautiful, eager to tempt, and enjoy associating with humans. They like to lure with their musical enchantments, creating sweet, intoxicating melodies with their harps, or singing pure, uplifting songs for those who are still and near enough to listen. Found wherever there is a natural source of water, the undines are responsible for the vitality within liquids and they also work with plants that grow underwater. All water upon our planet - rain, rivers, oceans, lakes, et cetera - has immense undine activity. Undines, like the gnomes, are subject to mortality, but they are more enduring. They are dependent upon humans for growth, and as we evolve, so do they.

One of the most famous of the Water elementals is the Lady of the Lake who features in the legends of King Arthur. This undine beauty rose from her lake to present Arthur with the sword Excalibur and captured the hearts of many of the Knights of the Round Table. The undines govern the realm of autumn and Water, the west, and the Cups in the Tarot deck. In many religions, water symbolises the initiation through baptism in the 'waters of life'. In ancient times all great rivers were considered holy and sacred, without which nothing could prosper; springs, wells, ponds, pools and fountains were regarded as holy places where great healing properties and energies could be found and prophecies foretold.

The Undines work to maintain the astral body of humans and to stimulate our feeling nature. This is associated with heightened psychic functions as well as emotional ones. Theirs is an energy of intuition, creation and birth. Undines guard and carry the secrets of the Dreamtime, inner visions, emotions, feelings and journeys.

Water is the springwell of life, and these beings are essential to our finding that springwell within. Essential to the gifts of healing, purification and empathy, they work with humans to help us discover both our inner and outer beauty. Human beings are made of around 75 per cent water, which acts as a channel or stream for all physical and chemical changes to occur; and the same percentage again is echoed by our planet's water composition - three quarters of the Earth's surface is covered by seas, rivers and oceans, which are governed by the Moon, which provides a natural rhythmical rulership over planetary phenomena. Folklore says that water gives to us what we give to it. The undines, who dwell in the Watery realms, will indeed do the same. The King of Water is Llyr or Nixa (or Necksa *), its archangel is Gabriel, its magickal tool is the Cup (which calls down the spirits into form), and its sacred ceremonial stones are Amethyst, Moonstone and Pearl.

* Necksa (or Nixa or Nicksa) is the Queen of the deep oceans who rides a chariot of pearl. Necksa is pulled by pure-white seahorses dressed in all the colours of the sea and has shells braiding her hair. She can endow the powers of good luck, granting wishes, fertility, love, marriage, reconciliation, peaceful endings and new beginnings, and psychic powers.

INVOKING THE WATER DEVAS

Water represents flow and change – in many myths crossing a stream signifies a shift in consciousness, all cultures regard water as the biggest life-giving source, and baptism is a rite of passage in some religions. Water is mysterious, moody and changeable, but is almost the easiest elemental to connect with as they are linked so strongly with human emotions. They are associated with compassion, inner harmony, gradual growth, natural cycles, unconscious wisdom, purity, peacemaking, and blessings for babies, children and families. Water devas embody all of these attributes and most are hauntingly beautiful. Water can be a tricky medium to work with, but overall they help to connect you with the wellsprings of your feelings, bringing sympathy, empathy and the bonds of human love, endowing their gifts of purification, healing and cleansing. If you are feeling raw, lonely, sad, uncared for or buffeted by life, ask the water devas for their help. They can be found in any body of water, the tides and the rains, in mists and in fogs, estuaries, springs, aquariums, floods plains, streams, oceans, pools and ponds, rivers and tidal rivers, whirlpools, marshlands, sacred wells, and waterfalls. To attract undines into your experience, you can use silver, copper, kelp, scrying bowls, crystal spheres, some essential oils ^, certain crystals *, wine offerings, steam, water features, misty mirrors, fish in tanks, and silver bells on cords. Undines will give you blessings when you are going into any situation that requires deep emotional strength.

^ Some essential oils you can use to attract water spirits are coconut, jasmine, lemon, lilac, orchid, lily, heather, sweet pea, orchid, violet, peach, passion flower, vanilla, strawberry, myrrh, eucalyptus, hyacinth, and apple blossom.

* Some crystals that can help to bring undines into your experience are calcite, fluorite, aquamarine, mother of pearl, jade, opal, coral, moonstone, selenite, and pearl.

God & Goddess Messages

ABOUT GODS & GODDESSES

Let us be silent, for so are the gods.

Ancient Saying

For thirty years I sought God. But when I looked carefully, I found that in reality God was the seeker and I was the sought.

Bayazid Bastami

It is not necessary to go off on a tour of great cathedrals in order to find the Deity. Look within. You have to sit still to do it.

Albert Schweitzer

Your zodiac gods and goddesses were chosen based upon your ruling luminary (the Sun or Moon) or your ruling planet, which were named after mythological gods and goddesses of the ancient world, making them effectively your governing entities. Your god or goddess has a special zodiac message for you, and through heeding their very special messages and embracing their archetypal energies, essences and symbolism, your journey can be illuminated and enhanced.

INVOKING YOUR GOD OR GODDESS

The word 'prediction' comes from the same root as *predicament*, which is nearly always something unpleasant; prophecy, however, implies collaboration with the Divine in order to co-create the most loving, ingenious and interesting life possible. True help is always reciprocal: whatever we help serves us. The word therapy means 'healing' but its original meaning was 'to serve the gods'. Similarly, the Mayan word for human meant 'one who owes the gods'. We serve the gods, internally and externally, in a dance of reciprocal generosity. When we work for the gods, they work for us.

Caroline W. Casey

The only way the gods and angels know we're asking for help is through ritual. One principle (of requesting help from the other-worlds) is that the invisible world would like to help, but spiritual etiquette requires that we ask. Help is always available. Operators are standing by.

Caroline W. Casey

The Goddess and the God can help us change our lives. Because the Deities *are* the creative forces of the Universe, we call upon Them to empower our rites and to bless our magic. This is what makes Wicca a truly satisfying way of life. We have direct links with the Deities. No intermediaries are needed; no priests or confessors or shamans. *We are the shamans.*

Unknown

To invoke a god or goddess is to send an appeal or petition to a higher power (or powers) to them and bring their essence and blessings into your own energy or experience. Invocation is also a method of establishing conscious ties with those aspects of the goddess and god that dwell within us. In essence, then, we seemingly cause them to appear or make themselves known by becoming aware of them. Be aware that if consistently call upon one particular deity power to the exclusion of all others, you will eventually begin to manifest characteristics of that energy pool within your personality. If this is done correctly in order to gain positive results, these changes will become an important part of your magical personality. You can call in beneficial, powerful entities and deities using: Cinnamon, Gardenia, Frankincense, Rose and Sandalwood.

THE PLANETARY POWERS, GODS & GODDESSES

Each planet has its own distinctive and original meaning which, according to its position in the zodiac, combines with the qualities that are inherent in each of the twelve astrological signs. If a planet is your sign's ruler, however, it exerts a significant influence upon your life, regardless of its birth chart or zodiacal position.

The birth chart is a symbolic map of one's contract with life. The planets represent different kinds of intelligence, different parts of the psyche. When we feed each part of ourselves, as represented by the planets, we bloom as individuals.

The planets move against the backdrop of the zodiac wheel, which is the outer circle of the chart. The zodiac signs give the planets their flavouring, their myriad permutations of expression, and tells us how they will express themselves in our lives.

Planetary Meditation

I am my Earth (my body), and my Sky (my transcendence)
I am my Sun (my spirit), and my Moon (my soul)
I am my Venus (my pleasure), and my Jupiter (my faith)
I am my Mars (my courage), and my Saturn (my lessons)
I am my Mercury (my thoughts), and my Uranus (my truth)
I am my Neptune (my dreams), and my Pluto (my transformation)

GOD & GODDESS MESSAGES FOR THE ZODIAC

ARIES

♈

MESSAGE FROM MARS

"I am your ruling planet Mars, and I am the great warrior, associated with Action, Drive, Competition, Desire, Courage, Force, Vitality, Impulse, Bravery, Passion, Initiative, Sexuality, Power, Ego, Achievement, Ambition, Wilfulness, Vigour, Assertion, Confidence, Territoriality, Conquering and Overcoming, Energy, Motivation, Aggression, Will, One's Masculine Side, Confrontation, Battle, Enthusiasm, Virility, Heat and Dynamism. Named after the Roman god of war and spring, I am the planet most concerned with the way we assert ourselves and what it is that drives us, propels us forward. I am always shown powerfully built and dressed for adventure and the battlefield. I am the great achiever god. I can and will perform any task you set for me. In order to attain your goals, you must let me know exactly what you desire - the more details you give me, the less I will be led astray. My force will work to bring your wishes to manifestation for as long as you hold the image firmly in mind, maintain your focus, and continue to work at it through your own initiates and actions also. And *work* is the operative word here, as I am no dreamer. My Martian energy and influence, throughout your whole life, bestows upon you the gifts of courage, independence, assertiveness, self-confidence, boldness, heroism, passion, directness, courage, endurance, initiative, willpower, determination, ambition, enterprise and mighty strength. The Mars-inspired Arian spirit will always triumph over any odds; after all, your motto is '*I*

Am', because quite simply, you just *are*, no frills, pretences or façades. How will you use my phenomenally powerful Martian influence in your life?"

DIVINE MESSAGE FROM THE GOD MARS ★ "Aries, I am the Warrior God and Brave Crusader, and I give you the gifts of strength, courage and an indefatigable optimism, that carry you through all life's inevitable battles with pure glory, a natural charisma, and an unwavering love that radiates from your innermost core. Being born under my Divine influence imprints your soul with my essence. I reside in you always, from birth through to death and beyond if you so desire and ensure that you operate through my best and highest qualities at all times. If it feels like I am not within you, then that may be because you are not honouring me properly, your Inner Warrior. You can invoke and thus honour me during the first dawn hour of a Tuesday, using a red candle, a piece of red coral, and the element of Fire."

To Invoke Mars

Day ★ Tuesday
Number ★ 9
Intelligence ★ Graphiel
Spirit ★ Bartzabel
Basic Energy & Magic ★ Action, Motivation
Colours ★ Strong Reds, Scarlet, Magenta, Autumnal Shades
Gods/Goddesses/Angel ★ Ares, Mars, Samael
Metals ★ Iron, Steel, Brass
Gems/Minerals ★ Ruby, Amethyst, Diamond, Red Jasper, Pyrite, Bloodstone
Malachite, Lodestone, Garnet, Flint, Carnelian, Hematite
Trees/Shrubs ★ Monkey-puzzle, Heather, Holly, Pine, Hawthorn
Flowers/Herbs ★ Nasturtium, Nettle, Allspice, Tobacco, Garlic
Wood ★ Mahogany
Fabric ★ Tweed
Animals ★ Tiger, Falcon, Wolf, Snake
Element ★ Fire
Zodiac Signs ★ Aries, Scorpio

★ OTHER GODS & GODDESSES ARIES CAN SUMMON FOR ASSISTANCE, GUIDANCE OR CONNECTION ★

Artemis, Bellona, Nerio, Minerva, Ares, Athena, Minerva, Mercury, Ashur

★ ★ ★

TAURUS

♉

MESSAGE FROM VENUS

"Taurus, I am your ruler, the beautiful Morning or Evening 'Star' Venus. I am The Lover, the Charmer, the Romantic and the Artist, associated with Love, Beauty, Unison, Harmony, Affection, Desire, Enjoyment, Relating, Relationships, Acceptance, Social Graces, Vanity, Sociability, Persuasion, Luxury, Aesthetics, Outward Style, Indulgence, Refinement, Values, Comfort, Resources, Art, Agreeableness, Good Humour, Symmetry, Proportion, Mutuality and Sympathy. I can tell you how you express affection and appreciate beauty and show the sort of relationships and people you attract, as well as your behaviour in love. I show you how you give and receive, appreciate, and merge with others. I influence your feelings and motivations and govern your more outer emotional self. Whether you regard the planets as springs of cosmic activity or as symbols, the astrological importance of my powers is easy to understand. I am commonly known as the *planet of love*, which is an over-simplification, but I do have a potent effect on your motivations, tastes, feelings, desires and what you are drawn towards. I also govern how you relate to other people socially and economically and have an influence on your attitude to money and possessions. Being your ruler, in the Taurean spirit I symbolise a strong need for comfort, nourishment, love and affection, and the desire for peace and balance deep within you. My Venusian energy and influence, throughout your whole life, bestows upon you the gifts of grace, equability, an easygoing nature, charm, accommodating to others' needs, cooperation, affection, tact, kindness, friendliness, refinement, appreciation for beauty, aesthetic awareness and placidity. Too much of this Venusian energy can make you vain, lazy, indecisive, weak-willed, dependent, careless, impractical, promiscuous, manipulative, possessive, overly romantic, self-indulgent and greedy. But the Taurean always knows what keeps her soul in perfect harmony; after all your motto is, '*I Possess*', and possession of all things beautiful to you, including relationships, gives you all the security you'll ever need. How will you use my phenomenally powerful Venusian influence in your life?"

DIVINE MESSAGE FROM THE GODDESS VENUS ✶ "Taurus, I am the Goddess of Love and Beauty, I give you the gifts of love, beauty, artistic appreciation, money and relating, gifts which carry you through all life's inevitable ups and downs with unwavering love, peace and acceptance, that radiates from your innermost core. Being born under my Divine influence imprints your soul with my essence. I reside in you always, from birth through to death and beyond if you so desire and ensure that you operate through my best and highest qualities at all times. If it feels like I am not within you, then that may be because you are not honouring me properly, your Inner Love Goddess. You can invoke and thus honour me during the first dawn hour of a Friday, using a pink or green candle, a diamond, and a symbol of a pentagram (which denotes the path of Venus in the cosmos)."

To Invoke Venus

Day ★ Friday
Number ★ 6
Intelligences ★ Hagiel, Beni Seraphim
Spirit ★ Kedemel
Basic Energy & Magic ★ Love, Sociability
Colours ★ Light Blue, Green, Pink, Soft Yellow, Pastels
Gods/Goddesses/Angel ★ Aphrodite, Venus, Raphael
Metals ★ Copper, Bronze, Brass
Gems/Minerals ★ Jade, Lapis Lazuli, Rose Quartz, Emerald, Kunzite, Peridot, Malachite (Copper Ore), Sapphire, Green Aventurine, Carnelian Chrysolite, Green Jasper
Trees/Shrubs ★ Peach, Pear, Alder, Ash, Birch, Cypress, Fig, Almond
Flowers/Fruits/Herbs ★ Rose, Carnation, Lilac, Pomegranate, Apple
Wood ★ Sycamore
Fabric ★ Satin
Animals ★ Cat, Dove, Sparrow
Element ★ Air
Zodiac Signs ★ Taurus, Libra

★ OTHER GODS & GODDESSES TAURUS CAN SUMMON FOR ASSISTANCE, GUIDANCE OR CONNECTION ★

Ceres, Lakshmi, Aphrodite, Eros, Freya, Brigid, Hymen, Vulcan, Kwan Yin (Quan Yin)

★   ★   ★

GEMINI

♊

MESSAGE FROM MERCURY

"I am Mercury, your ruler, the Great Communicator, Learner and Eternal Student. I am associated with Information, Communication, Movement, Mobility, Intellect, Change, Adaptability, Rational Thinking, Learning, Analysis, Dissemination, Synchronicity, Perception, Inventiveness, Correspondence, Short Trips, Transportation, Eloquence, Knowledge, Assimilation, Cunning, Coordination, Logic, Expression, Interpretation, Thought Deduction and Adaptation. I am the fastest planet and I guide your fluid, speedy Sun sign. In Gemini, I express myself in an experimental, eloquent, jubilant, open-minded and sometimes scattered but ever-luminous way of thinking. I make you conversational, intellectual, sociable and happy to share ideas with others on a wide variety of subjects. Always pictured with wings on my feet, to represent the speed of thought and the ceaseless activity of the mind, I symbolise all things intellectual and linked with communication. In some mythology, I am a direct descendent of Hermes, the messenger of Zeus, and the god of magic and travels. The deity of roads, protector of travellers, god of doorways, commerce and thievery, of good and bad luck, of treasure troves, of honest and dishonest gain, I am widely known as a cunning, clever trickster. Using the nimble wit for which I was always noted in the ancient world, I am the immortal go-getter, a lightning flash whose mental frequency is always switched to 'high'; in essence, I am a god who gets things done. I encourage you to listen, respond, learn and reflect and then finally, disperse the knowledge you have acquired for the benefit of others. Being a prominent principle in your life as your ruling planet, I give you the gifts of a quick wit, ingenuity, adaptability, humour and a love of study and learning. Watch that you don't take on my shadowy side, which can make you changeable, cunning, exaggerating, nervous, temperamental, quarrelsome, superficial or indecisive. My Mercurial energy and influence, throughout your whole life, bestows upon you the gifts of versatility, sharp perception, adaptability, intelligence, reason, cleverness and wit. Too much of this Mercurial energy can make you restless, critical, lacking in imagination, argumentative, inconsistent, non-committal, insubstantial, cynical, immature, overly mind-based, neurotic, tense, flighty, unreliable, and unable to see the forest for the trees. But the Geminian's key phrase is '*I Think*', and your thoughts are always off in the sky somewhere flying high as a kite in the Airy substance your element is made of, never quite touching the ground of earthly realities but always connecting with the Ethereal entities such as myself. How will you use my phenomenally powerful Mercurial influence in your life?"

DIVINE MESSAGE FROM THE GOD MERCURY ✯ "Gemini, I am the God of Mental Gifts, and I endow you with cleverness, high-mindedness, and an eloquent intelligence, that carry you through all life's inevitable ups and downs with pure wit, charm and Mercurial dazzle, that radiate from your innermost core. Being born under my Divine influence imprints your soul with my essence. I reside in you always, from birth through to death and beyond if you so desire and ensure that you operate through my best and highest qualities at all times. If it feels like I am not within you, then that may be because you are not honouring me properly, your Inner Genius. You can invoke and thus honour me during the first dawn hour of a Wednesday, using a yellow candle, a piece of emerald, and the element of Air."

To Invoke Mercury

Day ★ Wednesday
Number ★ 5
Intelligence ★ Tiriel
Spirit ★ Taphthartharath
Basic Energy & Magic ★ Speed, Communication
Colours ★ Yellow, Silver, Blue, Metallics, Mixed Hues, Checks, Plaids
Gods/Goddesses/Angel ★ Hermes, Mercury, Thoth, Raphael
Metals ★ Quicksilver, Zinc
Gems/Minerals ★ Citrine, Agate, Carnelian, Opal, Emerald, Tiger's Eye,
Topaz, Sardonyx, Chalcedony, Glass
Trees/Shrubs ★ Hazel, Forsythia, Filbert, Myrtle, Mulberry
Flowers/Herbs ★ Bittersweet, Fern, Lavender
Wood ★ Beech
Fabric ★ Linen
Animals ★ Monkey, Magpie, Hare
Element ★ Air
Zodiac Signs ★ Gemini, Virgo

★ OTHER GODS & GODDESSES GEMINI CAN SUMMON FOR ASSISTANCE, GUIDANCE OR CONNECTION ★

Hermes, Thoth, Apollo

★   ★   ★

CANCER

♋

MESSAGE FROM THE MOON

"I am the Moon, your ruler, and I am associated with the Emotions, Intuition, Habits, the Subconscious, Instincts, Moods, Fluctuations, Cycles, Memories and Feeling. I am planet Earth's nearest celestial neighbour and exert a great influence upon the Earth and all life that dwells upon it, including - and especially - *you*! There are four main phases in the Lunar cycle (New Moon, First Quarter, Full Moon and Last Quarter), each one an expression of energy reflecting a particular mode of activity and emotional response. The influence of each phase can be felt in two ways: in the formation of your personality and in your day-to-day life and magic. And because my Lunar pattern repeats itself every month, you will find that you can also pace yourself on a long-term basis, to achieve your highest self and greatest desires. This will enable you to effectively target your efforts and goals on periods of time that you know will be auspicious to you. My powerful but gentle energy can be such that there are certain phases during which you will notice you have abundant energy, feel inspired and can generate new ideas with ease. During this period, you should work towards the fruition of your efforts, bring your dreams into light and reach for the stars! My Lunar energy and influence, throughout your whole life, bestows upon you the gifts of sensitivity, adaptability, sympathy, receptivity, empathy and imagination. Too much of this Lunar energy can make one dependent, clingy, moody, prone to martyrdom, neurotic, withdrawn, inconsistent, and lack leadership and courage. But the Cancerian always listens to the quiet whispers of her inner lunar self, and trusts her heart and follows her intuition: after all, your motto is *'I Feel'*, because deep down, you really do *feel* your and intuit way through life, your face always turned towards light of the Sun. How will you use my phenomenally powerful Lunar influence in your life?"

MESSAGE FROM THE MOON ★ "Cancer, I am the Moon, the Celestial Illuminator of Feelings. I reach your aura through the Triple Goddess, and my gifts are three-fold. As the Universal Mother, I have three faces: the Maiden, the Mother and the Crone. I am the source of fertility, endless wisdom, and loving caresses. My threefold aspects encompass youth and enchantment (the Maiden), maturity and fulfilment (the Mother), and old age and wisdom (the Crone). I am omnipresent, changeless, eternal. I give you the gifts of intuition, loyalty, imagination, and a deep love of those you hold dear, that carry you through all life's inevitable ups and downs with empathy, understanding, and a signature luminescent charm, that radiate from your innermost core. Being born under my Divine influence imprints your soul with my essence. I reside in you always, from birth through to death and beyond if you so desire and ensure that you operate through my best and highest qualities at all times. If it feels like I am not within you, then that may be because you are not honouring me properly, your Inner Child. You can invoke and thus honour me during the first dawn hour of a Monday, using a silver or white candle, a pearl, the element of Water, and a symbol of the Triple Goddess."

To Invoke the Moon

Day ★ Monday
Number ★ 2
Intelligences ★ Chashmodai, Tarshism, Malcah Betarshisim Ve-Ad Ruachoth Ha-Schechalim
Spirits ★ Chashmodai, Shad Barschemoth Haschartathan
Basic Energy & Magic ★ Emotions, Intuition
Colours ★ Silver, Pastel Shades, White, Blue, Cream, Silvery Grey, Opalescent & Iridescent Hues
Gods/Goddesses/Angel ★ Artemis, Luna, Gabriel, Selene, Diana, Hecarte, Isis
Metals ★ Silver, Aluminum
Gems/Minerals ★ Moonstone, Opal, Pearl, Selenite, Emerald, Angelite,

Celestite, Diamond, Beryl, Clear Quartz
Trees/Shrubs ★ Willow, Hawthorn, Silver Birch, Lemon, Eucalyptus
Sycamore, Tamarind, Maple, Alder
Flowers/Herbs ★ Convolvulus, Watercress, Myrrh, Poppy, Jasmine,
Lotus, Clary Sage, Rosewood, Wintergreen, Ylang Ylang, Mimosa,
Freesia, Chamomile, Gardenia, Lemon Balm, Lily
Wood ★ Birch
Fabric ★ Silk
Animals ★ Crab, Owl
Element ★ Water
Zodiac Sign ★ Cancer

★ OTHER GODS & GODDESSES CANCER CAN SUMMON FOR ASSISTANCE, GUIDANCE OR CONNECTION ★

Diana, Selene, Isis, Luna, Hecate, Phoebe, Artemis, Mercury, Hermes, Neptune

★ ★ ★

LEO

♌

MESSAGE FROM THE SUN

"I am the Sun, your ruler, and I am powerfully associated with your Authentic Self, Essence, Identity, Ego, Creativity, Life Force, Will, Spirit and Life's True Purpose. I am the generator of life, the channel through which your self-expression is expressed outward, and the motivating force behind all your activities. As a Child of the Sun, you are the quintessential Solar-Powered Golden Child! In essence, I am your pure conscious self, your authentic, pure *be*-ing, as I am not veiled by superficialities or façades. Tear all your masks and pretences down, and you are left with me, your guiding light the Sun. I am your personal powerhouse, your genuine and essential self, before you were conditioned by external influences and the limitations and imposed fears of others. Through me, you always were and always will be. Before you 'become' your Sun however, I am the energy that holds together the disparate parts of your-self until these can be integrated as you develop and mature. You will grow into me, but I have always been in you, waiting patiently and lovingly as you gradually embrace me until I become your whole inner *and* outer self. Leo, my Solar energy and influence, throughout your whole life, bestows upon you the gifts of luminosity, benevolence, leadership, playfulness, nobility, magnanimity, generosity and an abundance of creative expression. The pure Leo is really just an overgrown, exuberant, bounding kitten with a heart wide enough to embrace many, and a strength that allows you to rule the kingdom and conquer the enemy; after all, your motto is *'I Will'*, because deep down, you undoubtedly *will*. How will you use my phenomenally powerful Solar influence in your life?"

MESSAGE FROM THE SUN ★ "Leo, I am the Sun, your Pure Life Force. I give you the gifts of love, charm, flair, charisma and leadership, which carry you through all life's inevitable battles with dazzling charm and determination, that radiate from your innermost core. Being born under my Divine influence imprints your soul with my essence. I reside in you always, from birth through to death and beyond if you so desire and ensure that you operate through my best and highest qualities at all times. If it feels like I am not within you, then that may be because you are not honouring me properly, your Inner Light. You can invoke and thus honour me during the first dawn hour of a Sunday, using a gold candle, a stone of ruby, and the element of Fire."

To Invoke the Sun

Day ★ Sunday
Number ★ 1
Intelligence ★ Nakhiel
Spirit ★ Sorath
Basic Energy & Magic ★ Will, Success
Colours ★ Gold, Orange, Deep Yellow
Gods/Goddesses/Angel ★ Helios, Sol, Apollo, Amun-Ra, Michael
Metal ★ Gold, Brass
Gems/Minerals ★ Diamond, Amber, Citrine, Topaz, Chrysoprase, Ruby, Hyacinth, Chrysolite, Yellow Sapphire, Goldstone
Trees/Shrubs ★ Juniper, Laurel, Palm
Flowers/Herbs ★ Marigold, Saffron, Sunflowers, Cinnamon, Peony, Musk, Frankincense, Yellow Poppy, Chamomile, Mistletoe, Almond, Heliotrope
Wood ★ Walnut
Animals ★ Lion, Hawk
Element ★ Fire
Zodiac Sign ★ Leo

★ OTHER GODS & GODDESSES LEO CAN SUMMON FOR ASSISTANCE, GUIDANCE OR CONNECTION ★

Apollo, Ra, Sol, Helios, Jove, Zeus, Jupiter

★ ★ ★

VIRGO

♍

MESSAGE FROM MERCURY

"I am Mercury, your ruler, the speediest planet and the archetypal Great Communicator, Learner and Eternal Student. I am associated with Information, Communication, Movement, Mobility, Intellect, Change, Adaptability, Rational Thinking, Learning, Analysis, Dissemination, Synchronicity, Perception, Inventiveness, Correspondence, Short Trips, Transportation, Eloquence, Knowledge, Assimilation, Cunning, Coordination, Logic, Expression, Interpretation, Thought Deduction and Adaptation. Always pictured with wings on his feet, to represent the speed of thought and the ceaseless activity of the mind, Mercury symbolises all things intellectual and linked with communication. In some mythology, he is a direct descendent of Hermes, the messenger of Zeus, and the god of travels. The deity of roads, protector of travellers, god of doorways, commerce and thievery, of good and bad luck, of treasure troves, of honest and dishonest gain, Mercury is widely known as a thief and a cunning trickster. Using the nimble wit for which Mercury was noted, he was an immortal go-getter, a lightning flash whose mental frequency was always switched to 'high', a god who gets things done. Mercury gathers the energy from any information we attract and compresses it into usable form; it can be likened to the wire through which the current flows. As such, I encourage listening and responding, learning and reflecting. However, Mercury's charm, quick wit and cleverness requires positive direction, for he can just as easily turn into a prankster and cheat as into a brilliant scientific genius. Being prominent in your chart as your ruling planet, Mercury gives you the gift of a quick wit, ingenuity, adaptability, humour, and a love of study and argument. If it is disharmoniously aspected, however, it can give you a changeable, cunning or exaggerating mind, a nervous and excitable temperament, and a tendency to be quarrelsome, superficial or indecisive. My Mercurial energy and influence, throughout your whole life, bestows upon you the gifts of logical thinking, rational thought, an above average intelligence, cleverness, attentiveness, sharp perceptions, and an inquisitive intellect. Too much of this Mercurial energy can make one restless, critical, superficial, lacking in imagination, argumentative, inconsistent, non-committal, insubstantial, cynical, immature, overly mind-based, neurotic, nervous, tense, flighty, unreliable, and unable to see the forest for the trees. The Virgo's key phrase is '*I Analyse*', which is a perfect banner for your refreshingly discerning nature and powers of breaking down the big picture into bite-sized, manageable pieces, but which can be your downfall or your greatest strength. How will you use my phenomenally powerful Mercurial influence in your life?"

DIVINE MESSAGE FROM THE GOD MERCURY ★ "Virgo, I am the God of Mental Gifts, and I bestow upon you the gifts of cleverness, high-mindedness, and an eloquent intelligence, that carry you through all life's inevitable ups and downs with pure wit, wisdom, and a signature Mercurial dazzle, that radiate from your innermost core. Being born under my Divine influence imprints your soul with my essence. I reside in you always, from birth through to death and beyond if you so desire and ensure that you operate through my best and highest qualities at all times. If it feels like I am not within you, then that may be because you are not honouring me properly, your Inner Genius. You can invoke and thus honour me during the first dawn hour of a Wednesday, using a yellow candle, a piece of emerald, and the element of Air."

To Invoke Mercury

Day ★ Wednesday
Number ★ 5
Intelligence ★ Tiriel
Spirit ★ Taphthartharath
Basic Energy & Magic ★ Speed, Communication
Colours ★ Yellow, Silver, Blue, Metallics, Mixed Hues, Checks, Plaids
Gods/Goddesses/Angel ★ Hermes, Mercury, Thoth, Raphael
Metals ★ Quicksilver, Zinc
Gems/Minerals ★ Citrine, Agate, Carnelian, Opal, Emerald, Tiger's Eye, Topaz, Sardonyx, Chalcedony, Glass
Trees/Shrubs ★ Hazel, Forsythia, Filbert, Myrtle, Mulberry
Flowers/Herbs ★ Bittersweet, Fern, Lavender
Wood ★ Beech
Fabric ★ Linen
Animals ★ Monkey, Magpie, Hare
Element ★ Air
Zodiac Signs ★ Gemini, Virgo

★ OTHER GODS & GODDESSES VIRGO CAN SUMMON FOR ASSISTANCE, GUIDANCE OR CONNECTION ★

Ceres, Hermes, Thoth, Demeter, Vesta, Chiron

★   ★   ★

LIBRA

♎

MESSAGE FROM VENUS

"Libra, I am your ruler, the beautiful Morning or Evening 'Star' Venus. I am The Lover, the Charmer, the Romantic and the Artist, associated with Love, Beauty, Unison, Harmony, Affection, Desire, Enjoyment, Relating, Relationships, Acceptance, Social Graces, Vanity, Sociability, Persuasion, Luxury, Aesthetics, Outward Style, Indulgence, Refinement, Values, Comfort, Resources, Art, Agreeableness, Good Humour, Symmetry, Proportion, Mutuality and Sympathy. I can tell you how you express affection and appreciate beauty and show the sort of relationships and people you attract, as well as your behaviour in love. I show you how you give and receive, appreciate, and merge with others. I influence your feelings and motivations and govern your more outer emotional self. Whether you regard the planets as springs of cosmic activity or as symbols, the astrological importance of my powers is easy to understand. I am commonly known as the *planet of love*, which is an over-simplification, but I do have a potent effect on your motivations, tastes, feelings, desires and what you are drawn towards. I also govern how you relate to other people socially and economically and have an influence on your attitude to money and possessions. Being your ruler, in the Libran spirit I symbolise a strong need for comfort, nourishment, love and affection, and the desire for peace and balance deep within you. My Venusian energy and influence, throughout your whole life, gives Librans the gifts of grace, equability, an easygoing nature, charm, accommodating to others' needs, cooperation, affection, tact, kindness, friendliness, refinement, appreciation for beauty, aesthetic awareness and placidity. Too much of this Venusian energy can make you vain, lazy, indecisive, weak-willed, dependent, careless, impractical, promiscuous, manipulative, possessive, overly romantic, self-indulgent and greedy. But the Libran always knows what keeps her soul in perfect harmony; after all, your motto is '*I Balance*', because deep down, you fear being out of kilter in any area of life regarding relationships, money and overall comfort. How will you use my phenomenally powerful Venusian influence in your life?"

DIVINE MESSAGE FROM THE GODDESS VENUS ✶ "Libra, I am the Goddess of Love and Beauty, and I give you the gifts of love, beauty, artistic appreciation, money and relating, gifts which carry you through all life's inevitable ups and downs with unwavering love, peace and acceptance, that radiates from your innermost core. Being born under my Divine influence imprints your soul with my essence. I reside in you always, from birth through to death and beyond if you so desire and ensure that you operate through my best and highest qualities at all times. If it feels like I am not within you, then that may be because you are not honouring me properly, your Inner Love Goddess. You can invoke and thus honour me during the first dawn hour of a Friday, using a pink or green candle, a diamond, and a symbol of a pentagram (which denotes the path of Venus in the cosmos)."

To Invoke Venus

Day ★ Friday
Number ★ 6
Intelligences ★ Hagiel, Beni Seraphim
Spirit ★ Kedemel
Basic Energy & Magic ★ Love, Sociability
Colours ★ Light Blue, Green, Pink, Soft Yellow, Pastels
Gods/Goddesses/Angel ★ Aphrodite, Venus, Raphael
Metals ★ Copper, Bronze, Brass
Gems/Minerals ★ Jade, Lapis Lazuli, Rose Quartz, Emerald, Kunzite, Peridot, Malachite (Copper Ore), Sapphire, Green Aventurine, Carnelian Chrysolite, Green Jasper
Trees/Shrubs ★ Peach, Pear, Alder, Ash, Birch, Cypress, Fig, Almond
Flowers/Fruits/Herbs ★ Rose, Carnation, Lilac, Pomegranate, Apple
Wood ★ Sycamore
Fabric ★ Satin
Animals ★ Cat, Dove, Sparrow
Element ★ Air
Zodiac Signs ★ Taurus, Libra

★ OTHER GODS & GODDESSES LIBRA CAN SUMMON FOR ASSISTANCE, GUIDANCE OR CONNECTION ★

Lakshmi, Aphrodite, Eros, Freya, Brigid, Hymen, Juno, Hera, Vulcan, Dionysus, Hephaestus, Pallas Athene

★ ★ ★

SCORPIO

♏

MESSAGE FROM PLUTO

"I am your ruling planet Pluto, the Powerful Undercover Agent of Change, Transformation and Regeneration, powerfully associated with Death, Rebirth, Power, Renewal, Passion, Penetration, Yearning, Elimination, Control, Metamorphism, Eruptions, Sex, Penetration, Insight, Self-mastery, Occult, Hidden

Secrets, Obsession, Transmutation, Charisma, Riches, Magnetism, Subversion, Psychoanalysis, Research and Compulsion. For eighteen years before it was discovered, Pluto was called planet X, a factor which was known to exist but could not be found. Pluto, or Hades as he was known to the Greeks, was the ruler of the dead and the underworld. He was the son of Saturn and brother of Jupiter and Neptune. Jupiter came to rule the skies and Neptune inherited power over the oceans, leaving Pluto to rule the underworld. The ancients associated Pluto with wealth and riches because underground gold and other precious stones and minerals were said to dwell in his domain and be in his custody. Greek mythology therefore depicted Pluto as the god of wealth and buried treasure, and the word 'plutocracy', which refers to a government ruled by a group of rich men, derives its title from Pluto. But when one's life is unbalanced and there is a total and absolute focus on the attainment of material wealth without the development of the spiritual wealth inside, Pluto can see to it that the slate is wiped clean and have devastating effects on the tides of fortune. Pluto rules intense energy and describes the areas in which you consciously or unconsciously seek to exercise power or control. It reveals the areas in which you must gain the deepest level of understanding. But it can also reveal contradictions in yourself. Pluto can present us with maddening paradoxes: it is both an annihilator and transformer, constructive and destructive, psychiatric healing and brainwashing propaganda, self-destructive and self-empowering, use and misuse of power, mass communication and mass hysteria, intense hatred and consuming love, toxic build-ups and swift disposal. Pluto tells us about our urge for transformation, penetration, power, self-mastery and how we access deep insights. Associated with renewal and rebirth, Pluto represents endings and new beginnings, as well as spiritual growth and transformative powers. Pluto's energy can be linked to many analogies and metaphors: a snake shedding its skin to allow its new self to emerge, the caterpillar morphing into a butterfly, autumn leaves decomposing so that a tree may grow from the resultant nutrients in the soil. In its role as the transformer, it brings about the end of one form so that another form may be brought to life. This sometimes requires total disintegration in order to rebuild from scratch. Pluto represents the change within - the earthquake, the volcano and the powerful seed. But first we must understand the nature of crisis, in that it is not always the disaster it may seem and offers opportunity for upward growth. In fact, the Chinese character is the same for both words: crisis = opportunity. Pluto reveals not only our purpose and powers of regeneration, but our style of evolutionary growth, self-destruction and renewal, and our interest or otherwise in the occult, black magic, release, purging, catharsis, resurrection, metamorphism, the underworld, obsessions, corruption and hidden powers. Pluto is the 'journey to empowerment', showing the path from unresolved pain into empowerment and freedom. By our very natures, and as a kind of self-protective survival mechanism, we tend to repress trauma, grief, loss, unresolved painful feelings or potentially damaging hidden secrets. All that is repressed is the domain of Pluto. Chaos, drama and betrayal can all ensue as a result of stored emotions. Though Pluto often puts us through this process of initiation by imposing loss, pain, grief and darkness, he also symbolises the rising up again through resurrection. And herein lies his greatest power: rebirth. The Plutonian descent is inevitably linked with a subsequent resurfacing. People with a strong Pluto in their chart are attracted to mysteries and probe to get to the bottom of things, and can often be found in police work, scientific and medical research, paranormal studies and psychoanalytical work where an essential quality is the courage to face pain and disturbing or difficult truths. Upon Pluto-ruled Scorpios, this planet endows a sense of dynamism, mystery, power, magnetism, intensity, secretiveness, courage, perceptiveness, and yearnings to transform oneself. Too much Plutonian influence can make one suspicious, secretive, malicious, controlling, piercing, vengeful, explosive, manipulative, ruthless and power-hungry. More than any other planet, Pluto symbolises the miraculous ability of the human will to triumph over all odds, like the mythological phoenix rising, reborn and renewed, from the ashes of the battleground. It is no coincidence that the phoenix is potent symbol for Scorpio. This mythological bird's metaphor, above all else, encapsulates the essence of the Pluto-inspired Scorpio spirit. How will you use my phenomenally powerful Plutonian influence in your life?"

DIVINE MESSAGE FROM THE GOD PLUTO ★ "Scorpio, as God of the Underworld, I give you the gifts of death and rebirth, resurrection, catharsis and purging. I rule over your hidden riches and personal power, which carry you through all life's inevitable battles with dazzling insight, perceptive brilliance and deep intuition, that radiate from your innermost core. Being born under my Divine influence imprints your soul with my vital and potent essence. I reside in you always, from birth through to death and beyond if you so desire and ensure that you operate through my best and highest qualities at all times. If it feels like I am not within you, then that may be because you are not honouring me properly, your Inner Truth. You can invoke and thus honour me during the first dawn hour of a Tuesday, using a deep purple candle, a Fire Opal, and any magical materials representing the elements of Fire or Water."

To Invoke Pluto

Deities ★ Hades, Persephone, Demeter
Basic Energy & Magic ★ Transformation, Personal Power
Colours ★ Dark Reds, Black, Dark Purple, Magenta, Violet, Ultraviolet (beyond sight)
Gems/Minerals ★ Jade, Pearl, Beryl, Smoky Quartz, Black Obsidian, Jet, Kunzite
Metal ★ Plutonium
Flowers ★ Narcissus, Daffodil
Tree ★ Cypress
Zodiac Sign ★ Scorpio

★ OTHER GODS & GODDESSES SCORPIO CAN SUMMON FOR ASSISTANCE, GUIDANCE OR CONNECTION ★

Hades, Persephone, Anubis, Hecate, Osiris, Mars, Ares, Vesta, Juno

★ ★ ★

SAGITTARIUS

♐

MESSAGE FROM JUPITER

"I am the mighty Jupiter, your ruling planet, the Great Benefic, Expander and Bringer of Joy. I am associated with Expansion, Luck, Abundance, Faith, Ethics, Morals, Wisdom, Ideals, Inflation, Generosity, Travel, Philosophy, Beliefs, Knowledge, Enthusiasm, Conscience, Religion, Trust, Hope, Vision, Justice, Opportunities, Joy, Benevolence, Optimism, Exploration, Education, Success, Well-being, Confidence, Indulgence, Creative Visualisation and Opulence. A giant planet shrouded in swirling cloud, Jupiter was considered the beneficent father of the gods by the ancients. Jupiter is indeed the largest planet orbiting the Sun and is bigger than all the other planets in our Solar system combined. Jupiter is the first of the transpersonal planets, which is less associated with the self but more involved with interactions with others - in other words, it can be classified as a 'social planet'. It is concerned with expansion in every form, the acquisition of knowledge and the desire to be free. Buoyantly optimistic, Jupiter's main function is to 'grow' and exaggerate everything it touches. However, he inflates and expands indiscriminately, making bad points worse and good points better. He not only brings material benefits but is also the source of philosophical wisdom and moral conscience. He imparts this knowledge frequently by coming to the rescue at the last minute, when all hope seems lost. Broad-visioned, Jupiter paints a big picture and impels you to think, act and dream large. Jupiter brings hope, honesty, spirituality and fortuity to your Sagittarian spirit. While the Sun may be regarded as the essential core of our being which directs us towards our true spiritual goal, it is through Jupiter that we make our goals *real* in a worldly sense. If it weren't for this expansive planet, our dreams may well stay within our core and feed our essence, but not necessarily be *achieved* or realised. Jupiter's optimism and striving helps bring them out. My Jupiterian energy and influence, throughout your whole life, gives you the gifts of generosity, philanthropy, flashiness, extravagance, liveliness, exuberance, and a happy-go-lucky attitude. Too much Jupiterian influence can lead to over-optimism, idealism, blind faith, inflated self-confidence, risk-taking, over-indulgence, arrogance, and being too big for one's boots. But the Sagittarian needn't worry about this too much, as just being born under the auspice of the Centaur's domain renders you lucky from the word go; after all, your motto is '*I Aim*' - and wherever you decide to direct your arrow, it seems to hit exactly the mark you were aiming for. How will you use my phenomenally powerful Jupiterian influence in your life?"

DIVINE MESSAGE FROM THE GOD JUPITER ★ "Sagittarius, as the Powerful Ruler of the Skies and King of the Gods, I give you the gifts of benevolence, expansion, wisdom, knowledge, generosity, tolerance, and an indefatigable optimism, that carry you through all life's inevitable battles with pure charm, a natural charisma, and an unwavering love that radiates from your innermost core. Being born under my Divine influence imprints your soul with my essence. I reside in you always, from birth through to death and beyond if you so desire and ensure that you operate through my best and highest qualities at all times. If it feels like I am not within you, then that may be because you are not honouring me properly, your Inner Wisdom. You can invoke and thus honour me during the first dawn hour of a Thursday, using a purple candle, a yellow sapphire, and the element of Fire."

To Invoke Jupiter

Day ★ Thursday
Number ★ 3
Intelligence ★ Yophiel
Spirit ★ Hismael
Basic Energy & Magic ★ Expansion, Faith, Philosophy
Colours ★ Purple, Deep Blue, Indigo
Gods/Goddesses/Angel ★ Zeus, Jupiter, Ammon, Sachiel
Metals ★ Tin, antimony
Gems/Minerals ★ Amethyst, Lapis Lazuli, Blue Diamond, Turquoise, Emerald, Jacinth, Green Jasper, Sapphire, Topaz, Aquamarine
Trees/Shrubs ★ Oak, Cedar, Ash, Birch, Linden, Chestnut
Flowers/Herbs ★ Sweet William, Sage, Nutmeg
Woods ★ Oak, Cedar
Fabric ★ Velvet
Animals ★ Horse, Eagle
Element ★ Fire
Zodiac Signs ★ Sagittarius, Pisces

★ OTHER GODS & GODDESSES SAGITTARIUS CAN SUMMON FOR ASSISTANCE, GUIDANCE OR CONNECTION ★

Zeus, Thoth, Hermes, Lakshmi, Fortuna, Artemis, Chiron, Apollo *

* Apollo was a Greek god of music, truth, prophecy, healing, poetry, light and the Sun. Apollo assumed various functions, all broadly interrelated. As seer, Apollo is patron of poetry and music and the leader of the Muses, and as prophet and magician he is patron of medicine and healing. Conversely, he can deal out death and as such is sometimes

represented as an Archer, the 'far shooter' who slays with his arrows. His portrayal as an Archer connects him powerfully with Sagittarius.

★ ★ ★

CAPRICORN

♑

MESSAGE FROM SATURN

"I am Saturn, your ruler, The Wise Teacher and Timeless Sage. I am powerfully associated with Time, Karmic Lessons, Practicality, Boundaries, Restrictions, Limitation, Ambition, Control, the Father, Authority, Obstacles, Reality Checks, Rigidity, Solitude, Caution, Duty, the Teacher, Discipline, Perseverance, Austerity, Inhibition, Frustration, Thrift, Consolidation, Direction, Denial, Responsibility, the Shadow, Endurance and Patience, and the profound wisdom gained through life experience. I am one of the least understood energies in the astrological matrix, for although my principles can be seen in part as difficulties, obstacles and limitations, I am also a sage, a teacher, and it has been said that when the student is ready the teacher appears. And Saturn always appears in a timely manner, although this may not be apparent to the uninitiated. It could be said that each of us has a soul which has chosen to wrestle with the difficulty of expressing spirit through the base material of a human body, and Saturn represents that battlefield. The apparent difficulties experienced on this harsh plane can be transmuted into qualities which can enhance our soul's journey. But to achieve this, Saturn's deeper side needs first to be understood. Cold, hard and stern, Saturn deals with issues of discipline, boundaries, focus, maturation, patience, obstacles, inhibitions and frustrations, and shows how we face and deal with limitations, setbacks, authority and restrictions. He points the way along the path of both duty and destiny and provides firm direction and important lessons along the way. As the way-pointer, Saturn shows us where our soul must dwell in order to fulfill our inner purpose and destiny. Representing rules and lessons on many levels - personal, collective, societal, cosmic and karmic - if we allow it, Saturn can be a great sage-like presence in our lives. Saturn is the archetype of the judge. Many approach him with fear and trepidation as a result. Saturn limits you. Saturn says "No." Saturn punishes you. Saturn is unmoved by your pleadings and protests that life is unfair, as he sagely knows that you always have a choice: to accept responsibility for your actions, or to resist authority and necessary restrictions placed upon you to your detriment. Saturn knows that you can reclaim your power at any time and stop playing the victim, for you have only imposed this label on yourself and no one else is to blame for the consequences. When you stand respectful and humbled before Saturn as judge, devoid of excuses, you will discover that he is in fact, merciful. He may even turn a "No" into a "Yes." Saturn is our wise inner voice. It is the planet that determines your maturity. The position of Saturn in your birth chart has an important effect on how you listen to and interpret your inner voice. It is all about how far we expand our horizons and how we become aware of our own limitations. We become mature when we become able to collect our thoughts, cultivate wisdom learned from tough lessons, and master our actions. We can master the elements of our destiny and take responsibility for the consequences of our desires and actions. We can discover our real motivations. In fact, we become an individual in our own right. My Saturnian energy and influence, throughout your whole life, bestows upon you the gifts of wisdom, perseverance, stability, structure, realistic application of ideas, tenacity, a sense of duty, sensible caution, wise discernment, patience and lucidity. Too much of this Saturnian energy can make one cold, unfeeling, controlling, tight, unmoved, harsh, selfish, mistrustful, cynical, indifferent, fatalistic, resentful, sterile, mean, severe and authoritarian. It can also indicate enduring periods of hardship, depression, sorrow or chronic ill-health. But the Saturn-ruled Capricornian always knows how to use her best qualities to achieve her ambitions and goals in life; after all, your motto is '*I Use*', because in your amazingly shrewd, direct and no-nonsense way, you *do* use everything you can to your full advantage. And like the mountain goat that represents your sign, you keep putting one hoof patiently in front of the other until you reach the peak. How will you use my phenomenally powerful Saturnian influence in your life?"

DIVINE MESSAGE FROM THE GOD SATURN ★ "Capricorn, I am the Divine Tester and Way-Shower, I give you the gifts of persistence, ambition, steadfastness, and a brilliant business mind, that carry you through all life's inevitable battles with a dazzling success and single-mindedness, that radiate from your innermost core. Being born under my Divine influence imprints your soul with my essence. I reside in you always, from birth through to death and beyond if you so desire and ensure that you operate through my best and highest qualities at all times. If it feels like I am not within you, then that may be because you are not honouring me properly, your Inner Wise One. You can invoke and thus honour me during the first dawn hour of a Saturday, using a black candle, a blue sapphire, and the element of Earth."

To Invoke Saturn

Day ★ Saturday
Numbers ★ 4 and 8
Intelligence ★ Agiel
Spirit ★ Zazel
Basic Energy & Magic ★ Authority, Banishing, Stabilising
Colours ★ Black, Midnight Blue, Green, Grey, Dark Brown
Gods/Goddesses/Angel ★ Cronos (sometimes spelt 'Kronos'), Saturn, Cassiel
Metals ★ Lead, Iron, Steel
Gems/Minerals ★ Onyx, Jet, Diamond, Green Calcite,

Obsidian, Garnet, Deep-hued Sapphires
Trees/Shrubs ★ Cypress, Elm, Buckthorn, Willow, Aspen, Pine
Flowers/Herbs ★ Patchouli, Myrrh, Holly, Ivy
Wood ★ Birch, Ebony, Alder
Animals ★ Crow, Wren
Element ★ Earth
Zodiac Sign ★ Capricorn

★ OTHER GODS & GODDESSES CAPRICORN CAN SUMMON FOR ASSISTANCE, GUIDANCE OR CONNECTION ★

Cronus, Ceres, Athene, Vesta, Hestia

★ ★ ★

AQUARIUS

♒

MESSAGE FROM URANUS

"I am Uranus, the Great Awakener and Powerful Agent of Revolution. I am associated with Intuition, Electrifying Force, Innovation, Disruption, Higher or Psychic Functions, Individuality, Cosmic Consciousness, Inventions, Shock, Sudden or Unexpected Change, Originality, Electricity and Revolution. Uranus offers a welcome change from its neighbouring planet Saturn, giving us a chance to seize our freedom, break free, be progressive and enhance our creativity. Uranus is an astronomical maverick, alone in rotating horizontally, and on a personal level, its electrically charged energy is reckoned to denote individualists, reformers, outsiders and intellectual brilliance; people who break the norms of a cultural or political mould. People born under the sign of Aquarius are particularly sensitive to its influence and being born with an (often) emphasised Uranus factor makes them susceptible to being extremely stimulated most of the time, living in a constant state of wired or other-worldly energy. Most of all, this planet's role is to break down the established 'order' and replace it with experimental, novel or idealistic regimes - whether these are applied to the wider world, or in our personal lives. It acts to break up the crystallisation that Saturn has imposed, and stands for originality, shock, inspiration, dynamic self-expression, will and the ability to synthesise. It also acts to electrify, galvanise, vivify, awaken and mobilise, often working in a spasmodic, unexpected fashion, but highly effective as an agent of change nonetheless. It signifies unusual characters, inventors, electricians, and those with transcendental interests. Uranus is a political planet which seeks to change and maneuver the world into new ways of thinking and *being*. Uranus, as one of the three outer or generational planets, is regarded as a 'planet of a higher octave', along with Neptune and Pluto. These higher octave forces account for those flashes of inspiration we are occasionally jolted with, when we become especially aware of our life's purpose, albeit usually only very fleetingly - unless of course you are an Aquarian! Uranus never seeks to put up boundaries around your soul or spirit, allowing you to more easily build and create things according to your own inner visions, ideals and views of the world. A legacy of your ruling planet, chaos to you is actually beneficial; in fact, it produces a bubbling, creative cauldron in which you can create the most useful, innovative and magical of transformations. Uranus also gives its Aquarian charges the tendency to need more change and serendipity in your life than other zodiac signs. Uranus teaches you that you have a bigger job to do and there is no time for sitting still, which suits you fine. Commotion is your forte, and when things get dull you deliberately shake them up by rattling the status quo. In this way, Aquarians and Uranus work in very sudden and unexpected ways, which is why this planet is called the Great Awakener, and why its offspring are so rebellious. Uranus is the planet which embodies the sixth sense, and Aquarians are often gifted with the flashes of insight that are characteristic of the higher, spiritual faculties of the mind. Uranian individuals are therefore blessed with the futuristic and brilliant intellect that a strong Uranian influence implies, especially if at the time of your birth Uranus was well-placed in the sky in relation to Mercury, the two combining forces to indicate genius. The Uranus influence upon the Aquarian soul urges the Water Bearer to enlighten others and certainly to pour the waters of knowledge onto all fellow humans. Uranus, along with Jupiter, is associated with lightning, and bestows the Aquarian with those lightning bolts thinking processes. However, these thoughts may never make it to earth, and the sense of frustration that the soaring Aquarian spirit so often experiences, is due to its flying high among the nebulae, keenly aware of the universal order of the cosmos, but trapped in an earthly body that is typically restricted and tied up in chains. My Uranian energy and influence, throughout your whole life, bestows upon you the gifts of vision, originality, futuristic thinking, and eccentricity, giving the potential to be the impactful 'outsider', and the bringer of hope and messages society most needs to hear. Too much of this Uranian energy can make one anarchistic, fanatical, contrary, unpredictable, inflexible and overly eccentric, to the point of 'dropping out' of or being rejected by society. But the Aquarian always knows what's best for his own soul; after all, your motto is *'I Know'*, because deep down, you really do *know*, even if you can never quite manage to articulate *what* it is exactly that you know. How will you use my phenomenally powerful Uranian influence in your life?"

DIVINE MESSAGE FROM THE GOD URANUS ✶ "Aquarius, I am the Divine Rebel and Powerful Agent of Personal Revolution, I give you the gifts of sudden flashes of insights, well-placed rebellion, brilliant genius, and an indefatigable quest for the truth, that carry you through all life's inevitable battles with a dazzling originality, uniqueness and unmatched individuality, that radiate from your innermost core. Being born under my Divine influence imprints your soul with my essence. I reside in you always, from birth through to death and beyond if you so desire and ensure that you operate through my best and highest qualities at all times. If it feels like I am not within you, then that may be because you are not honouring me properly, your Inner Awakener. You can invoke and thus honour me during the first dawn hour of a Wednesday, using an electric blue candle, a lapis lazuli crystal, and the element of Air."

To Invoke Uranus

Numbers ★ 4 and 22
Basic Energy & Magic ★ Invention, Innovation, Change
Colours ★ Light Blues, Electric & Glaring Hues, Stripes
Metal ★ Uranium
Gems/Minerals ★ Amber, Jacinth, Jargoon, Chalcedony,
Aquamarine, Azurite, Sapphire, Lapis Lazuli
Zodiac Sign ★ Aquarius

★ OTHER GODS & GODDESSES AQUARIUS CAN SUMMON FOR ASSISTANCE, GUIDANCE OR CONNECTION ★

Caelus, Saturn, Cronus, Thoth, Juno, Hera, Jupiter

★ ★ ★

PISCES

♓

MESSAGE FROM NEPTUNE

"I am your ruler Neptune, the Great Artist, Mystic and Dreamer. I am powerfully associated with Inspiration, Dreams, Imagination, Mystical Longings, Sensitivity, Mysticism, Higher or Psychic Functions, Other-worldliness, Escapism, Delusions, Artistry, Enigmas, Compassion, Intrigues, Cloudiness, Unreality, Spirituality, Subtlety, Idealism, Deception, Creativity, the Subconscious, Illusions and Fantasies. The ocean has always been the symbolic keynote of Pisces, and we attribute the sign's rulership to Neptune, who was the god of the sea. Artists and mystics are able to reach into the deep ocean of images that this sign's symbolism evokes, connecting Pisces with psychics and dreamers, artistic types and idealists; after all it is precisely from these watery depths that they garner their visions, poetry and melodic symphonies. Neptune is the planet of altruism, dreams and deep faith, and as such engenders great compassion, insight and inspiration, as well as a profound sensitivity to beauty. Its trident symbol, Poseidon's pitchfork, symbolises the threefold parts to each person: body, mind and spirit, the greatest of these being spirit. Being prominent as your ruling planet, Neptune gives you a heightened sensitivity, misty nature, a strong imagination and powerful psychic potential. Being an outer planet, Neptune is an impersonal energy, and can be difficult to understand or even describe. It presides over artistry, music and illusion, the kinds created by lighting, film and photography, colour, clothing and conjuring. It is also linked with religious miracles and mysticism of the mediumistic and psychic varieties. Neptune dances somewhere on the mystical side of life, and is prone to fantasising, daydreaming and idealising. Seeing the world through rose-coloured glasses a lot of the time, it compels its subjects to believe in magic, dreams, fairytales and happy endings. The typical Neptunian is otherworldly, her vision tuned to an inner reality which may create fantastical castles that delight, or which can lead him or her into a dark, swirling undercurrent of undesirable emotions. With so much tenderness and sensitivity, most Neptune-influenced individuals don't survive very well in the outside world. But in time they figure out that they are not of this world and, most importantly, that they don't have to be. Their challenge in life is to keep in touch with their inner spiritual centre while continuing to function on the material plane, a process similar to that represented by the two fish swimming in opposite directions. Both their strength and their weakness, Pisces and Neptune have the ability, beyond all other signs and planets, to absorb everything around them, therefore blessing them with a refreshing absence of ego, but at the same time cursing them with an oft troublesome lack of boundaries. Neptune's energy is dreamy, mystical, fantastical, delusional and magical. This planet pulls the veil of dreams over our eyes, but it can just as readily pull it away. Its influence often coincides with both mystical and romantic experiences. Its adverse side can cause carelessness, impracticality, foolish decisions, needless worrying, and the tendency to live in either a fantasy world or under the influence of substances. Neptune's actions are to loosen, to dissolve, to etherealise, sensitise, idealise, make intangible, refine, expand, inflate and distort. It also falls within the sphere of chaos and dissolution. Neptune in its highest form brings the blessings of a creative imagination. The positive side of Neptune ultimately leads to inspiration - which manifests itself as truth, light and wisdom. My Neptunian energy and influence, throughout a Piscean's whole life experience, bestows upon you the wondrous gifts of creativity, illumination, dreams, spirituality, visions, intuition, and the potential to be the dream manifester and the bringer of the spiritualism, compassion and universal love that the world so desperately needs. Too much of this Neptunian energy can leave one confused, intoxicated, vague, secretive, indecisive, a little bit mad, weak-willed, in denial, and unable to cope with the practicalities of life, to the point of succumbing to escapism and fantastical paths. But the Piscean always manages to intuit what's best for her own soul; after all, your motto is 'I Believe', and deep down, you really do *believe*, even when all hope seems lost. After all, Neptune's force encapsulates the essence and role of the pure Piscean - that of the humble, selfless, saintly saviour. Sometimes though, you must remember to save yourself. How will you use my phenomenally powerful Neptunian influence in your life?"

DIVINE MESSAGE FROM THE GOD NEPTUNE ★ "Pisces, I am the Dream Creator of your Wildest Imaginings, I give you the gifts of dreams, spiritual connection, Universality, and a sense of the other-worlds, that carry you through all life's inevitable ups and downs with pure belief in magic, the unknown and the unseen, and a gentle, all-pervading love that radiates from your innermost core. Being born under my Divine influence imprints your soul with my essence. I reside in you always, from birth through to death and beyond if you so desire and ensure that you operate through my best and highest qualities at all times. If it feels like I am not within you, then that may be because you are not honouring me properly, your Inner Magician. You can invoke and thus honour me during the first dawn hour of a Friday, using a violet candle, a fluorite crystal, and the element of Water."

To Invoke Neptune

Numbers ★ 7 and 11
Basic Energy & Magic ★ Dreams, Fantasies, Magic
Colours ★ Lavender, Mauve, Aquamarine, Sea Green,
Etheric Colours, Indigo, Violet
Metals ★ Neptunium, Platinum
Gems/Minerals ★ Coral, Aquamarine, Amethyst,
Fluorite, Jade, Coral, Sugilite, Apophyllite
Zodiac Sign ★ Pisces

★ OTHER GODS & GODDESSES PISCES CAN SUMMON FOR ASSISTANCE, GUIDANCE OR CONNECTION ★

Poisedon, Jupiter, Zeus

★ ★ ★

★ DIVINE AFFIRMATIONS ★

"Infinite Spirit of the Universe, open the way for great abundance of all good things for me. I am an irresistible magnet for all that belongs to me by Divine right."

"Infinite Spirit of the Universe, open the way for the Divine Design of my life to manifest; let the genius within me now be released; let me see clearly the perfect plan".

"The Universe is my unfailing supply, and all that I request and desire, comes to me at the right time, under graceful conditions, through clear channels, and in perfect ways."

"Infinite Spirit of the Universe, open the way for my immediate supply, let all that is mine by Divine right now reach me, in great avalanches of boundless abundance."

"May I be now freed from that thing which has held me in bondage throughout my life or recent experience, standing between myself and my own, and know the Truth which will set me free – free to fulfill my destiny, bring into manifestation the Divine Design of my Life, Health, Wealth, Love and Perfect Self-Expression."

"All is well."

"Thank you, thank you, thank you!"

★ ★ ★

✶ SPECIAL MESSAGE FROM ALL YOUR GUIDES ✶

The Path is in yourself, and Truth is in yourself, and Mystery is in yourself.

P.D. Ouspensky

"You are never alone. Throughout your life you will have our company in everything of significance that you do and feel. We are always near enough to hear and respond to your requests. Solitary suffering is needless, and is the result of insufficient faith, for all you need to do is ask for help or advice and one of us will be sent to shelter, guide or comfort you. We will surely bring rays of energy to help make things easier for you. A relationship between a human and a guide is a mutually beneficial phenomenon. We are always within hailing distance, just as your calling on our help renders us loved and useful. You may be attempting to contact us, but meanwhile we've been watching you for many years, long before you were even aware of our existence. Even prior to your birth we began examining your life plans to see if you were The One we were looking for and if it was therefore our purpose to share in your Path *. If we did indeed choose you, you became a member of our tribal family and we made a commitment to act as your guardian and guide during your lifetime. Although we may not be continually hovering over you, we are with you always, and especially in your deepest times of trouble. We never abandon you and stay ever-tuned to your life situations. While we only make contact once in a while, when it's especially needed or called for, we do approach you periodically to check in and see how you're doing. We are always arranging events that will help you to grow and transform, and you will bump into us in the sometimes cryptic, encoded, disguised messages that we bring to you at regular intervals. Know that events are continually being created, by you and by us, to bring the light of Truth into focus. With regards to events of your future, it is very hard for us to supply precise information about things to come, firstly, because we know that such information contravenes your sense of free will, your power to shape your own life, and may therefore be detrimental to your growth. Secondly, because your Earthly clocks are bound by different dynamics and laws to our own, it is difficult to always be perfectly attuned to your time schedule with any exactitude. When unsure about anything at all, you can come to us for guidance, illumination, advice or corroboration, and if your need is great enough, you may even obtain help from an Archangel or your Oversoul who will be sent to assist you. When you are on your proper spiritual Path, we give thanks, for your life and its successes are also ours. Remember that this is a mutual partnership we share, and by appreciating us, you contribute to the fullness of our existence and presence as well. Furthermore, you assist us in building the evolutionary mechanisms that allow reciprocal pathways to open up and unfold on both sides. Each time you affirm and avow your beliefs in the reality and existence of the Divine spirit world, you open the gate through which we can both freely move a bit more, and your beliefs will begin to bloom into revelation, knowledge, awakening, and enlightenment. Whenever you feel abandoned or lost, re-connect yourself to our realm through practising the four ways of transcendental living: Affirmation (prayer), Meditation, Love and Forgiveness. We are all in this together. All is well. Trust."

* Sometimes a guide can come to you in the form of a Master Guide. Otherwise known as an 'Ascended Master', a Master Guide seeks you out, not the other way around. Master Guides strengthen your creative courage and their principal teachings revolve around love. People who link up with such wise old beings begin to appreciate themselves more profoundly and to demonstrate kindness, compassion and wisdom. A Master Guide is a loving gift of the highest order. You can trust that if one taps you on the shoulder, the Universe knows that you're worthy and ready to receive this special gift. While our roles are transitory (writer, wife, artist, traveller, etc.), the calling of a Master Guide has permanence. Because Ascended Masters choose us rather than us seeking them out, it is usually futile to search for one with whom to connect (although if you have achieved high levels of spiritual connection with other guides, you can ground and clear yourself, then humbly request that a meeting take place). Instead, by making full use of the interaction with your regular spirit helpers, you raise your chances that sooner or later a Master Guide will choose to communicate with you.

★ SPECIAL MESSAGE FROM THE UNIVERSE
FOR ALL ZODIAC SIGNS ★

Believe in the 'Plan' guiding all evolution, in yourself becoming 'more than you are', and truly realise that you are an evolving Star.

C. L. Weschcke & J. H. Slate

For You, Dear Child of the Universe

"Ultimately, the highest power of all is that of me - the Universe, All That Is, the Absolute, the Eternal Circle Spiral - an eternal, powerful, all-pervading, all-knowing, omnipresent, omnipotent presence / entity that eludes description, explanation or definition. All we know is that I exist at all times, on all levels, and everywhere, from within the tiniest of atoms to the largest of the planetary bodies, and that I do not have a conceivable end, nor a discernable beginning. I have no boundaries, for I stretch into an infinite expanse of boundless space. The Universe in this context - space - according to quantum physicists, extends forever and ever into infinity. No one can even grasp my essence, yet every-one and every-thing lives through me constantly. I, the Universe, am within you all and pervade your being as a Divine holographic concept, with each part of everything containing the whole. So, from me, the Universe, to you, my Divine Child, my message is simple and clear: '*Trust. Love. Flow. Be.*' I am always here, around you, but most of all, I am within you, as well as in every other direction and space imaginable. I wish you all the best with your journey, wherever it may lead, for however your own personal voyage unfolds, it is always and ever for your highest good and most powerful of lessons. Accept adversities with grace, successes with gratitude, and victories with humbleness. May the wellspring of abundance, love, health and Divine fulfillment be eternally and infinitely yours. You hold the key to my vast kingdom. I will never let you fall. All is unfolding as it should be, and you are in exactly the place you are meant to be. You are loved. You are safe. You are free. You are *home*.

Yours faithfully and forever,
The Universe.

★ ★ ★

You are endless galaxies - and you have seen but one star.

Temple of Thebes

★   ★   ★

ABOUT THE AUTHOR

Lani is an astrologer with 34 years-experience, published author of 18 books, mother, witch, spell-caster, tarot expert, healer, crystal therapist, Akashic Record reader, teacher of esoteric subjects, metaphysician, ardent dream believer, light-worker, eternal student of magic, channeller of cosmic forces, and Divine messenger, whose spiritual home is in the exquisite tropical north of Australia. She is an accredited member of the World Metaphysical Association and the Australian Astrologers Federation. Her greatest passions are writing, astrology, reading, esoteric studies, spiritual evolution, personal development and weaving magical spells on behalf of herself and others, using the powers of pure belief, faith, crystals, the cosmos and the Universe. She wholeheartedly believes that the power of the written word has the potential to transform lives, change the world one page at a time, and enhance the mind, body and spirit of everyone who seeks it. By creating *Divine Zodiac Messages* and other spiritually-themed books, she hopes to instill a sense of deep, timeless and enduring magic in her readers. You can connect with more of Lani's inspiring work on her Facebook pages *Lani Sharp Author* & *Astrology Magic*, on Instagram at *lani_sharp_author*, or by email at astrologymagick@gmail.com.

☆ ☆ ☆

www.ingramcontent.com/pod-product-compliance
Lightning Source LLC
Chambersburg PA
CBHW071902290426
44110CB00013B/1242